HOW PHILANTHROPY IS CHANGING IN EUROPE

Christopher Carnie

First published in Great Britain in 2017 by

Policy Press
University of Bristol
1-9 Old Park Hill
Bristol BS2 8BB
UK
t: +44 (0)117 954 5940
e: pp-info@bristol.ac.uk
www.policypress.co.uk

North American office:
Policy Press
c/o The University of Chicago Press
1427 East 60th Street
Chicago, IL 60637, USA
t: +1 773 702 7700
f: +1 773-702-9756
e:sales@press.uchicago.edu
www.press.uchicago.edu

British Library Cataloguing in Publication Data
A catalogue record for this book is available from the British Library.

Library of Congress Cataloging-in-Publication Data
A catalog record for this book has been requested.

ISBN 978-1-4473-3110-0 (paperback)
ISBN 978-1-4473-3112-4 (ePub)
ISBN 978-1-4473-3113-1 (Kindle)
ISBN 978-1-4473-3111-7 (ePdf)

Cover design by Andrew Corbett
Front cover: image kindly supplied by Getty

Printed and bound by CPI Group (UK) Ltd, Croydon, CR0 4YY

I have met many, many good people in my work in philanthropy, but I am only going to name three, who have shown me what good, tough, love really means; thank you Jordan, Greer and Crinan.

"People start off in philanthropy, usually modestly, and then find out how much fun it is. As others have observed, you never meet an ex-philanthropist."

Theresa Lloyd, interviewed 8 December 2015, Bath, England.

'Le doute n'est pas un état bien agréable, mais l'assurance est un état ridicule.'
'Doubt is not a pleasant condition, but certainty is an absurd one.'

Au prince royal de prusse, le 28 novembre, in M. Palissot (ed), *Oeuvres de Voltaire: Lettres Choisies du Roi de Prusse et de M. de Voltaire*, Tome II. Paris: Chez Baudoiun, 1802. p 419.

Contents

Acknowledgements

It was Martine Godefroid who first introduced me to the wonders of continental European foundations and philanthropy, and I am eternally grateful to her for giving me an interest that has shaped my working life.

This is a book about people being good to other people, so it must begin with the people who have been good to me – people from NGOs, universities and foundations, philanthropic people who have helped me learn about philanthropy, including the many who gave time and mind to the interviews that shaped this book. I have been a slow learner; despite the many years as a fundraiser, a prospect researcher and now a consultant and teacher I still cannot say that I really understand that deep, bright place in our hearts and minds that drives us to do good. What I have understood is all here, in this book; the views, and the errors, are mine.

I would like to thank Laura Vickers and Ruth Harrison at Policy Press for taking on a book with 'Europe' in its title at a moment when England seems to have swung away from the continent, for their patience, their many suggestions, and their clear guidance.

Acknowledgements

PART ONE

Introduction

ONE

Introduction

Giving, evolved

We are in Bilbao, northern Spain, at the headquarters of a mid-size Spanish NGO (non-governmental organisation). In the meeting is a board member. He is a lawyer at a leading Madrid law practice, on the point of retiring from the firm. At home he serves as a local councillor for the Partido Popular, the right-of-centre political party. He supports the NGO with time – lots of it – professional advice and money, and he has done so for years. I ask him about his philanthropy. He says it is his duty (*"mi deber"*) to be philanthropic; it's something necessary for him, and something private. No one has asked him to be philanthropic – it is just something that he feels the need to do. Nor is his philanthropy something he talks about with others. It is not a topic for dinner-time conversation, except in the most general terms.

Here is another philanthropist from Italy, who has a family foundation. He's in his 40s, the successful scion of an Italian engineering family, who runs one branch of the family's investment empire. The investment holding company donates 1% of its profits and 1% of the founder partners' salaries to a family-run foundation that supports people with disabilities. Why is he philanthropic? He recalls his childhood, the big villa in the mountains north of Milan and his mother who each August invited a group of orphans to holiday there. He inherited his mother's sense of duty. He is talking to me about his philanthropy, and I sense that he is a bit more willing to do so than is my Spanish lawyer. But philanthropy is still a largely private affair.

These are examples of how philanthropy largely is across Europe. The Spanish lawyer and the Italian entrepreneur fit the pattern of many, perhaps most, of Europe's philanthropists. The private duty to be philanthropic is embedded in the minds of millions of people across Europe, an inherited moral standard that is an accepted tax on wealth. These morals are not necessarily religious, although religion does provide part of the explanation of this suite of beliefs about philanthropy, including the sense that when one has money one has a duty to do some good with it. They are ancient – we can see examples of philanthropy in Europe right back to the beginnings of history – but they are evolving. Look more closely at the Spanish lawyer and you will find that he is on the board of a network of foundations in Spain – philanthropists coming together to try to improve their ways of giving. The Italian entrepreneur is in fact a 'philanthropic investor', using a combination of social enterprises and non-profits to target specific social changes he seeks to encourage.

Philanthropy is evolving right now, in Europe. William Beveridge, a renowned early 20th century welfare reformer in the UK, said in a 1942 report (Penn, 2011) that 'philanthropy has shown its strength of being able perpetually to take new forms', and Europe today feels like a crucible of ideas, products, projects, forms and fiscal inventions for philanthropy. The research laboratory for these ideas is the world of high-value philanthropy, where people have the money, the experience and the influence to test out the sometimes weird and the often wonderful.

The objective of this book is to capture and illustrate the evolution in high-value philanthropy in Europe and to provide a practical map for people working in the field.

Definitions and frontiers

Philanthropy

This book will use the same definition as Pamala Wiepking in her seminal 2008 work on the sociology of giving: 'The literal translation of the Greek word philanthropy is "the love of mankind", "*philo*" meaning "love of" and "*anthropos*" meaning "mankind."' (2008, p v)

There are many ways of expressing one's love of mankind, including a wide range of acts of generosity and some of abstinence: reducing one's carbon footprint by taking the train rather than the car (or the plane), is mild abstinence for the love of mankind. Helping out in accidents or disasters can also be philanthropy: a bandage for that child who has just scraped his knee in the playground, or a month volunteering at one of Europe's new refugee camps. This is philanthropy as a human response to things going wrong, as Professor Michael Moody describes it (Payton and Moody, 2008). This book will focus on one specific segment of philanthropy, the use of money to help others. That does not limit us solely to giving – as we will see, there are many ways of using money to help others – but it does provide a focus for this work.

It is worth noting that in continental Europe there is a selection of other words related to 'philanthropy':

Alms: Giving to God, to benefit the poor. This occurs across many religious groups (*zakat* is its approximate equivalent in Islam). The history of almsgiving illustrates the ways in which philanthropy changes. As Eliana Magnani (2009, p 111) points out, 'almsgiving developed as a result of the creation of the social category of the poor' between the 4th and 6th centuries. We had to be told that there were people in poverty in order to understand that we were meant to give.

Charity, and words from the same Latin root: In continental Europe 'charity' is used to refer specifically to a gift or entity with a religious purpose, to help the poor. In the UK 'charity' is used to refer to any public benefit non-profit – legally, a 'charitable trust' as well as the act of doing good. The continental European view of charity is illustrated in this 19th century poem by a Spanish author (Arenal, 1894):

> Beneficence sends the sick person a bed
> > Philanthropy comes to aid him
> > Charity takes his hand.

Donation: In the UK this refers to any kind of gift. In the context of this book, for example, it might be used in the phrase "I made a £50 donation to the Red Cross last week." In some countries in continental Europe a donation can mean a pledge, in some cases made before a notary, to give a certain amount to a non-profit over a certain time period. The 'donation' in this sense is an irrevocable pledge, equivalent to a 'covenant' in the UK.

Foundation: See below for the various words and definitions used here.

Maecenas, and words from the same root: Rarely used in the UK, these words ('*mecenazgo*' in Spanish for example, '*le mécénat*' in French) are derived from the name of Gaius Maecenas (68 BC–8 BC) who was a patron of poetry and the arts. In continental Europe they are used mainly to refer to giving that supports the arts, but as Virginie Seghers (2009, p 15) points out, the words can have a wider meaning: 'we talk today of "*mécénat des entreprises*" to define donations by [businesses] to public benefit causes, not only cultural [causes] but also social, scientific or in favour of the environment.' Some authors (for example Parés i Maicas, 1994) distinguish between Maecenas meaning support for culture, and sponsorship meaning support for sport or television, but this frontier is not clearly defined across Europe.

Sponsorship: This word carries broadly the same set of meanings on both sides of the Channel, referring either to business support for an activity (sports sponsorship, arts sponsorship) or for defined types of individual giving (sponsoring a student, child sponsorship)

Profits, or not

There are many ways of describing what in the UK would be called a 'charity' and in continental Europe might be called a foundation or an association. In this book I am not going to use 'charity' except where I mean an entity that has a specific religious purpose to help the poor – the European version of 'charity'/'caridad'/'carità'. To refer to the sector I will use the term 'non-profit'. This is an unsatisfactory term, because the frontiers between the 'for-profit' and 'non-profit' worlds are disappearing, with the space being occupied by organisations called 'social enterprises', although even that term is applied to a very wide range of life-forms. But I want to be able to distinguish between organisations with a primarily social or environmental purpose (the 'non-profits') and those with a primarily financial purpose (the 'for-profits').

The space between non-profits and for-profits is a continuum that includes non-profits that run businesses (the fair trade operations of Oxfam for example, or the corporations owned by Danish foundations), social enterprises, businesses with a strong social purpose (La Fageda, the Catalan dairy products firm that largely employs people with learning difficulties), and for-profits that are linked to non-profit foundations (the publishing businesses of Bertelsmann Stiftung in Germany, for example).

Charities, foundations and associations

For people outside continental Europe there is often confusion over the words 'foundation' and 'association'. Are they both 'charities' in the sense that word is used in England or in the US? Is a 'fondation' in Paris, France the same as a 'foundation' in Paris, Texas? The answer to both questions is a measured 'no'. In summary:

- The non-profit entity called a 'charity' in England – full name 'charitable trust' – shares the characteristics of continental European foundations *and* associations.
- An association, in continental Europe, is 'a grouping of people around a non-profit objective' whereas a foundation is built around 'an irrevocable donation of assets in order to achieve a non-profit goal that is of public interest' (Anon, 2015a).
- An association can defend the interests of a segment of the population whereas, at least in theory, a foundation in continental Europe has to serve the wider public interest.
- To confuse matters, associations can be declared 'public interest' bodies; in most of continental Europe this entitles them to offer tax reductions to donors.
- An association shuts down if its members withdraw, whereas a foundation is permanent, surviving its founders.
- An association is governed by the vote of all of its members, one person, one vote, whereas a foundation does not have members and is governed by a board.

Note that there is nothing in this list which says that a foundation has to make grants. Continental European foundations may do many things – ranging from running projects to owning businesses, but they are generally not required to be grant making, unlike their US sisters.

The limits of knowledge

"There is no systematic collection of data [about philanthropy]. We don't even know the precise number of foundations in Italy", says Marco Demarie, Head of Research in Philanthropy at Compagnia di San Paolo in Turin, Italy, interviewed for this book.

We know very little about what is happening in the world of high-value philanthropy in Europe. There are few studies and many rely on interviews with those who give. As Theresa Lloyd wryly points out, "finding out about the people who do not give is very difficult. You come along as a researcher with a label, and often your research is supported by a philanthropic foundation. 'Why don't you support charitable activities?' is not likely to lead to a constructive conversation." The statistical studies, such as those in the Netherlands, tend to lump together donors of anything over €1,000, with the result that we cannot determine whether those who give more than €25,000 are materially different. In this book I will try to draw together some of these studies but they come accompanied with a warning: be careful about extrapolating beyond the data, and bear in mind, if you do, that you are out in the wilds of risky assumptions.

Here, now, Europe

This book is a snapshot of Europe, now. A Europe that is emerging slowly from the global economic crisis that began in 2008, that is in political turmoil as populist parties gain votes across the continent and formerly sensible politicians court the extremists, that is having to regroup and heal wounds after the divisive 2016 referendum vote by England to leave the EU, a Europe that has caught itself in a tailspin over its humanitarian responsibilities toward the migrants escaping wars that were fuelled, in part, by its own national governments, and that has a range of longer term worries including climate change and its ageing population.

These uncertainties must have an effect on philanthropy, including on high-value philanthropy. As Marco Demarie pointed out to me, "we have been experiencing economic decline here in Italy. There is a tendency to treasure your money to set it aside for a rainy day. Those rainy days are almost every day now."

I can hope that by the time you read these words, the Europe you live in or visit has begun to find its way again. But I will be cautious, throughout the book, about looking into a misty future from a foggy present.

The money frontier

The scope of this book is limited by money. I am not going to touch on the millions of typical donors to our hundreds of thousands of non-profit organisations. I am going to focus on the big or at least bigger money: the private sector donors – principally people and foundations – who make gifts in the range from €25,000 upwards. This is entirely pragmatic; it is the market that I know, and it is a market of a size that permits a study the size of a book. The wider market, the millions of generous people who donate €10 to their favourite NGO, is the stuff of a much deeper study than I could undertake. Which is not to say that this wider market is not touched by the changes in attitudes to philanthropy. There is evidence that it is: the success of Kiva (www. kiva.org) in Europe, for example, is built on the back of thousands of normal donors and donations, and yet Kiva shares many of the elements of new-style European philanthropy, including an innovative financing mechanism, and a direct contact between donor (or in the case of Kiva, lender) and recipient.

The (American) gorilla in the corner

This book is firmly about Europe. Open almost any book about philanthropy and you will find references and research from the USA. There are many reasons for this, including the size of the non-profit sector, public awareness of the sector and of star figures such as Bill and Melinda Gates, and the continuity of private philanthropy throughout the 20th century (differing, here, from Europe's more on-off relationship with philanthropy).

There is a great deal more data on philanthropy, including on high-value philanthropy, from the USA than from Europe. In part this is because, of the 153 research centres in philanthropy listed by the International Society for Third-Sector Research (http://istr.site-ym. com) just over one-third (53), are based in one country – the USA. The next nearest country in terms of numbers of centres is the UK, with 11 (followed, perhaps surprisingly, by Mexico and Brazil, with seven each). In total, Europe has just 36 such centres.

This book will not – could not – ignore that wealth of US information. But the examples used here and as far as possible the research and data used here will be European. In putting down that frontier the author is aware of the gaps that will leave; at the simplest level, for example, there is no comparison between the levels of data on philanthropic foundations held by the Foundation Center in the USA and those held by the European Foundation Centre in Brussels. The former is terabytes ahead of the latter. In the author's view these gaps are important; we need to know, in Europe, what we know and what we don't, and this book will illustrate many of the don'ts.

The USA and Europe do philanthropy differently. We have different cultures, and different social models. At least, that is the viewpoint of many who work in the field. The interviewees featured in this book illustrate some of the subtleties of this view. But as Nicolas Guilhot notes in 'Pratiques du don' (quoted in Peretz, 2012), 'Comme toutes les oppositions tranchées entre des modèles abstraits, celle qui nous est proposée – la philanthropie privée d'un côté, la solidarité et la justice sociale garanties par l'État de l'autre – est à la fois globalement fondée et en partie trompeuse' [Like all entrenched opposing positions on abstract models, that which is proposed to us – private philanthropy on the one side, solidarity and state-guaranteed social justice on the other – is broadly based and in part misleading].

Bouleversement, metamorphosis, revolution?

Guilhot claims that philanthropy in the US and Europe is undergoing a revolution (he calls it the '*bouleversement du monde philanthropique*') as the practices of the financial sector are applied to the institutions of philanthropy.

Referring to an earlier age, Alison Penn describes a 'metamorphosis' in philanthropy in her 2011 review of Beveridge's report on voluntary action. The Observatoire de la Fondation de France, an august and serious institution, talks of 'revolution' (Thibaut, 2008) and a 'change in the social model' as the French state reforms the relationship between citizen, state and philanthropy. Steven van Eijck, Chairman of the SBF (Samenwerkende Brancheorganisaties Filantropie, or Netherlands Cooperative Association for Philanthropy), says that we are in the middle of 'a great revolution in the philanthropic sector' (Scheerboom, 2013). In Chapter Two we hear the views of many of those interviewed for this book on whether or not this is a 'revolution'.

Whatever word you wish to apply, the evidence of change is all around. The launch of the European Venture Philanthropy Association in 2004, the creation of New Philanthropy Capital in London in 2002, legislation in France (2006–2009) to permit the creation of eight different forms of foundation (see Anon, 2015a for a brief explanation), legislation to require transparency for foundations in Catalonia, Spain (2014), the boom in the registration of new foundations across Europe, and the rapid rise of the social enterprise, all indicate that philanthropy is changing. Foundation growth is one of the clearest indicators, because there is substantial historic data. Nothing there matches the rapid growth of recent years; currently an average of four new foundations are being created each week in the UK, around two per week in the Netherlands and one a day in Germany. The growth in the numbers of paid professional fundraisers is also indicative of change – 200% growth in the last eight years in France, for example, and a similarly dramatic growth in academic studies from European universities.

All of these are evidence that philanthropy in Europe is not what it was, and that it will be yet more different soon. In this book I will examine the evidence for change, seek out its causes, and help the reader to find and track the new forms of philanthropy. My aim is to provide a guide that you can use both to understand philanthropy in Europe and to find your way around it, so the book includes a substantial appendix of sources.

The book, summarised

The central idea in *Part two* is that there are *new people in Europe with new ideas on philanthropy*. In this section we examine the new people in philanthropy in Europe. Here you will find more on the generational shift in wealth and philanthropy, on trend-setting philanthropists, on women and philanthropy, and on new circles, groups and networks in philanthropy. People are, of course, the principal force behind philanthropy and it is the shift in attitudes amongst a new generation of people of wealth that is a major driving force behind the changes in philanthropy in Europe.

In *Part three* we show how *governments have encouraged, or tried to encourage, philanthropy in Europe*. There is clear evidence that European governments like philanthropy and the things it can do – even if some attempts to catalyse it, such as former UK Prime Minister David Cameron's 'Big Society' initiative appear ham-fisted. Other governments have been more agile – the Dutch with new regulations on transparency that are forcing a tranche of foundations out into the public eye, the French with a comprehensive foundation law and very attractive new fiscal regimes for donors, the Spanish and Italian with their privatisation programme for 'social' savings banks and, perhaps by the time you read this, the European Commission in Brussels with a Europe-wide foundation statute. The courts have been busy too, with a remarkable case that overnight transformed the tax treatment of cross-border gifts.

Transparency is the subject of *Part four*. The central idea in this section is that *increasing transparency has led to changes in philanthropy in Europe*. Transparency is uncovering philanthropic practice in Europe. If you had tried just a few years ago to research a foundation in Switzerland, you would have found nothing. Not even a registration number. Try the same research today and you will find a range of information including at least some clues on their finances, their board and, with luck, their interests. The same can be said in Spain, where the Spanish Foundation Association published the first more-or-less complete directory of foundations in 2007. Transparency is a work in progress in Europe. Foundations and philanthropists are still largely invisible in Italy, and their finances remain a hidden mystery in Belgium, for example. But the wave of transparency that is opening up Europe is creating change in our attitudes to and our understanding of philanthropy.

In *Part five* we meet the professionals – the people who work in and with philanthropy – and suggest how, and why, they have *changed the way we do philanthropy in Europe*. There are many new faces amongst the professionals in the sector. The philanthropic adviser in the private client area of Rabobank in the Netherlands was formerly a fundraiser at Worldwide Fund for Nature, and the new adviser at of UBS (formerly the Union Bank of Switzerland) Philanthropic Services was last seen at Scope, the UK disability charity, where he devised an ingenious system for investing in social housing. The numbers of professional advisers in philanthropy has rocketed in the last five years, and in Part five we meet them and find out what they do. The growth in the numbers of hunters of philanthropy – the professional fundraisers – started slightly longer ago but has been equally meteoric, with national fundraising associations now counting hundreds, and in a few cases thousands, of members. Are these two groups, the philanthropy advisers and the philanthropy hunters, relevant in the shifts on philanthropy in Europe? Yes they are, and we will see evidence of how this works.

In *Part six* we look at the ways in which we are redesigning giving in Europe. New structures such as the fast-growing easy-access endowed foundations of France are encouraging philanthropists to organise their giving. Financial products such as bonds and loans are adapting to the needs of philanthropists who increasingly talk of 'social investments' and look for better ways of measuring their 'social return'.

Part seven is designed to help people find their way around the sector. There is a list of sources in the Appendix, so Part seven focuses on how to find philanthropy and philanthropists, and how to use the new transparency to understand them. The section includes a chapter on prospect research, the process of finding and understanding philanthropists.

Finally, in *Part eight* I draw some conclusions on the philanthropy that is being uncovered in Europe – traditional, silent philanthropy and the noisier variety of philanthropic investment that is sweeping across the continent. I attempt to link the changes that we can see to the forces that are active in the market, and from here to extrapolate into the future.

Throughout the book I refer back to the interviewees who have helped shaped the ideas that are expressed here. I spoke to people in Belgium, Denmark, France, Germany, Italy, the Netherlands, Spain, Switzerland, Turkey and the UK. People in foundations, philanthropists, fundraisers, investors and advisors, working in or focused on animal rights, culture, education, the environment, faith, health, human rights, human services and international development. They are witnessing change on the ground, and they describe how they, and their organisations, are responding to the shifts in high-value philanthropy in Europe.

The book includes an extensive indexed *Appendix* of sources to help you find your own way through the philanthropic revolution. Whether you are a philanthropist, a wealth manager, a fundraiser or a student of philanthropy you should find a source here that will help you find out more than I can squeeze into these pages.

TWO

Is philanthropy changing?

In developing this book I had the opportunity to talk to people involved in philanthropy across Europe. The interview guide – these were conversations, not rigidly structured interviews – is given in the Appendix: Interview questions. The viewpoints of these interviewees are included throughout the book, but as an introduction to the interviewees, their responses to the first question in the conversation are shown here.

Is philanthropy in Europe changing?

Is philanthropy in Europe changing? This was the first question that was put to each of the people interviewed for this book. The answer, overwhelmingly, was 'yes'. But there were experienced voices who dissented from this majority view. We will start with them.

It is a continuation

Theresa Lloyd is a philanthropy expert and adviser to non-profit boards. She is the author of four books including *Why Rich People Give* (2004) and, with Dr Beth Breeze, *Richer Lives* (2013). She is more cautious about the level of change:

> 'I don't think it's a revolution. There have always been people who have tried to fill the gaps. It is a continuation. But the focus has changed. For example, in the nineteenth century there was a focus on their employees, and philanthropic factory owners built houses. But now the wealthy say that housing is the role of the state.'

For Theresa Lloyd there is much in philanthropic motivations that has stayed the same:

> 'I do not think that the narrative has changed. There is a passion for the cause, conviction that the organisation will make a difference. There is the focus of giving, with family foundations supporting education, research, the arts. People may use philanthropy as a way of inculcating values in their children. The Sainsbury family for example; each family generation is encouraged to set up trusts and foundations – now there are 20 such trusts. The values are those to do with having respect for others. You want to ensure that your kids have some idea of obligation, morality, of the kind of society they should be living in.'

But Theresa Lloyd acknowledges at least one "significant change, in the UK at least": "For some the priority placed on discretion, and having a low profile, has changed".

David Carrington, a UK-based independent philanthropy professional is also sceptical about some of the 'new' in 'new philanthropy'. "There is a certain amount of reinventing the wheel." He reminds us that, as Professor Adrian Sargeant has repeatedly pointed out "the level of giving is not dramatically changing." The manager of a group of family foundations in the Netherlands agrees with David Carrington's suggestion that we might just be reinventing the wheel; "Yes it is changing. But a lot is new words for old stuff – old wine in new bottles. Impact, for example – what do you call impact? If you ask ten people you will get ten different answers."

The lack of clear data restrains some from pronouncing on the issue. "I really don't know", says Dr Pamala Wiepking, Assistant Professor, Department of Business Society Management, Rotterdam School of Management, at Erasmus University in the Netherlands. "I do have the impression that more major donors are coming out of the closet. Whether they are actually being more generous I don't know."

Marco Demarie, Head of Research in Philanthropy at Compagnia di San Paolo in Turin, Italy, is also not convinced that there is measurable change:

'The public discourse is more aware of private generosity
and there are more ways to give. But actually measuring
what you get? Then you are likely to be disappointed.
There are many more players asking for public generosity.
This has created a small change in the minds of people but
I don't think that this has meant a move from one stage
to another in philanthropy.'

He notes that the change in mind-set is positive toward philanthropy:
"If you had come to Italy 20 years ago you would have seen no
grant making at all. Now people speak highly of philanthropy and
foundations ... there is a professional community that did not exist
in the past."

It is a big yes

The majority of interviewees, however, were convinced that something
substantial is changing in high-value philanthropy in Europe.

Barbara de Colombe, Executive Director, Fondation HEC, the
foundation supporting the leading French business school HEC (École
des Hautes Études Commerciales), was emphatic in her answer:

'Yes! The main changes are that more and more people
give, give larger amounts, and give to new sectors.
Traditional sectors of philanthropy were humanitarian,
social, unemployment, homeless, children ... We now
have more and more people who in the last ten years give
time and money to new sectors, especially education and
higher education.'

Miquel de Paladella is the CEO (Chief Executive Officer) and
co-founder of UpSocial and a Professor at the Institute for Social
Innovation at ESADE (Escola Superior d'Administració i Direcció
d'Empreses), Barcelona. He teaches, with the author, at the University
of Barcelona on the Postgraduate Certificate in Fundraising. He was
formerly with Ashoka, UNICEF and Plan International. "Yes, it is
changing. The important change has been from '*buonismo*' [roughly
translated as a slightly cynical 'goodness'] to an empirical view" that
emphasises impacts and outcomes. "There is frustration that the

problems are unending", says Miquel de Paladella. "Saving the life of one child is not enough – people don't want to help just one. They want system change. People are thinking bigger than before."

Marie-Stéphane Maradeix is CEO (Déléguée générale) of the Fondation Daniel et Nina Carasso, a philanthropic foundation based in Paris and Madrid which derives from the family that owned Danone, the dairy foods company. In her view there has been "a very, very fast evolution of philanthropy in France, since 2003", when the Minister of Culture created a new law offering attractive fiscal concessions for giving.

Arnout Mertens is General Director of the Salvatorian Office for International Aid Support Services (SOFIA) at the Salvatorian Fathers and Brothers, and is responsible for fundraising at this Catholic religious order. Is philanthropy changing in the faith-based sector in Europe? "Absolutely. I have been in sector for eight years. In that time the whole landscape has changed drastically. At a slower pace perhaps [than amongst the rest of the sector] – the faith-based sector is more conservative."

Edwin Venema is Editor in Chief of *De Dikke Blauwe* ('The Big Blue', formerly *Filanthropium Journaal*) in the Netherlands. "It is very clear in my opinion. It is a big yes." The evidence of change in philanthropy is "completely in line with the trends we are monitoring in the last couple of years. There is a big transformation from giving to investing. It is not a total transformation – old school philanthropy is still a very important factor in Dutch philanthropy – but there is a very clear movement toward investing." There is a "whole new dynamic in the market", with old and new organisations seeking private funding and "the new philanthropists, and companies, responding by forming foundations. Everything is moving at the moment."

Jean-Marie Destrée is Assistant Director General of Fondation Caritas France. He underlines the family values of philanthropy, but sees change here also. "Traditionally one left everything to the children. Today people realise that you don't make your children happy simply by passing on the money. It's the transmission of values that matters. Many of the founders of our funds have created them with the hope of transmitting the family values to their children and they involve their children in the boards of the funds."

Marc Wortmann is Executive Director at Alzheimer's Disease International and a former Vice-Chair of the European Fundraising

Association. Is philanthropy changing? "Yes I would think so. Philanthropy is a broad topic. What we see in the Alzheimer's field is that we have been approached by foundations, not us going to them but the other way round. People look over the borders more than they used to." He notes the growing openness of the foundation sector. "They want to be more proactive, be involved in projects and do press releases. Not everyone – some want to be anonymous."

Ulrik Kampmann, director at The National Council for Volunteering and at the Danish Disability Council, is the former Director of Development at Realdania, a philanthropic organisation focusing on bettering the quality of life by improving the built environment. For him, "philanthropy is changing very fast. I have worked in two large Danish foundations and seen that increasingly we are being more strategic. Foundations are focusing on fewer and fewer areas of support – we are eager to create impact."

Serge Raicher is co-founder of EVPA, the European Venture Philanthropy Association. Is philanthropy changing?

> 'Yes it is. The big change is the generational change within the philanthropic community. The second or third generation in a family want to do their own philanthropy. Industrial, tech people are becoming philanthropic. That is an enormous change. This has led to a complete rethinking and a change of mind-set.'

Sophie Vossenaar is Director, Fundraising Europe, at African Parks and serves on the boards of Stichting De Vondelbrug and of FIN, the Dutch Foundations Association. She makes three points about the ways in which philanthropy is changing: the growing interest in social impact investments, the wider social viewpoint of organisations, and the shift from a primarily religious motivation for giving.

> 'Yes, philanthropy is changing. But there is also a lot going on with social investment, where there is a lot of interest in new formats. There is also much more looking at societal issues, not just the cause or the charity. Some charities are responding – for example the Dutch Lung Foundation (Longfonds, http://research.longfonds.nl/)

are looking for a much broader sense of health issues, not just pulmonary health.'

"A lot of philanthropy used to come from old money buying their way into heaven", says Sophie Vossenaar. "The Church had much more influence in the past. Now people have started to realise it is fun to do this."

Karen Wilson is the founder of GV Partners, an adviser on entrepreneurship and investment, and Senior Fellow in the Bruegel (www.bruegel.org) economic think tank in Brussels. Is philanthropy changing?

'Absolutely. The whole social entrepreneurship movement has developed over the last two decades. Across Europe, USA, and the world. People have realised that these social entrepreneurs need financing. At the same time philanthropists are finding that they can't get the impact they want. Philanthropists want to be more proactive – they are asking "Are our grant programmes the best way to leverage their resources?"'

In Karen Wilson's view it is the combination of these ideas – the need for impact, the frustrations over grant programmes, and the new focus on impact investing – that is creating change led by family offices and some foundations. Loans and investments are now seen as better tools than donations: "from the foundations' point of view even if we just get our capital back then that's better than a grant."

Dr Lisa Hehenberger, former Research Director at the European Venture Philanthropy Association and now a professor at ESADE, the Barcelona business school, also gives a clearly positive response when I ask whether high-value philanthropy in Europe is changing.

'Yes it is. Different types of players are entering the space with a philanthropy strategy and an expectation of some spectrum of financial returns. That is new in philanthropy. In the past many foundations were interested in social issues, but their focus was on how much money was dedicated to each area, not on impact. Philanthropy is becoming much more resource oriented.'

Dr Arthur Gautier is Executive Director and Researcher at the ESSEC (formerly l'École Supérieure des Sciences Économiques et Commerciale) Philanthropy Chair in Paris. For him "philanthropy is becoming more mainstream in Europe. People and politicians are advocating for wealthy donors to get involved. There is a growth in interest in this area of philanthropy."

Luis Berruete is Coordinator of Creas, a social investment enterprise in Spain. Is philanthropy changing?

> 'In Spain it is slow. I was many years in fundraising [for Fundación Vicente Ferrer] when what you did was to ask for a donation. Now it is called an "investment". In my view it is moving slowly because there is not yet a track record [for new methods such as social impact investment].'

Change is slow in France, too, according to a philanthropist living there whose billionaire father created a foundation, and who spoke off the record. "France has been terrible at being innovative. Wearing my progressive foundation hat I would say that there are only four really progressive family foundations here." But this did not mean that nothing was happening. "Since 2008 it has definitely changed. There are changes in the fiscal climate and in our culture, with a new generation. It is slow, but definitely moving." (There is more on the legal changes in France in Chapter Eight.)

Judith Symonds is a strategy and philanthropy advisor based in France and working in Europe and in the USA. She teaches New Philanthropy and Social Investing to Master-level students at Sciences Po. Is philanthropy changing?

> 'It's changing, but in different places it is changing in different ways, and at different speeds. In Europe, particularly in France, there is a much greater awareness and interest in the social investing sphere (microfinance, impact investing, social business) and it is important to put it in that context. Impact investment, microfinance and philanthropy have had a tougher ride because of the culture here.'

For Judith Symonds, "it had to do with the culture and the dominant role of the state. There is such '*pudeur*' [modesty] about talking about money in the philanthropic sense. The social investment movement has been one of the watersheds; it's easier when you talk about investment."

Stefania Coni is International Projects Coordinator at the Fondazione CRT (the 'CRT' refers to its former bank, Cassa di Risparmio di Torino) in Turin, Italy. The foundation is one of a group of foundations there created from regional savings banks (see Chapter Eight).

> 'Of course it is changing. You can feel it strongly in Italy. Previously, philanthropy was considered as a donation, to do good to people. This approach has moved toward something different in Italy. I remember we decided to be part of EVPA; it was difficult to talk about non-traditional philanthropy with the board. It was difficult to switch approach. It meant uncovering what you don't know.'

My colleague Martine Godefroid, Managing Director of Factary Europe, formerly with JP Morgan, distinguishes between changes on the surface and the core motivations.

> 'Motivations for philanthropy have not changed. But the perception of responsibility for social change has emerged along with the perception of what philanthropy brings to the donor. When they were motivated principally by religious beliefs, donors felt that getting something back meant that they were not completely disinterested. Now donors say that philanthropy brings a lot to them.'

There is, says Martine Godefroid, a "change in the way people do philanthropy, in the number of people involved, the size of the grants, the fact that very large gifts are made public. A more professional and structured philanthropy is emerging."

Marita Haibach is a consultant, author and trainer, and the co-founder of the Major Giving Institute in Germany. "Yes it has changed. There are mega gifts, at least some €200 million gifts. You also hear about million euro gifts." That is new in Germany – people did not talk about their philanthropy, and it can still be the subject of public criticism. Reflecting a trend that is happening across Europe, and that is reviewed in Part five, she points out that the key measurable trend in Germany is that "people are creating their own foundations".

Dr Atallah Kuttab is the founder of Saaned (www.saaned.com), the philanthropy advisers in the Arab region. He is the founder of the Arab Foundations Forum, and a founding member of the Arab Human Rights Fund. Dr Kuttab has experience in philanthropy across Europe and the Arabic-speaking world, and I invited him to reflect on philanthropy in Europe. He reminded me that the countries of Europe are different, each coming from different traditions – "100 years ago the Prussians were in power in Germany and they build a partnership between philanthropists and the government to run hospitals." He cited the wealth gap as a key driver for change: "the wealth gap has existed for many years in the Arab region. We have the richest and the poorest – think about Qatar and Mauritania, Sudan, and Egypt." (The wealth gap is covered in Chapter Four.)

Wolfgang Hafenmayer is Founding Partner of Challenger73, an impact investment advisory group. His response to my question about change? "I hope so! Philanthropy has been done in a very unprofessional way and not a very impactful way for a long time. It's time it changed." According to him:

> 'the key driver in the sector is professionalism. Businesspeople are entering the sector, people who are much more interested in outcomes, and who structure organisations accordingly ... We still have 18th century patriarchs who just hand out money. But on the other hand we now have professional advisers who say "if you want impact you have to invest".'

But he emphasises that he is not criticising traditional philanthropy: "the old ways of doing philanthropy are still OK – they are not good or bad. You just can't compare those forms of philanthropy with today's impact investors." He underlines the segmentation in the sector. "Philanthropy has lots of different segments – from small gifts to multi-million euro investments. I hope that philanthropy changes in that we become aware of the different [traditional and modern] segments."

It's not science

This collection of views is not scientific proof of change. As we will see throughout this book, there is very little of that – we just do not have the data in Europe to be scientific about high-value philanthropy. But it is, I hope, a faithful reproduction of the views of experts from across Europe, views that include 'no', 'yes', 'somewhat' and 'don't know'. The rest of the book includes more from each of these standpoints; you, in the end, must make up your own mind.

THREE

Not new philanthropy

Introduction

The term 'new philanthropy' is debated in the academic world, but meanwhile it is being used by practitioners in fundraising and philanthropy. Is there a 'new philanthropy'?

Not new philanthropy

The phrase 'new philanthropy' is widely used and abused across the non-profit sector – a Google search on the phrase comes up with 78,400 hits. More than 20 years ago the Salzburg Seminar heard about 'The New Philanthropy for the New Europe' (Brademas et al, 1993). A year later Manuel Parés i Maicas published *The New Philanthropy and Social Communication* in Barcelona (1994). Lilya Wagner at the renowned Center on Philanthropy at Indiana University asked in a 2002 paper if the 'new donor' was the result of 'creation or evolution', and linked the idea of 'new philanthropy' to the practice of 'venture philanthropy'. *The Economist* described 'new philanthropists' in a 2006 special edition (Anon, 2006) on 'The birth of philanthrocapitalism'. 'Charity is history, here comes the new philanthropy', said Miren Gutiérrez in a 2006 article for Inter Press Service. The phrase 'new philanthropy' is the title of Virginie Seghers' 2009 book on high-value philanthropists in France, of a 2015 book by this publisher (Morvaridi, 2015), of blogs on philanthropy (Sibille, 2008 for example). Mark Zuckerberg's 2015 announcement that he was shifting his investments toward social purposes caused a flurry of articles on the 'new philanthropy' in newspapers across Europe, including the Canaries (Anon, 2015b). It is applied retrospectively, for example to the 'new philanthropy of the Edwardian Age' (Laybourn, 2015).

Only a little bit of research will tell you that most of the clever-sounding philanthropic ideas have been tried before. Take social enterprises, for example; it sounds like a new idea, but in fact it has been around for a very long time. Frances Hines (2005) describes social enterprises as 'a well-developed part of the Victorian social landscape', but we can go much further back. For example, the Haseki Sultan Imaret, built in Jerusalem in 1552 and established as a *waqf* or endowed foundation, provided food and shelter for homeless people. It was funded by the rental income from 25 villages and several shops as well as a range of social enterprises including bath houses, two soap factories and 11 flour mills (Peri, 1992). The Imaret is also an example of women's philanthropy: it was commissioned by Haseki Hürrem Sultan and may have been built using her dowry.

'Do you believe in the new philanthropy?' asks a 2011 article (Anon, 2011a) in Ethic, a blog on sustainability. 'No', says Dr Beth Breeze (2011) in *Understanding the Roots of Voluntary Action*, where her chapter on the new philanthropy neatly demolishes any claim you might ever want to make to a 'new philanthropy'. Breeze asks: 'why have claims of a "new philanthropy" gained credence?' In her view the fantasy of a new philanthropy is the result of a 'loss of historical memory', a 'preference for novelty' and 'a desire by contemporary givers to appear distinctive and to distance themselves from the negative connotations of the traditional meanings of philanthropy'.

Breeze lists more past claims for a new philanthropy – going back at least as far as 1934, when Elizabeth Macadam published *The New Philanthropy*. Breeze notes that many – perhaps most – of the characteristics of 'new philanthropy' can be found in 19th century London, when a group of philanthropists created the Society for Bettering the Condition and Increasing the Comforts of the Poor (SBCP), with the objective of developing 'a new legion of scientific philanthropists' – meaning people who approach their philanthropy from an analytical standpoint. As Jonathan Fowler (2011) points out, the SBCP aimed to measure scientifically and systematically 'those things which experience hath ascertained to be beneficial to the poor'; in other words 'impact' writ differently.

Timothy Ogden, who serves on the board of Give Well (www.givewell.org/), debunks the idea that today's donors are different. In an article in *Alliance* in 2015 he questions the common statement that 'today's donors are different … they care about measuring impact'. He asks: 'did earlier philanthropists really NOT care about impact?' and demonstrates that they did indeed care. These earlier philanthropists used different business models to measure impact and Ogden argues that 'today's donors are different when it comes to impact – not in how much they care about it but in how they approach it'. They define and measure impact using tools and data that were simply unavailable 20 years ago. He takes a critical view, noting the irony that the impact movement has not yet provided evidence of its own impact on the wider philanthropic community. The assumption that donors wanted more information to enable them to measure impact was behind the creation in 2002 of New Philanthropy Capital, the London-based non-profit sector think tank, research centre and consultancy. But Tris Lumley, the organisation's Director of Development, admitted in a 2015 article (Milner, 2015), 'that turned out to be a shaky assumption. Donors who were actively seeking out the highest social returns from their giving were in the minority, as were charities that were able to clearly communicate their impact.'

And yet we know of younger donors who are clearly doing their philanthropy in ways that differ from their parents. People who are thinking differently about impact, about organisational sustainability, and about their engagement in the organisations that they support. There is evidence for a segmentation of the high-value philanthropic market, for the emergence of groups with identifiably different attitudes to giving (see Chapter Four).

Given this history and the 'shaky assumptions' about what, precisely, 'new philanthropy' is, it makes no sense to use the term. It is more useful to adapt the phrase that the venerable Lester Salamon uses in his 2014 book, where he writes about 'the revolution on the frontiers of philanthropy'. If we consider a revolution in the sense of a wheel turning then we are indeed in the midst of a revolution, another revolution, in high-value philanthropy in Europe.

Previous revolutions

There have been at least three previous revolutions in philanthropy in Europe – or rather in Christian Europe. Spain of the 'Moors' had demonstrated philanthropy in health, education and poverty at least since the 10th century (Carballeira Debasa, 2012). This had in turn been 'influenced by earlier civilizations including ancient Mesopotamia, Greece, Rome and pre-Islamic Arabs' (MacDonald and Tayart de Borms, 2008, p 22). Models for charitable trusts and foundations in Europe may be based on the *awqaf* (endowed foundations, *waqf* in the singular) of Islam; 'Oxford University would seem to represent the quintessential English academic institution' writes Monica Gaudiosi (1998, p 1231), 'yet, in its early phases of development Oxford may have owed much to the Islamic legal institution of *waqf*, charitable trust.' Charles Debbasch (1987) gives foundations a Catholic Christian heritage, saying that the Edict of Milan, 313, suggested the creation of foundations via donations, but says that it was Pope Innocent IV in the 13th century who created foundations with legal personality in order to help hospitals.

In Christian Europe, the first of the philanthropic revolutions came between the 4th and 6th centuries with the 'invention' of poverty and the church's role in institutionalising the 'charity' that supported it (Magnani, 2009). If philanthropy in the Middle Ages was the purview of religious elites (Bekkers and Wiepking, 2015), then the second revolution was when it emerged as a subject for merchants and industrialists. At that time philanthropy began to be regulated by the state; in 1601 the Statute of Charitable Uses Act was passed by England's Queen Elizabeth I, 'An Acte to redresse the Misemployment of Landes, Goodes, and Stockes of Money heretofore given to Charitable Uses'. These were regulations that 'sought to rationalize the administration of private charities – to specify the purposes for which funds could be devoted to charity, to ensure such funds were applied to the uses specified by donors, and to place the private charity under the supervision of the State' (Seel, 2006).

The third revolution was the development of the welfare state. As Bekkers and Wiepking (2015, p 2) point out, the Dutch government during the early part of the 20th century:

> introduced several laws for social security arrangements, including arrangements for those who could no longer work because of an injury (1901), those who fell ill (1913 and 1930), those of older age (1919), and those in need of general assistance (1965). These laws slowly diminished

the need for private poor relief organized by religious institutions and made welfare a responsibility of the state.

This pattern was repeated elsewhere in Europe to varying degrees.

But 'these changes were by no means the end of philanthropy in the Netherlands. The existing religious charities remained active, but shifted their focus to groups in society that the state found difficult to reach, such as the homeless, the addicted and the mentally ill. The second half of the twentieth century also saw a surge of new religious and secular philanthropic organizations, who focused their attention on public goods and services that were perceived to be outside the realm of core government tasks: for example, in the areas of human rights, international relief, culture, sports, and recreation.'

We should not be surprised if we are now facing the fourth revolution in European philanthropy. The wheel has turned before, but it is spinning faster today. We had better be prepared.

New people

PART TWO

New people

FOUR

The philanthropists

This section argues that there are new people in Europe with new ideas on philanthropy.

Sitting on the floor

European Foundation Centre (EFC) conferences used to be very starched events, full of older white men in suits and ties, exchanging knowing nods. A closed shop for the elder statesman. Come to an EFC conference now, and you will see a very different range of people. The old guard is still there, but today you will find delegates in their 20s sitting on the floor between a sharp-suited Swiss banker and a French investment manager. The people involved in philanthropy in Europe are changing, or at least that is how it looks.

There is anecdotal evidence from fundraisers, wealth advisers and foundations that there is a new generation of philanthropists, people with self-made wealth. Beyond the anecdotes, there is also evidence of change: the growth of venture philanthropy in Europe, the emergence of women as a force in philanthropy, and the rapid growth in the numbers of foundations in Europe. This new generation is said to have views on philanthropy that differ from those of their parents or grandparents, to want to be strategic with their giving, to 'invest' rather than 'give'. This shift in thinking reflects a wider social change in which:

> people and organisations active in civil society increasingly view themselves as a 'source of inspiration and ideas for social change'. Dedicated citizens have become more impatient and no longer wait for others to provide

solutions, and instead take the initiative, develop solutions themselves, and put them into practice. (Anon, 2015c)

In Part two I will focus on these people. I will review the forces that appear to be shaping high-value philanthropy in Europe, look at research in this field, and try to understand what is happening with wealth, and attitudes to wealth, in Europe.

The existence of circles and networks of philanthropists is evidence of change in philanthropy in Europe. To come out about your philanthropy, your motivations, your wealth and your feelings in a circle of peers – none of this would have been possible, or polite, in the older traditions of giving in Europe. People learn about philanthropy, and learn how to be strategic with their philanthropy from others in their circle, and this desire to learn is an important ingredient in the revolution in philanthropy in Europe. Circles and networks of philanthropists are growing across Europe and in Chapter five I will review who they are and uncover the challenges they face.

After a period in which women's philanthropy flourished in the 19th and early 20th century the topic slipped quietly away from view. Today the situation of women in Europe is very different; women's rights are protected by law – or at least some of them are – women are a potent force in the economy as generators of wealth and as consumers, and women are confirming that the social changes are here to stay. Is this new female social and economic capital being turned into philanthropy? Are women in Europe approaching philanthropy differently? In Chapter Six, we will look for answers to these questions, and make a brief comparison with the situation in the USA where networks of women philanthropists such as Women Moving Millions have become so prominent.

One of the most significant evolutions in philanthropy in Europe has been the arrival of the 'venture philanthropists'. The model was originally devised at Harvard University (Letts, Ryan and Grossman, 1997) in the late 1990s and turned into practice by the Community Foundation of Silicon Valley, California. In venture philanthropy, the philanthropist applies many of the techniques relevant to venture capital investment to their philanthropy. The aim is to generate measurable social or environmental impact with tailored finance including grants, debt and equity, and to provide non-financial organisational support to strengthen and grow the social purpose organisation. While the numbers of organisations practising venture philanthropy is small – the European Venture Philanthropy Association had just over 200 members in 2016 – their impact is disproportional, with a number of large, and some very large European foundations adopting parts of the venture philanthropy model. Venture philanthropy – at least as it is defined in Europe – merges at the edges with impact investment and this has the potential to unleash very large sums of money into the social and environmental fields. We will review what is happening in venture philanthropy in Europe in Chapter Seven.

High-value philanthropy is very welcome, almost all of the time. But it does create some problems. One of them is the Direct to Beneficiary problem. Instead of giving to a northern NGO in order that they support a partner and its project, some donors are getting on a plane to the Global South and giving directly to projects. There is an apocryphal tale of the well-meaning scions of a wealthy family travelling business class to the Democratic Republic of the Congo, hiring a 4x4 and donating cash to the first project they found. Is this a threat to the model that has supported Europe's NGOs since the 20th century?

And there are questions, many of them, about high-value philanthropy. Is it right that people who have the means should be, or could be, influencing the directions of social or environmental action? I will summarise the arguments in this section.

Back to the future

As we saw in Chapter One, the Introduction to this book, there is a revolution happening in philanthropy. It is not a revolution in the 'to the barricades!' sense, but it is certainly a revolution in the literal sense – the turning of a circle so that we are shown an edge that we, in our lifetimes, have not seen before. New people are trying out new ideas – with ancient and traceable roots – in the hope that these will do more good for humankind than the charity of their parents and grandparents. In the process they are uncovering a philanthropy that was private, secretive, anonymised.

Four people have created much of this revolution, three from the present and one from the past. Bill and Melinda Gates and their friend Warren Buffett have become flagship philanthropists, pledging the bulk of their huge wealth to the cause and creating a gargantuan foundation.

'With their substantial funding and assertive manner, they have shaped the public perception of foundations on an international level in recent years', said one recent report (Anon, 2015c).

Many of the interviewees who participated in the preparation of this book mentioned the Gates and their giving. "Bill Gates is the model for Europe", says Miquel de Paladella in Barcelona. "His personal involvement, his ability to choose causes in a more scientific way ... Bill Gates would have had impact even if his foundation had been five times, ten times smaller." Ulrik Kampmann agrees, and explains the nuances from a Scandinavian perspective.

> 'The Danish foundations' primary inspiration is from the USA. When I first started it was Gates' seven big challenges to global health (http://grandchallenges.org/). We have not managed to meet that grand challenge in the way Gates has done. They [the US foundations] are very strategic. We are trying to be catalytic in our approach and that is also inspired by the USA. We are not following the US model but we are inspired by it.'

There is one other, a man who links 19th century philanthropy with today's revolution.

Andrew Carnegie was born in Dunfermline, Scotland on 25 November 1835, the elder of two sons of William and Margaret Morrison Carnegie. William had been a hand-loom weaver but the new water-powered looms led to him losing his job and with Andrew aged just 13 the family migrated to Allegheny, Pennsylvania. Andrew Carnegie's first job was as a bobbin boy in a cotton mill; he worked as a messenger and then, aged 17, became personal telegrapher for Thomas A. Scott, superintendent of the Pennsylvania Railroad's Western Division. He advanced rapidly through the railroad hierarchy, eventually taking over from Mr Scott as district superintendent. In 1865, Carnegie left the railroad and went into business for himself. A decade later he moved into the steel industry, becoming the most powerful partner in the country's largest and most successful steel company, Carnegie Steel. In 1901 he sold his interest to J.P. Morgan for US$200 million. Mr Morgan told Carnegie that he was now 'the richest man in the world' (Carnegie, 2006, p vii).

Mr Carnegie bequeathed to us his Gospel of Wealth. Originally written as an essay on 'Wealth' for the June 1889 edition of the *North American Review*, it caused so much interest that it was reprinted in England for the *Pall Mall Gazette* as 'The Gospel of Wealth'. Talk to philanthropists today – especially venture philanthropists – and you will find that many have read the Gospel of Wealth and base much of their thinking on the ideas that Mr Carnegie left us.

Mr Carnegie had made his wealth in his lifetime. He believed that wealth was not something that should be passed from parent to child: 'great sums bequeathed oftener work more for the injury than for the good of the recipients'. He encourages the wealthy person to:

> set an example of modest, unostentatious living … to provide moderately for the legitimate wants of those dependent upon him; and after doing so to consider all surplus revenues which come to him simply as trust funds which he is called upon to administer … to produce the most beneficial results for the community.

Great wealth should be used in the person's lifetime to carry out the good works that she or he felt strongly about. We can see the roots of The Giving Pledge (http://givingpledge.org), the public commitment to give half of one's wealth to philanthropy, in the writings of Andrew Carnegie. At the date of writing 148 billionaires had signed up to the Pledge, which has been mirrored in one European country with *De Blauwe Belofte*, the Blue Pledge (www.deblauwebelofte.nl), funded by the Lenthe Foundation aiming to persuade wealthy people in the Netherlands to donate or socially invest at least 10% of their fortune.

Mr Carnegie believed that the wealthy person should not just respond to whatever charitable whims came her way, but should seek out causes that match her interests. (I am using 'her' deliberately and provocatively here; my compatriot Carnegie refers solely to 'the wealthy man' and 'him' throughout his Gospel.) This is strategic philanthropy, a term not used by Mr Carnegie but in common use amongst the crème de la crème of European giving today.

Why are people changing their philanthropy?

There are many forces shaping high-value philanthropy, some working in conjunction, others in conflict with each other. Karen Wilson illustrates some of these forces amongst Millennials (born 1982–2000). Talking about the Social Enterprise Initiative at Harvard University she says that "the Millennial generation wanted to act socially. At the same time, government budgets were being cut. These factors combined with improved communications [the Internet], meaning we could hear from all around world." Edwin Venema, Editor in Chief of *De Dikke Blauwe* in the Netherlands, illustrates the effect of the new generation in the Netherlands:

> 'It is partly a generational thing. I meet a lot of major donors. Businessmen who want to approach philanthropy in a more business-like manner, looking for social profit and financial profit. On the demand side, it is not only charities that are asking for contributions; a lot of new social enterprises are also fundraising, and they are becoming a big thing in the Netherlands. Social enterprises are becoming a competitor for the [traditional] non-profit sector. There is also a big grey area of all the possible mixes and combinations of giving and investing – it's very fluid, at the moment. It is very difficult to establish whether something is old school giving, or 100% investment. It is a bit of a semantic thing. There is a complete new range of intermediary stages between the two.'

Edwin's description highlights two of the themes that recur in any analysis of high-value philanthropy. First, our knowledge is based on perceptions, not evidence. This is not meant as a criticism of Edwin's views but simply reflects the fact that in Europe we have very little objective evidence that applies to high-value philanthropy. The Netherlands is a possible exception thanks to the Giving in the Netherlands Panel Survey (GINPS) but even here the data is limited; the definition of a 'high net worth' household is one where the 'income and equity combined is at least €60,000' (Bekkers, Boonstoppel and de Wit, 2013) – some way from the income or asset wealth that would be required to make a gift that we might take to be 'high-value philanthropy'. Second, Edwin emphasises the issue of definitions: "old school giving, or 100% investment". The lack of definitions dogs the study of high-value philanthropy. What is a 'major gift' for example? One study in Holland defines a major donor as anyone giving €1,000 or more (Peerdeman, 2015). As Professor Adrian Sargeant has pointed out, there is:

> no universally accepted definition of what constitutes a major gift. This is seen as a relative concept which is largely dependent on organizational size. Some non-profits may consider a major gift to be $1,000, while others will only accord donations worth $1 million (or more) the same status. (Sargeant, Eisenstein and Kottasz, 2015)

The threshold for high-value philanthropy is undefined and the result is that the market, and the forces that shape it, are hard to measure objectively.

Money, mind or society?

Pamala Wiepking's doctoral thesis is one of the clearest descriptions of the forces around philanthropy in Europe, and the ways in which academics have tried to understand them. She reviews the three main lines of research into charitable giving; economic, psychological and sociological (Wiepking, 2008).

Economic research has focused on income, finding that people on higher incomes give more, and on price effects, showing that where the price of giving to charity is reduced by tax relief, people give more. Economists have also studied the motivations for giving as an equilibrium between private benefits (the warm glow one gets when one makes a donation) and public benefits (the child who is inoculated or the homeless person who is fed as the result of your gift).

Crowding out and crowding in

Economists have attempted to measure private versus public benefits by considering state expenditure. If you are a donor who supports your local hospital and who donates, say, €100 per annum to the hospital, what do you do in the (admittedly unlikely) situation in which the government increases its grants to the hospital? Economists argue that if you were solely motivated by private benefits (the warm glow) then you would continue to give €100 despite the increase in government grants. If you were only interested in public benefits then you would reduce your gift. This is the effect known as 'crowding out', where private donations are 'crowded out' by public expenditure. This book is not the place for a detailed analysis of an argument that has run through economics since the 1970s. The debate rages over the cause of changing levels of donation; can this be attributed to increasing or decreasing government expenditure?

Abrams and Schmitz (1984), using US data from 1979, found that the neediness of beneficiaries and the level of governmental aid play a role in determining private charitable contributions. But James Andreoni and Abigail Payne (2010) say that 'a growing body of evidence from both experimental and survey data, however, questions this assumption'. As they and others point out, 'the theory [that individual donors will reduce giving to charity by the amount of government grants] also requires that donors are aware of the fluctuations in government grants received by the charity and respond accordingly'. In Europe we can state categorically (see Part four, Transparency) that it is highly unlikely that donors know much at all about the levels of government grants. In their 2010 paper Andreoni and Payne do find crowding out, but say that most of it 'is the result of reduced fund-raising'. In other words, in their view, winning government grants means that organisations engage less in private sector fundraising. Three years later, and now joined by Professor Sarah Smith of the University of Bristol, the researchers continued to show the subtleties at play in this over-simple model: reviewing grants from a UK lottery grant programme they find that 'grants do not crowd out other sources of income' and in fact that 'grants may improve a charity's chances of survival' (Andreoni, Payne and Smith, 2014, p 85).

Bruce Kingma's 1989 study of crowding out is often cited, because it uses household data (again, from the USA) on donations to public radio to establish 'an accurate measurement of the crowd-out effect'. But when, 15 years later, Sonia Manzoor and John Straub (2005) used the same methodology on very similar data they found that Kingma's estimate of crowding out was 'not robust'. These questions of methodology appear in a 2016 paper by Arjen de Wit and René Bekkers (de Wit and Bekkers, 2016) who find differences in results depending on whether the researchers include income from government grants or that from government contracts, and find reversals of crowding-out under different experimental conditions.

This substantial effort by economists seems designed to provide an answer to a question that is self-evident. When the economists find that, yes, we do enjoy the private benefits (the 'warm glow') of giving, they describe us as 'impure philanthropists'. We are all, it seems, impure. In an interview with Pamala Wiekpking for this book, I asked her about this research:

> 'I don't like many of the studies on crowding out. Economists think that altruism can be tested. I don't believe people think like that. All this crowding out literature is to prove altruism, but we already know that people are not "pure altruists". So they call it "impure altruism". I'm interested in that aspect, in the warm glow.'

She reminds me that "people typically have no clue what the government is contributing to those causes", so the supposed motor behind crowding out may not exist at all.

Psychologists have looked at prosocial behaviour, acts that are defined by some part of society as beneficial to others, such as volunteering. Donating to a non-profit is one specific type of prosocial behaviour in which there is normally an intermediary (the non-profit) between the donor and the beneficiary. There is some evidence that the presence of the intermediary diminishes the perceived benefits of giving; people feel happier when they give to a person connected with the cause (Aknin et al, 2013). This is the fundraising strategy used in much high-value philanthropy, where fundraisers aim to put the donor into direct contact with the beneficiary; many NGOs organise site visits for their high-value donors for example, and universities offer events for high-value scholarship donors where donors meet scholars. The Direct to Donor issue (see below) may be linked to this effect.

Sociologists, according to Wiepking, have dedicated little time to individual charitable giving. Wiepking argues that there are good theoretical models in sociology that can help us understand philanthropy. First, people who participate in social groups with positive norms for charitable giving act according to those norms. Rotary Club members give more because their fellows do. This has of course become a strategy in fundraising: create a group with a new higher norm for giving and encourage your donors to join it. These groups have various names, but you might recognise 'The President's Circle', or 'The Founders Club' or similar vehicles at your *alma mater*, or 'The Conductor's Circle' at your local theatre. Madrid's Teatro Real, for example, currently offers four circles for donors – Benefactor, Collaborator, Sponsor and Maecenas.

Second, sociologists argue that people use philanthropy to distinguish themselves from the rest of society, as an elite. In sociological terminology this is using cultural and economic capital to create and reproduce social inequalities. This idea is recurrent through research into philanthropy: that by making a donation, especially a large donation, an individual cements their place in society as a member of the elite.

Third, the more social capital we have – the larger our network of friends, for example – the more likely we are to be asked, and the easier (and thus cheaper) it is for us to check the credentials of the person or organisation asking us. Studies such as Brown and Ferris (2007) in the USA seem to show that people with wider associational networks, and greater trust in their community, are more generous. In recent years fundraisers have turned to network research and the increasing volumes of public domain information on personal connections, to identify people of wealth with large networks of contacts (my own company, Factary, has conducted many such research projects using its 'Factary Atom' tool).

Finally, sociologists measure confidence and trust in others, elements that affect whether we give and who we give to. René Bekkers (2006; Bekkers, R. et al., 2010) emphasises the importance of confidence in the fundraising organisation, especially where it provides intangible services (cultural or religious organisations for example) or services far away such as development NGOs. I shall return to this topic – trust in the fundraising organisation – throughout this book because it is both a brake on the development of high-value philanthropy in Europe, and the focus of much concern in fundraising.

Wiepking describes the idea of a 'giving standard' – the norms about levels of giving in specific situations that people in different income groups share. One explanation of what is happening in philanthropy in Europe is simply that this giving standard amongst people of wealth is shifting. Review a database of regular donors to any of Europe's leading

NGOs and you will find, with a bit of hunting, tens or hundreds of people of wealth. Their donations, in the main, will be very modest. For example, an analysis of the database of regular donors to a NGO in Spain revealed four UHNWIs (Ultra High Net Worth Individuals) each with over $30 million in investible assets. These donors were giving an average of €25 per month. Their 'giving standard' was €25, not €25,000 or €250,000. We suggest in Part four that this may be the result of a gap at the top; Europeans in the highest income groups are not sharing information about their gifts, and thus are not creating a 'giving standard' for high-value philanthropy.

Possible causes of change

We might speculate across a huge range of social changes, from the emancipation of women to the decline in organised religion, to explain the evolution of philanthropy in Europe. Here is a selection that has appeared in past research:

- The personal situation of the philanthropist
  - Wealth
  - Demographics (for example, age at which people start high-value philanthropy)
- Her or his beliefs
  - Religion, political views and personal tastes and preferences
  - The influence of easier travel, internet and connectivity on these beliefs, values and taste
- Engagement and personal experience
  - Engagement in volunteering
  - Awareness of need
  - Solicitation (asking – being asked more, or asked differently)
  - Awareness of impact
  - Perception of efficacy, or value for money
- Information and advice
  - Transparency in the social sector in Europe
  - The growth in the numbers of professional philanthropic advisers
- The economic environment
  - Economic stability
  - The wealth gap
  - Fiscal encouragement of giving

- New structures and tools (or tools from other sectors now applied to philanthropy) such as social enterprises, donor circles, venture philanthropy, Social Impact Bonds, loans.

There is no room here for so much speculation, so I am going to focus on those that appear most relevant to high-value philanthropy in Europe, starting with wealth and its corollary, poverty. We will see that the market is segmented, with philanthropy having evolved in different ways in various social groups.

The personal situation of the philanthropist: wealth

Wolfgang Hafenmayer, founding partner of Challenger73, an impact investment advisory group, puts wealth into context. "Until the late 1970s people did not make billions by the time they were 30. Very few people, then, could stop working for money before their 40th birthday. All of a sudden you had people who made large amounts of money early in life." For Hafenmayer this is the:

> 'main driver that explains why the philanthropy industry has grown so much. Why was venture philanthropy (VP) started by [people from] private equity? Because they had made money fast and young. Once they had satisfied their material needs, they started to look for meaning; the third or fourth car was not going to make them more fulfilled … They started working not for money but for fulfilment.'

Theresa Lloyd agrees, comparing the 1989 Sunday Times Rich List, which was 75% inherited wealth, with today's list, which is 80% self-made wealth. This shift in how wealth is made "has a profound difference on the questions that people ask and their expectations", she says.

Marie-Stéphane Maradeix, CEO (Déléguée générale) of the Fondation Daniel et Nina Carasso, summarised the changing nature of wealth. "Recently, people have become rich very rapidly, thanks to the dot-com boom, finances, telecoms … they have made their fortune fast, and it may have nothing or little to do with their parents. They have built a fortune by the time they are 50." The first thing they do, says Maradeix, is to "safeguard their children. Once they have done that they decide: 'I will step back [from business] and create pleasure for me, and pleasure for others.'" The attitudes of new wealth to the world that surrounds it may be different, she says, because many have come from families that were not historically wealthy: "the new rich are better connected to the society around them ... They have lived through the economic crises of recent years."

Often, says Wolfgang Hafenmayer:

> 'they start quite traditionally, volunteering with a charity. Then they go and help an NGO. They find a community of like-minded people in the Venture Philanthropy space – they want to use their skills to make an impact. All through their working life they have absorbed certain assumptions about efficiency, risk, investment, change ... The type of discussion they can have within the venture philanthropy field is a very logical discussion for them.'

A Fondation de France study (de Laurens and Rozier, 2012) showed that between 2000 and 2012, 67% of people setting up philanthropic foundations in France had made their wealth in their own lifetime, making the point that new wealth is a strong driver to philanthropy. There are many implications in this relatively simple shift. Being philanthropic during a lifetime (as opposed to leaving a vast sum to charity in a legacy) means, for many European philanthropists, direct engagement with the cause. "I wanted hands-on involvement – my two brothers and my sister too", said a member of a wealthy Dutch family, philanthropist and social investor who was interviewed for this book.

For richer for poorer: the wealth gaps

But wealth is a precursor for high-value philanthropy; to give a lot you must have a lot. How much is a lot? The answer is relative. In 2016 we crossed a Rubicon: the share of the wealth of the richest 1% of the population exceeded that of the remaining 99% of people for the first time in history (Cukier, 2015).

There is an uneasy relationship between wealth and philanthropy. A philanthropist living in France whose father created a foundation, and who spoke off the record, reminded me of the "complex relationship that the French have with money. It was not chic or elegant to boast about philanthropy; if you boasted publicly then you'd get the *huissiers* [law court officers who serve injunctions, in this case for tax]". People who are philanthropic, and wealthy, are aware that there is a wide gap between rich and poor, and that this is not a healthy situation. Warren Buffett told a Senate Finance Committee meeting in 2007 that "in a country [the USA] that prides itself on equality of opportunity, it's becoming anything but that as the gap between the super-rich and the middle class is widening". A tax on inherited estates is necessary, in Mr Buffett's view to "curb the movement of a democracy toward a plutocracy" (www.reuters.com/article/us-buffett-congress-idUSN1442383020071114).

Aside from concerns over plutocracy, there are more mundane concerns about the growing wealth gap, and they relate directly to poverty, the object of much of philanthropy. As the OECD has shown, 'higher inequality lowers economic growth. Increasing income inequality by 1 Gini point[1] lowers GDP per capita growth by 0.1% per year' (Cingano and Förster, 2014). The growing wealth gap deserves a moral and political critique too, which we can understand by simply pointing out the charitable dilemma that while donations from people of wealth are welcome, many non-profits exist to eradicate the poverty that is the obverse of that same wealth.

"There is a growing concern about inequalities," says Dr Arthur Gautier, Executive Director and Researcher at the ESSEC Philanthropy Chair.

'Everyone knows that the wealthy got wealthier in recent years. There is more pressure on wealthy people to justify their wealth, to think about how their wealth is making a positive difference, more pressure now for the financial elite to play a bigger role in addressing these inequalities. Elites are openly challenging their peers to do something. This is changing the way people think about their philanthropy.'

'Wealth' and 'poverty' are relative terms. At the top end the word is generally defined by the HNWI/UHNWI measures: High Net Worth Individuals are defined as having US$1 million or more in investable assets, and UHNWIs as having US$30 million or more. As commonly applied it is a fixed measure. At the bottom end, poverty is defined in terms of median (mid-range) income. This is 'relative poverty', meaning, in the OECD (Organisation for Economic Co-operation and Development) definition (www.oecd-ilibrary.org/sites/factbook-2010-en/11/02/02/index.html?itemId=/content/chapter/factbook-2010-89-en), living below the 'poverty line' – taken as half the median household income. The 'poverty gap' is the percentage by which the mean income of the poor falls below the poverty line.

The poverty gap

To clarify these mathematical terms let us take two tiny EU states, Ricadonia and Povronia, each with 100 people living in them. In Ricadonia, 60 people earn €20,000 per year, 30 earn €15,000 and 10 earn €7,000. The median (mid-range) wage is thus €15,000 and the poverty line is half of that – €7,500. The poor – the 10 citizens of Ricadonia who earn less than €7,500 – earn €7,000, which is 7% below the poverty line. That 7% represents the depth of poverty in Ricadonia. It also shows how much would be required to bring a poor person in Ricadonia out of poverty – in this case, €500. Meanwhile, over in Povronia 60 people earn €20,000, 20 people earn €7,500 and 20 earn €2,500. The median wage is now €7,500 and the poverty line is €3,750. The poverty gap is thus 50% - the poorest people would have to earn an additional €1,250 to catch up with half the median wage. Notice that the number of wealthy people in Povronia (60) is the same as in Ricadonia. Driving through the two countries you might not notice the difference. Poverty is often invisible.

Measuring inequality

Ricadonia and Povronia are fictional. But the poverty gap is not so far from the truth. In 2010 the poverty gap in Spain was 42% and in the UK 35%. Meanwhile in Finland it was 19% and in France 24% (OECD, 2014).

Thomas Piketty's 1997 book about the economy of inequality is now in its seventh edition (Piketty, 2015). Piketty takes us through the economy of inequality and shows that the ratio between the lowest

10% by income and the highest 10% grew by almost half in the USA, from a multiple of 3.2 to one of 4.5 between 1970 and 1990. The ratio grew by 32% in the UK, with most of that growth in the decade 1980–1990. Meanwhile, Sweden's ratio did not change during the same period, remaining substantially lower than that of the US and UK, and in France the ratio decreased over the period, from 3.7 to 3.2.

The poverty gap and philanthropy

It appears, on the basis of these (selected) figures, that countries which in 1990 were developing as active markets for high-value philanthropy (principally the USA and the UK) were countries with a wide gap between those on low incomes and those on high incomes. Given (a) that 'poverty' is a relative term with 'relative poverty' being defined with reference to a median salary, and (b) that we know there to be a relationship between donation size and income, it is very tempting to postulate that high-value philanthropy may be closely linked to the ratio of high incomes to low incomes.

Edward Wolff found in 2001 that for the richest 1% of households in the USA, changes in inequality are related to the 'degree of philanthropic giving relative to personal income'. Since this group make around half of all charitable contributions in the USA, the effect is notable. In a study in Canada, Payne and Smith showed in 2015 that increases in income inequality correlates to increases in giving. Yen-Sheng Chiang (2015) studied this process using laboratory experiments in which 'wealthy' and 'poor' people interacted in different networks. In networks that 'link together very rich and very poor actors, and thus create profound income discrepancies in actors' local neighbourhoods', people respond by giving more. 'We suspect that egalitarian sharing is triggered when (local) inequality is large enough', says Chiang. This process may be driven by an 'automatic sense of morality', according to Carolyn Declerck, a University of Antwerp researcher quoted in *New Scientist* (Pearson, 2009).

Behind this are two connected ideas: that the 'supply' side of high-value philanthropy is stronger with a larger income gap (people of wealth simply have more) and that the 'demand' side is also stronger with a larger income gap (poor people, in greater relative poverty, are in greater need).

Serge Raicher debated this point. Is the wealth gap a driver of philanthropy?

> 'I would assume intellectually you'd think yes. Nevertheless, just five or ten people living in poverty are already too many. The crisis in Spain [Serge knows the country well] reminds us that we are not just looking at those guys who don't want to work. The coexistence of people of wealth with people in poverty has clearly been an element. Increasingly we are saying "there are people in my own city who are in need". Need is getting closer and closer.'

Andrew Carnegie, writing his 'Gospel of Wealth' in 1889, describes the gap between rich and poor in terms of a lack of understanding. As the result of industrialisation, he says, 'rigid castes are formed, and, as usual, mutual ignorance breeds mutual distrust. Each Caste [sic] is without sympathy for the other, and ready to credit anything disparaging in regard to it' (Carnegie, 2006, p 2).

A culture of wealth, and of philanthropy?

Why are some countries more equal in wealth than others?

Thomas Piketty writes about this in terms of taxation. He argues that the 'principal characteristic of contemporary redistribution via taxation, which one can observe in all the Western countries ... [is that] it does not actually create any significant financial redistribution between working people'. Tax in the modern Western economies is not moving funds from rich to poor. Tax is not closing the gap. Piketty continues: 'those countries in which the household revenue gap is small are the countries where the inequality in salaries is slight, and vice versa'.

In other words, it is the society itself, not the tax system, that defines the size of the gap. Could it be that those social attitudes – in Sweden for example – that create a more equal society are attitudes contrary to the development of a substantial high-value philanthropy market? Or the obverse (and slightly more understandable): could social attitudes that allow for the creation of more wealth (and thus, by definition, more poverty) encourage the creation of a high-value philanthropy market?

The existence of these social attitudes favouring equality or favouring wealth is at the heart of a constant debate in Europe. The debate often starts with a rejection; "No, we can't do major donor fundraising here; it is not in our culture." The speaker goes on to say that "we don't have a culture of that kind of philanthropy" or "it just would not be accepted here". I have spent many years rejecting this argument and demonstrating that, indeed, you can do major donor fundraising in almost any country (and certainly in any country in Europe). I have used examples from history (there are many) to demonstrate that whether you are in Cadiz, Chartres or Cambridge you live with a long history of high-value philanthropy and that therefore there is no cultural barrier to starting a major donor programme.

Perhaps I have been wrong. By implying that it is social attitude, not the fiscal state, that determines the revenue gap, Piketty argues that there are cultural differences – that Sweden is indeed different from England. And if you will follow me to the next wobbly stone out on this very rocky voyage of speculation and accept, for the sake of argument, my postulation that a larger poverty gap means a larger market for high-value philanthropy, then you have to say that I am wrong: that there is, indeed, a "culture of that kind of philanthropy" and that some places have that culture in abundance (UK, USA) and some barely at all. There are exceptions to this argument – for example, Spain has a substantial wealth gap but, until recently, was not known as a market for high-value philanthropy. But the coincidences between European countries with larger wealth gaps and better developed high-value philanthropy markets is interesting, and may be worthy of further research.

Do I like my wealth?

Philanthropy is one way of making wealth an easier burden to bear. Professional advisers and wealth managers know this and, especially with younger inheritors, use philanthropy as a way of coming to terms with wealth.

The relationship between an individual and her, perhaps especially her, wealth in Europe is not an easy one. Many people of wealth across Europe regard the expression of that wealth as vulgar or uneducated and some of our wealthiest citizens lead lives so private, so 'normal', that their wealth is invisible to even their closest neighbours. Author and consultant Marita Haibach co-founded Pecunia, the German network of women with inherited wealth. "Many of the women were not positive about their wealth", she said, "it was bad money." Sophie Vossenaar made a similar point; passing wealth on to the next generation is not going to help the youngsters build their own lives. "People did not want to burden their kids with wealth."

But it is not all negative. People are coming out about their wealth, says Vossenaar.

> 'In the mid-1990s in the Netherlands there was the first wave of exits from IT businesses. This was new money. In the past people were "well to do", but now they had more money than they were ever going to be able to spend in their lifetimes. We had the start of the Quote 500 [the Dutch rich list] – wealth was much more out there.'

Wealth in Europe is increasingly 'out there' in the form of philanthropy – think of the Coutts Million Dollar Donors Report (Anon, 2015h) or the publication by French business school HEC of the names of key donors to their campaign.

Religion as a motivation

In broad population studies, religion and religiosity appear to be linked to giving. (For a compilation of research see Bekkers and Wiepking, 2011. For detailed analysis of a potential link with wealth see Bekkers and Smeets, 2014.)

In Europe we are becoming a more secular society. "Philanthropy is moving from religious causes to humanistic causes, even though the religious driver in donation is by no means disappearing", says Marco Demarie. As Bekkers and Wiepking (2015) point out:

> the Netherlands is secularizing rapidly. While in 1960 only 18% of the population reported no religious affiliation, 44% of the population reported the same in 2009. The remainder of the population that year was 28% Roman Catholic, 18% Protestant denomination, and 5% Muslim. Furthermore, only 17% of the Dutch population attends religious services once a week or more.

In just one generation (1960 to 2009) the percentage of the population reporting no religious affiliation had more than doubled. But this appears to have had no noticeable effect on the total value of charitable giving.

People with experience in fundraising share this view: "Religion? It is not the majority. We are less and less religious", says Marie-Stéphane Maradeix. But Serge Raicher argues that "religious involvement must make you stop and think". He describes the shift in values as "not a rejection, but an evolution. People are giving less through the Church, and are adhering to morals that are more contemporary. They are making the old values theirs, and adapting them."

Despite these changes in beliefs, faith-based giving remains strong in Europe, including amongst high-value philanthropists. At least in one case, faith-based giving appears to be adopting some of the ideas of venture philanthropy. Recently the Salvatorian Fathers and Brothers, in Rome, created an Advisory Board. Arnout Mertens, General Director at the organisation takes up the story:

> 'The board includes two philanthropists. One is an ex-Salvatorian who became wealthy through real estate investments in the USA. He has given us money for [marketing and] promotion. Another is a Swiss-UK individual with investments in high tech. He has donated money to cover our overheads for four years. Their motivation is certainly religious. The *spiritual return on investment* is very important; the return for them is spiritual. These donors are trying to make us think long term.'

The same word – spiritual – was used by Wolfgang Hafenmayer, but in a broader context than the religious.

> 'If it makes you happy then you might just focus on making money. A lot of people are afraid of self-development. But some people focus on a spiritual part, a philanthropy, for personal development. We have more people now who live through various "lifetimes" in one lifetime. For many people philanthropy is a first step on a journey back to their own spiritual development.'

He sees potential here for the growth of philanthropy in emerging markets: "we will see a huge shift in the emerging markets which will go the same route. Once they have made money they will also look for meaning in their lives."

Note

[1] The Gini coefficient is a measure of statistical dispersion intended to represent the income distribution of a nation's residents and is a commonly used measure of inequality.

FIVE

Evidence and effects

What is the evidence that people are changing?

Philanthropy as a strategy

The phrase 'strategic philanthropy' is widely used, from the 'Erasmus Centre for Strategic Philanthropy' to various papers and books such as Peter Frumkin's (2006) 'Strategic Giving: The art and science of philanthropy'. There are websites dedicated to the topic and companies that use the phrase in their names. The term is applied to corporate social responsibility programmes (an early – 2002 – article by Porter and Kramer uses the phrase 'strategic philanthropy' in this sense), to the activities of foundations, and to individual philanthropists. It is used – for example by Maas and Liket (2010) – to mean corporate giving that has two objectives: 'benefitting social welfare and financial profitability'.

Writing in the *Stanford Social Innovation Review*, John Kania, Mark Kramer and Patty Russell (Kania, Kramer, & Russell, 2014) describe the core principles of strategic philanthropy as 'clear goals, data-driven strategies, heightened accountability, and rigorous evaluations'. Some authors, such as Shaw (2015), add a public policy lobbying element to strategic philanthropy – in other words using philanthropy to change government policy (in education, health or women's rights, for example).

Mark Kramer had been one of the co-authors of the paper attributed as the origins of strategic philanthropy, but by 2014 he, Kania and Russell were ready to criticise the approach.

Strategic philanthropy assumes that outcomes arise from a linear chain of causation that can be predicted, attributed, and repeated, even though we know that social change is often unpredictable, multifaceted, and idiosyncratic. It locks funders into a rigid multi-year agenda, although the probability and desirability of achieving any given outcome waxes and wanes over time. ... The forced simplicity of logic models often misleads funders to overlook the complex dynamics and interpersonal relationships amongst numerous nonprofit, for-profit, and government actors that determine real world events.

Ulrik Kampmann, the former Director of Development at Realdania, knows these complex dynamics in grant-making: "As a foundation we have to move a scale or two up in complexity. We cannot know all the steps from input to impact. We have a large degree of uncertainty." "You have to set on the goal. But it is not a business strategy, it is more loose."

These writings leave little room for what is happening in Europe. Yes, some corporate CSR appears to be more strategic (witness the activities of the Shell Foundation, www.shellfoundation.org/ for example), and certainly foundations across Europe are working on and applying strategies.

Some individual donors in Europe may be becoming more strategic with their giving. "Charity came with a tear in the eye and a big wallet", paraphrases Serge Raicher. "Social investment comes with those but also with a strategic mind-set." One of the explanations for the growth in the numbers of foundations across Europe is that these are ways of formalising and managing an individual's philanthropy, of making it more strategic.

Are people of wealth becoming more strategic about their philanthropy? There are many who say that they are, and the rapid growth in the number of philanthropic advisers and consultants seems to support the idea that people want to discuss, plan and target their giving. Beyond the world of wealth there is the wider social movement of 'effective altruism', led by Peter Singer and by Toby Ord and William MacAskill, both of Oxford University and linked to organisations including the Centre for Effective Altruism (www. centreforeffectivealtruism.org/), Give Well, a charity rating project (www.givewell.org/), Giving Evidence (https://giving-evidence.com/about/), and Giving What We Can (www.givingwhatwecan.org/).

One of the reasons for the apparent growth in interest in strategic philanthropy may be the fact that the donor is still alive. "There is a trend toward lifetime giving", says Dr Pamala Wiepking, reflecting a widely held view that people of wealth are now choosing to give during their lifetimes rather than leave a fortune to endow a foundation after their death.

The idea of applying strategy to giving is still a minority sport. Theresa Lloyd estimates that "probably it's still a low percentage of those who could give who do give as a strategic commitment to philanthropy." A 2015 study of a group of 91 private bank clients in Italy (Li Perni, 2016) showed that 16% had planned a defined annual budget for their giving – evidence of strategy in their giving. Amongst clients with investable assets of more than €30 million this number increased to 43%. For this group of people, more wealth meant a more strategic approach.

Luis Berruete, Coordinator of Creas, a social investment enterprise in Spain warns that the sector is "moving slowly because there is not yet a track record".

> 'The mentality [of giving] is not really changing in Spain. There are still many investors who put their philanthropic money into donations rather than in investments with a social return. Even when they invest socially, they are not valuing their investments for their economic return.'

In Europe the evidence for strategic philanthropy is anecdotal.

Segments

Philanthropic people are not one homogeneous mass; you may safely challenge the person who says "rich people are all the same" or "wealthy donors all like their name on a project". The varied nature of people of wealth has emerged from various research studies around Europe.

A paper from the Fondation de France offered early evidence that at least in France things were changing (de Laurens and Rozier, 2012). 'Until the summer of 2010, with Americans Bill Gates and Buffet launching their Giving Pledge, the French media were struggling to show the face of French philanthropy and its importance, its directions.' It states, cautiously, that 'if a new era is perhaps in the process of being born, the evidence shows that it will be a complete break with respect to centuries of history'. The paper cites the 'prickly relationship' between Christianity and money and the particularly French 'avowed hostility toward wealth'. This complicates philanthropy in France, 'especially in making any communication on the subject'.

The paper, based on a survey ($n = 1,200$) by Mediaprism and on interviews with 18 of the country's most generous philanthropists, broke some of the stereotypes that people had about philanthropists. They were not the scions of ancient family dynasties, but rather entrepreneurs and senior managers who have built their own wealth. 'Driven by strong personal convictions, they chose to share their wealth with society rather than leave the whole of it to their children.' In making this choice they are looking for impacts that will change the world. The questions they ask themselves are 'What use am I?' and 'What use is money in the world?'

There is evidence from this survey of a shift in attitudes to philanthropy amongst the general French public, caused in substantial part by the Giving Pledge of Bill Gates and Warren Buffet; one-third of survey respondents could name a philanthropist but none could name a French philanthropist. The names they gave were 'Gates' and 'Buffet'. According to the survey, most French people in 2012 believed that there were fewer than 100 philanthropists in France (in fact the report identifies more than 600), with half of the public believing there were fewer than 50.

In 2012, 40% of foundations and donor-directed funds in existence had been created in the previous 12 years. The sector was expanding rapidly. It has continued to do so. The surge of new foundations and funds is driven by people who are younger than the stereotypes might suggest, with the largest segment (39%) being created by people aged 50-64 years old, and 28% by people younger than 50. Most of these people have built their own wealth – just 34% are inheritors.

But the most interesting part of the study, the part that evinces the 'complete break' with the traditional model of French philanthropy is the analysis of the attitudes of philanthropists. The study identifies four segments of the philanthropic market:

- 'Inheritors of Philanthropy', from the 1950s
  - Slogan: 'To give is a duty'
  - Influences: parents, grandparents
- 'Children of the Republic', from the 1970s
  - Slogan: 'The same world, for everyone'
  - Influences: anonymous volunteers out in the field
- 'Solidarity Entrepreneurs', from the 1980s-1990s
  - Slogan: 'Invest for a better world'
  - Influences: Pasteur, Warren Buffet, Bill Gates
- 'Field Militants', from the 1990s to 2000s
  - Slogan: 'Change the World'
  - Influences: Bernard Kouchner, the founder of Médecins Sans Frontières, and Pierre Rabhi, the ecologist and leader of the 'oasis in any place' movement

The Inheritors of Philanthropy have been handed the duty to give along with the family wealth. The duty is arduous, because they are taking over from charismatic ancestors whose mythical status forms part of the founding histories of these dynasties. By contrast the Children of the Republic have fought their way up from modest or often challenging childhoods – for example, loss of a parent, migration. They acknowledge the role of education in social improvement. Theirs is an obligation to share wealth: 'a profound sense of the collective'.

The Solidarity Entrepreneurs are all self-made, and they apply their business skills to their philanthropy. Initiative, risk and innovation have combined with an innate sense of philanthropy, and in some cases with troubled lives. Philanthropy is a place of liberty, of experimentation and of human contact.

The youngest group – typically between 32 and 45 years old in 2012 – are the Field Militants. These people know the non-profit sector well; they have volunteered for organisations in their youth or have organised international humanitarian or cooperation projects. Wealth (self-made or through an inheritance) has given them the chance to create a foundation. This group is focused on finding 'new models and then new systems' for the world. This group appears throughout Europe. For example, social entrepreneur Ramón Bernat, based in Barcelona, might call himself a 'Field Militant'. He paraphrases Bill Drayton, founder of Ashoka (http://usa.ashoka.org/social-entrepreneurs-are-not-content-just-give-fish-or-teach-how-fish): "I am a social investor.

I don't want to give fish to people, or even to teach them to fish. I want to revolutionise the fishing industry."

These two younger groups – Solidarity Entrepreneurs and Field Militants – are evidence for a radical departure in philanthropy in France. The choice they make of:

> causes, amounts, [and] geographical areas for their [philanthropic] investments are generally based on a single criterion that is central for them: the efficiency of their action. To give in an area where there is little impact, over-invested with private or public money, makes no sense to them. Thus the choice of sector, of the objectives of their foundation, is not only based on the concerns of the founder. It is also defined in function of the state of 'competition'. (de Laurens and Rozier, 2012, p 26).

These philanthropists focus on smaller organisations; one is quoted as saying: "I believe in the virtue of the small, in the fact that the return on investment of the organisation is much bigger in the end than for the largest organisations" (de Laurens and Rozier, 2012, p 26). They understand the difficulties of smaller organisations, and will thus finance structural, functional costs where older philanthropists would have insisted on funding operational projects. They engage themselves in the organisation and its activities, offering it flexible finance or guaranteeing loans. Some of these philanthropists put their own networks to work for the organisation, bringing new expertise to the non-profit. These characteristics, described in detail in the 2012 report, sound very much like the characteristics of the venture philanthropists.

A study in the UK by New Philanthropy Capital confirms the existence of segments based on differences in attitude and motivation (Bagwell et al, 2013). This report defined seven segments, with 'Ad-Hoc Giver', 'Loyal Supporter' and 'Engaged Champion' representing more than two-thirds of all HNWI donors. These groups exhibited different levels of interest in the cause, of concern for impact and of willingness to go public about their giving.

Thinking of the high-value philanthropy market in terms of segments helps us understand many of the conundrums in the market, and especially the very varied attitudes to philanthropy across the continent.

Circles and networks

One of the features of contemporary high-value philanthropy in Europe is the existence of donor circles and networks – more or less formal groups of people sharing information and sometimes money for philanthropy. As we are finding in other areas of philanthropy, this is not new; Ladies' Circle (now Ladies Circle International, www. ladiescircleinternational.org) was founded in 1932 in Bournemouth by the wives of Round Table members.

Marjan Sax, previously Director of Mama Cash in the Netherlands and one of its founders, helped me to understand how circles and networks of women are relevant to high-value philanthropy.

There are two main types of structure:

1. *Donor networks or donor circles* whose main purpose is philanthropic giving. The dynamic of these organisations and the motivation of their members are first and foremost directed towards philanthropy. Alongside their philanthropic activities these organisations also give support and networking opportunities to their members.
2. *Support and exchange networks* whose main purpose is networking, mutual support and information sharing. These networks, such as the networks of women with inherited wealth, influential women's networks and women's business networks, can lead to philanthropy but this is not their original goal and not the primary motivation for members to join.

Donor networks

In donor networks individual philanthropists come together to pool their money for the support of NGOs, projects and campaigns. The networks have a strong learning component. The members learn about the organisations they can support, about the non-profit sector, and learn how to become effective philanthropists. As well as sharing information about philanthropy, sharing experiences, bonding and personal histories are important elements in these networks, according to Marjan Sax. Examples include the Network for Social Change (http://thenetworkforsocialchange.org.uk) and the Women Donors Network (www.womendonors.org/). Another is the Philanthropy Workshop (www.tpw.org) created by the Rockefeller and Hewlett

Foundations and the Institute for Philanthropy, active in the UK and USA.

Donor circles

Donor circles may form under the umbrella of an NGO (as did The Circle, led by singer Annie Lennox, initially under Oxfam UK) or a mother organisation such as Giving Women (based in Geneva, www.givingwomen.ch/) or the Women Donors Network www.womendonors.org/), active in the USA. Women Moving Millions (www.womenmovingmillions.org/), which is active in the USA and in Europe, is focused on high-value philanthropy, with 230 members pledging over US$600 million to advance the rights of women and girls around the world.

Donor circles are very diverse in the way they are organised. Giving Women, for example, creates 'Project Circles' to support selected projects with funds, time, expertise and skills. The organisation has supported more than 23 projects with over CHF589,365 since its inception in 2008. The Global Fund for Women has run donor circles that were formed around a particular theme or a region, such as the Middle East or North Africa, with a minimum level of annual commitment and regular calls with a programme team member or other expert. The Circle, created initially under the umbrella of Oxfam, has catalysed a number of other related circles including a Scottish Circle, a Lawyers' Circle and a Music Circle.

Some donor circles concentrate on giving and support, while others have a learning objective.

One of the problems with donor circles is that they can occupy a difficult space between donor and project. Donor circles find it hard in Europe to raise the funds required to administer their own organisation and pay for employees, so it is difficult for them to take on the NGO roles of project selection and management; conversely, participants in donor circles find it hard to act as the subsidiary of an NGO because the larger organisation imposes rules, limitations and bureaucracy on the smaller circle.

Support and exchange networks

Support and exchange networks include networks of women with inherited wealth, such as Pecunia in Germany (http://pecunia-erbinnen.net/) and Erfdochters in the Netherlands, co-founded by Marjan Sax (http://history.mamacash.nl/nl/theme/408/). These networks have been created for women who have inherited or who expect to inherit in the future. Marjan Sax comments that "unlike many male inheritors, [women] often have been ill-prepared for the financial and emotional requirements that lay ahead". Both networks concentrate on supporting women of wealth to become more at ease with their wealth and to encourage women to become active in managing their inheritance. This includes managing their philanthropy, but philanthropy is not the primary purpose of these networks.

These networks focus on sharing experiences with other inheritors, and empowerment. "By meeting other women in comparable situations possible feelings of shame and loneliness are changed into a positive attitude towards their wealth and active management of their finances", says Marjan Sax. "By exchanging information about their history, attitude and ideas about money, the women in the network develop close friendships and trust, which stimulate personal growth."

Some of the networks of professional women are active in philanthropy. The main roles of these networks are to connect members, provide support in personal and professional growth, and to advance more women into leadership positions. There are many such networks active in Europe – examples include the Professional Women's Network (www.pwnglobal.net/), Women's Forum for the Economy and Society (www.womens-forum.com/) and 100 Women in Hedge Funds (www.100womeninhedgefunds.org/). The Women's Forum for the Economy and Society (www.womens-forum.com/), founded in 2005 by Aude de Thuin, was ranked amongst the top five influential forums worldwide by the *Financial Times* in 2007; it is neither a professional nor a philanthropic circle, but discusses topics relevant to both.

Networks and circles appear, and occasionally disappear, all over Europe. Some are encouraged into existence by fundraising organisations or supported by private banks or wealth managers. Others are more informal. The revolution in women's philanthropy in Europe is the creation of circles and networks that only focus on wealth and philanthropy. Philanthropy is a part of what 100 Women in Hedge Funds does, but it is not the whole raison d'être. By contrast, it is the central purpose of Giving Women.

Direct to donor

Caroline Hartnell, reporting on a 2015 Robert Bosch Stiftung-sponsored meeting of foundations, wrote that 'mistrust of NGOs was a common theme at the meeting. NGOs may be seen as agents of government (because they sometimes run government programmes) or as a conduit for funds from abroad or simply as inefficient – or even corrupt' (Hartnell, 2015). As a consequence, she said, Russian philanthropists prefer to give directly to people in need, and endowed Spanish foundations are evolving into operating foundations, preferring to act directly and direct their own programmes. 'New donors', she says, 'often assume that the skills that made them successful in business will work for social change.' She quotes Firoz Ladak of Edmond de Rothschild Foundations who says that the wish for direct engagement sometimes 'stems from the fact that philanthropists wish to implement new ideas and solutions that do not yet exist'.

Northern NGOs based in the Europe and managed by a largely white European staff look increasingly like an anachronism, at least to sophisticated high-value philanthropists. Their principal marketing activity, fundraising, is seen as an expensive, inefficient way of generating income and venture philanthropists have been in the forefront in pointing out the high cost of capital from charity fundraising, compared to the cost of capital raised through loans or share issues. The experience of philanthropists who try to work with NGOs has been, to put it mildly, frustrating; many talk about traipsing around NGO offices, seeking involvement and participation alongside their proposed donation, and finding only one response: "We'll take your money but no, sadly, we can't let you play any role in how it is used."

Alongside these internal European factors there is an external influence – the Internet. "The world has become smaller", says Sophie Vossenaar. "People ask, 'where can I make a difference?' Some are becoming global citizens." It is becoming easier for projects in the Global South to project their activities directly to donors, or at least with minimal intermediation such as via Kiva. A project in Ghana that previously relied wholly on Northern NGO intermediaries can now launch its own website and gather donations directly. For philanthropists this looks like a better deal – why pay expensive European staff to sit in a costly office in central Amsterdam when you can pay much less for skilled, locally connected staff in Accra?

European NGOs are generally not prepared for this shift amongst donors. The impression is that high-value philanthropy is not important enough to them to catalyse change in the way they are organised. Largely reliant on their own national government funding and on tens or hundreds of thousands of individual donors they do not see the need to adapt to the demands of a few noisy philanthropists who are giving up on the NGOs in order to give direct to Southern recipient organisations. This illustrates the chasm between the pretensions and interests of philanthropists and the interests of the NGOs.

Is this all right?

Philanthropy and power

Is it right that wealth, through philanthropy, should exercise power over society? This debate has swung around and around without a clear compass. "Philanthropy used to be dirty money", says Dr Arthur Gautier, talking about the situation in France. "But today we don't have the luxury of having debates about money. Pragmatism trumped ideology."

As a 2015 report pointed out, the growth of large foundations led by people of wealth has:

> given rise to a debate that primarily centres around the power of foundations which questions the legitimacy of their activities in light of tax breaks and a lack of 'mission', and increasingly calls for more transparency. Founders and foundations that, in the future, rise to the societal challenges and want to take on a 'more prominent' role need to clearly articulate their position and legitimacy. (Anon, 2015c)

Legal theorist and judge Richard Posner is cited in Reich (2016, p 468) as describing the US model of a foundation as 'a completely irresponsible institution, answerable to nobody ... The puzzle is why these foundations are not total scandals'.

What right has a billionaire to influence policies in health or education, ask Matthew Bishop and Michael Green (2010) in the second edition of *Philanthrocapitalism*. Should it not be governments, democratically elected and responsible to their voters, who decide on the priorities in these areas, and in culture, environment, heritage, international development, women's rights and all the other areas in which philanthropists get involved? Bishop and Green (2010, p 11) ask whether it would not be better to 'tax the rich more heavily and let governments solve the world's problems?' They note that 'the previous golden ages of philanthropy all ended with the state significantly increasing its role in areas where philanthropists had tried to find solutions' for poor people, and in education. But they argue – and this is a line that would support the political philosophies broadly described as 'neoliberal' – that the ability of governments to raise taxes and thus to finance the sort of social support that poor people need is limited by the geographic mobility of the wealthy, and by the need not to stifle economic growth.

The first point, the geographic mobility of people of wealth, is highlighted by media reports about the tax exile of a few celebrity tax evaders – led by the purchase by Gérard Depardieu of a home in a former Customs post just metres into Belgium on the Franco–Belgian border in order to avoid the unpopular ISF (Impôt de Solidarité sur la Fortune) wealth tax. But while Depardieu and ageing rocker Johnny Halliday left France in order to avoid ISF, more than 342,000 ISF taxpayers did not (for the number of people who paid ISF in 2015, see Pluyette, C., 2016). Even an unpopular wealth tax is not enough to make people leave home.

The evidence from France is that people of wealth are not so geographically mobile, so it makes sense for governments to tax the rich more heavily and to apply the extra income raised to programmes (health, education, the environment) chosen by their electorate. Whether this would 'solve the world's problems' is much more debatable and here there is a further case for philanthropy, as an agile, rapid, experimental tool for trying out solutions to world problems. This was the point being made by Warren Buffett when he made his US$30 billion pledge to the Bill & Melinda Gates Foundation, saying that the Gates would "do a far better job in terms of maximising the good that comes out of that money than [could] ... the federal Treasury".

Philanthropy and me

There is a well-rehearsed argument that philanthropy, while it purports to support the poor, is really of benefit to the wealthy. In a December 2013 op-ed for *Salon* magazine, Robert B. Reich, Professor of Public Policy at the University of California at Berkeley, said that 'the wealthy aren't donating to food shelters. They're giving to Yale and fancy theatres' (Reich, 2013). In his view:

> a large portion of the charitable [tax] deductions now claimed by America's wealthy are for donations to culture palaces – operas, art museums, symphonies, and theatres – where they spend their leisure time hobnobbing with other wealthy benefactors. Another portion is for contributions to the elite prep schools and universities they once attended or want their children to attend.

Pamala Wiepking (2010) cites Ostrower (1997) to argue that 'elites will want to distinguish themselves by making donations to organisations that are less accessible to people in lower social strata such as…cultural institutions'. Teresa Odendahl (1989) made the case that HNWI giving went to institutions that served the interests of the upper class during the Reagan years. Charles Clotfelter (1992) examined the issue with colleagues in painstaking detail (and with data that would simply not be available in Europe) and concluded, with many cautionary notes, that state schools and health centres do indeed appear to serve the poor while non-profit schools and health centres serve the poor slightly less. In the same volume, Lester Salamon (1992, p 147) found that 'quite clearly, the non-profit human service sector does not appear to be primarily engaged either in providing the kind of material assistance most needed by the poor or in serving the poor in other ways'. He shows (p 156) that 'as the share of income from private charitable sources increases, the focus on the poor goes down', meaning that those receiving philanthropy are less likely to focus on the poor.

People of wealth in Europe *do* give to leading business schools, to Oxford or Cambridge Universities, and to the Concertgebouw, or the

Tate. But they also give to food banks, projects for people who are homeless and to the many humanitarian emergencies in the Global South. We can say the same of revenue generated through taxation; some of it goes to inner city homelessness, and some of it pays for the opera. Societies need all of this – social support and culture, business schools and food banks – and Europe meets these needs with a mixture of state support and philanthropy.

New people

Chapters four and five have reviewed some of the main forces that appear to be shaping high-value philanthropy in Europe, from the growing numbers of people who chose do good during their own lifetimes (rather than leaving it all to the trustees of their estates), to the gap between wealth and poverty. None of these elements is the single cause of shifting attitudes to giving, and none of them affect all donors; the evidence from research of segments in the market is the most convincing sign that there is change, but that it is patchy.

SIX

Women[1]

Philanthropy amongst women of wealth in Europe is not new. Marita Haibach, in 'Contemporary Women's Philanthropy in Germany' (1999) cites as an example Hedwig Heyl (1850-1933), a female entrepreneur based in Berlin, who not only contributed a significant part of her wealth to the women's rights movement but also raised funds from individuals and businesses. We can go much further back than that in tracing women's philanthropy. For example, as Filiz Bikmen points out, citing Murat Çizakça (2000), women established almost 40% of the 2,860 foundations in Istanbul, in the Ottoman Empire of the 16th century (MacDonald and Tayart de Borms, 2008).

But there seem to be differences between the evolution of philanthropy in Europe amongst women and that amongst men. In this chapter we will attempt to describe these differences, and – a harder task – explain them.

A brief review of research

The numbers of women of wealth in Europe

Wealth is a precondition for high-value philanthropy, so wealth held by women is an important measure. Frustratingly, data on the numbers of women of wealth in Europe are scarce. The most widely read report on global wealth, the annual World Wealth Report did not mention women of wealth in any of its editions of 2010 to 2014 and makes only an oblique reference to women in its 2015 report (Anon, 2015d). This report estimates a global population, men and women, of 14.6 million HNWIs,[2] 139,300 of whom are UHNWIs. It estimates that 4 million HNWIs live in Europe.

The Wealth-X/UBS Ultra Wealth Report 2014 (Anon, 2014a) estimates that the global UHNWI population in 2014 was 211,275 people. Wealth-X does not disclose the methods that it used to come to this estimate beyond claiming that it has a 'database of global ultra-high net worth individuals ... that is the largest in existence', but the difficulties in estimating wealth are illustrated by the fact that while the World Wealth Report estimates that in 2014 there were 139,300 UHNWIs on the planet, the Wealth-X report counts 211,275. That is a difference of almost 72,000 people; we might say that the authors of the Wealth-X report are one and a half times as optimistic as those who wrote the World Wealth Report.

How many of these wealthy people are women?

The Wealth-X/UBS Ultra Wealth Report 2014 reviews the situation of women of wealth globally, finding that 13% of UHNWI population are women, and that they hold 14% of UHNWI wealth.

Data from the USA shows that the proportion of women amongst the wealthiest 1% of the population has declined slightly since 1969, but still (according to data from 2000) accounted for two out of every five of the wealthiest 1% (Kopczuk, 2015). Note that the wealthiest 1% goes far beyond the UNHWIs, who represent just 0.017% of the world's adult population, into the relatively impoverished HNWIs. Meanwhile, a 2015 analysis by Factary on data from UK-published wealth lists over the last ten years found that 18% of wealth holders were women.[3]

Bearing in mind that these various percentages encompass different populations and three different methodologies (the UHNWI entry barrier of US$30 million in investible assets, the 1% wealthiest, and those who meet the various entry requirements of UK-published wealth lists), so we are in the land of guesswork. To estimate the numbers of women of wealth in Europe we will take the most conservative of these proportions (13% of the population) and the more conservative of the European population estimates – 4 million HNWIs, of whom 40,000 are UHNWIs. This would equate to a European population of 520,000 HNW women of whom 5,200 are UHNWW (Ultra High Net Worth Women).

This may explain one commonly noted phenomenon: women in Europe make fewer large philanthropic gifts than men. Perhaps it is simply that there are fewer HNW women than men.

How do women give, and is it changing?

US bias

If it is difficult to estimate the population of wealthy women in Europe, it is just as hard to establish from the academic literature why women give. Many of the studies in the academic literature are based on exclusively US samples. The frequently cited 2011 study by Debra Mesch is based, for example, on the 2002 and 2004 General Social Survey and the 2008 Knowledge Network data sets, all exclusively gathered in the USA (Mesch et al, 2011). They are also general population studies, not focused on the demographic segment that is at the heart of this study – women of wealth. The findings are interesting but may be irrelevant to Europe.

Men and women

Some studies, including a recent study in the Netherlands (Wit and Bekkers, 2015), find that men give more than women, although this is not a universal finding. According to a literature review by Mesch (2009, p 2) 'several studies find that while females are more likely to give, males give higher amounts'.

The cause could simply be differences in income, and a 2015 study in Spain reminds us that women's salaries are 77% of those of men, and finds that on a like-for-like salary basis, women are more generous (Rubio Guerrero, Sosvilla Rivero and Méndez Picazo, 2015).

Studies show that the pattern of giving differs between men and women, with some studies finding that women give to more causes, and to a broader range of causes than men (for example Wit and Bekkers, 2015). Mesch reports that 'males tend to concentrate their giving among a few charities, whereas females were more likely to spread the amounts they give across a wide range of charities'.

Women in structures of philanthropy

Research by Factary in England has shown that in the last 10 years women have remained in the minority on the boards of grant-making foundations (Carnie, 2015). The research, based on data covering 2,312 foundations created between 2005 and 2015, shows an average of one woman per foundation board. Women are in the majority on the boards of just one foundation in six (16.6%). These findings reflected earlier research into venture philanthropy funds in the UK, where Factary reported that just 27% of VP fund trustees were women (Carnie and Whitefield, 2013).

Women – at least in England – appear not to be joining the formal structures of philanthropy. Is this in part because they do not want to be publicly recognised as philanthropists?

The recognition motivation

In the USA, studies have noted differences in the need for recognition: 'Women donors ... want to see the results of their giving more than the recognition that accompanies it', according to a consultant quoted in *Women and Philanthropy* (Shaw-Hardy, Taylor and Beaudoin-Schwartz, 2010, p 10). The focus on results reflects the findings from qualitative research in 2012 amongst High Net Worth women who invest in sustainable green industries: 'a majority would accept lower returns in exchange for the certainty that their fortune is indeed invested into something sensible' (Anon, 2012a).

The lack of a 'women's cause'?

There is circumstantial evidence that women as philanthropists are not connecting with causes relevant to women. This is more obvious from the point of view of the causes. The women's rights sector is an example.

AWID (www.awid.org) has published a number of reports about resourcing women's rights. AWID describes itself as 'an international, feminist, membership organisation committed to achieving gender equality, sustainable development and women's human rights'. It has 4,781 members in 163 countries and around 46,000 subscribers to its weekly newsletter. AWID's 2013 study, graphically entitled 'Watering the Leaves, Starving the Roots' (Arutyunova and Clark, 2013), showed that the combined incomes of 740 women's organisations around the world was US$106 million in 2010. AWID makes the comparison between this global total for 740 organisations and the same year's total income of US$2.6 billion for just one NGO, World Vision International. Donors are not connecting with women's organisations.

The AWID findings are reflected in one of the few studies that has looked in depth at foundations' funding for women and girls in Europe, 'Untapped Potential: European Foundation Funding for Women and Girls' (Shah, McGill and Weisblatt, 2011). This study, jointly managed by Mama Cash, the European Foundation Centre and the Foundation Center, analysed funding for women and girls. It covered 145 foundations from 19 countries. These were substantial foundations, with €9.2 billion in total assets, and including 65 foundations with at least €50 million in assets. The study researchers obtained data on more than 9,100 grants awarded by 42 foundations.

The majority of foundations surveyed (58%) allocated less than 10% of their expenditures in 2009 to programmes benefiting women and girls. This includes one-quarter that did not designate any funds for women and girls. In 2009, the median percentage of total grant monies allocated by foundations in support of women and girls was 4.8%[4] (Cantwell, 2014). The median percentage of the total number of grants allocated by foundations was 4.1%.

Nearly half (45%) of all grants identified as benefiting women and girls were in the area of human services. The second largest share of grants focused on human rights (21%).

'Untapped Potential' characterised the market in 2009 as big on potential – 90% of foundations expressed an interest in at least one issue relevant to women and girls – but small on delivery, with just 4.8% of grant money, and 4.1% of grants, going to programmes for women and girls. The study does not analyse the reasons for this gap, but the authors speculate that 'one possible reason might be that foundations, despite their interest, have not found a tangible point of entry into this work' (Shah, McGill and Weisblatt, 2011, p 32).

The authors also focus on communications, saying that 'efforts to further articulate and communicate the value of consciously applying a gender lens to grant making and other programmatic activities could increase the percentage of foundations taking an intentional approach to funding women and girls'. The untapped potential appears to arise from a lack of understanding and of contact between foundations and women's funds; it is a communications (using this word in its widest sense) problem.

Talking the language

The issue of communications, identified by the authors of 'Untapped Potential' also emerges in a paper, the 'Business Case for Women's Economic Empowerment' (Hagen-Dillon, 2014), which includes a subsidiary study, 'Corporate Sector Funding and Women's Rights – Perceptions, Language, and How to Increase Engagement'. The research study – funded by Oak Foundation – was carried out by Assemblyfor (www.assemblyfor.com/, then known as Witter Ventures). 'The language of women's rights', the author notes, 'seems to be limiting rather than enabling communication.'

Alongside the communications issues 'most interviewees [including women's rights organisations, corporates and INGOs] found it difficult to name a single achievement of the women's movement beyond increased visibility'. Despite years of work, gender equality is still an issue, and violence against women has not, apparently, decreased. In other words, there are questions about demonstrating the impact of the women's movement.

Reviewing relationships between women's organisations and companies in 1999, Marita Haibach pointed out that in Germany 'both sides [women's organisations and companies] are suspicious of each other but at the same time they do not know much about their opponents'. She links the issues of communication and impact by noting that women's organisations in Germany rely on state funding:

> a major consequence of the government dependency is the fact that women's issues disappeared from the public agenda. At the same time, the achievements of the organisations have by and large remained invisible. Because the organisations did not engage in raising funds from individual women and other private funders, they failed to build a constituency of supporters.

Across the European non-profit sector there has been a remarkable lack of initiative to build a constituency of women supporters. Review the fundraising literature of many – perhaps most – development cooperation NGOs and you will see a raft of material on the central role of women in these NGOs' programmes: women as micro-entrepreneurs, women in health systems, women farmers. Examine the data and you will find that around half (the percentage varies slightly) their donors are women. But search for a fundraising programme specifically aimed at women and you will struggle. Ironically, this is the case despite the fact that the majority of fundraising staff in NGOs are women.

Women and philanthropy – still not visible?

We have in Europe a substantial number of women of wealth – perhaps 5,000 UHNW women. We have evidence from research in the Netherlands that women are giving less than men. We have evidence from Spain that this 'less' may be related to income – it may be that men and women give the same percentage of income.

We can see evidence from the UK that women are less likely to join the structures of philanthropy, and from the USA comes the suggestion that women do not seek public recognition as donors. All of this would militate against women's philanthropy in Europe being recognised.

The cause that might be regarded as a natural home for some women's philanthropy – women's rights – is clearly not getting the funding. This may be because women's rights organisations are not communicating with this constituency of philanthropists. And, specifically, because they are not communicating their impacts.

There is a contradictory surprise: despite focusing on women as the recipients of their programmes, and despite having fundraising teams majority staffed by women, very few NGOs have developed fundraising programmes aimed at women.

High-value philanthropy by women, and especially that by women, for women, is a challenge and an opportunity for non-profits, advisers and wealth managers in Europe.

Notes

[1] I am grateful to Mama Cash (www.mamacash.nl) and the Oak Foundation (http://oakfnd.org/) for commissioning the research that forms the basis of much of this chapter.

[2] HNWI is commonly defined as a person with US$1 million or more in investable assets (that is, excluding their principal residence). Ultra HNWI (UHNWI) is defined as a person with US$30 million or more in investable assets.

[3] Factary carried out an analysis of data in UK wealth lists (such as the Sunday Times Rich List) published over the last ten years. We found 13,852 men,

and 2,489 women. We are fully aware of the limitations of this type of source, so this data should be treated as an estimate.

[4] This is remarkably similar to the figure cited in '21st Century Barriers to Women's Entrepreneurship' (Cantwell, 2014). This report found only 4% of the total dollar value of all small business loans goes to women entrepreneurs.

SEVEN

Venture philanthropists

Introduction

One of the most significant evolutions in philanthropy in Europe has been the arrival of the 'venture philanthropists'. The current "big thing in France is impact investment and venture philanthropy", says a philanthropist living in France who spoke off the record for this book.

What is venture philanthropy?

The venture philanthropy model was described in a paper in the *Harvard Business Review* (Letts, Ryan and Grossman, 1997), and turned into philanthropic practice by the Community Foundation of Silicon Valley, California.

Referring to the $10 billion (1995 figure) in grants made by foundations, Christine Letts (Harvard University), William Ryan (then a consultant, now a Research Fellow at Harvard) and Allen Grossman (then CEO of Outward Bound, now a Professor at Harvard) commented that:

> many social programs begin with high hopes and great promise, only to end up with limited impact and uncertain prospects. ... In the process of making a grant, foundations often overlook the organisational issues that could make or break the nonprofit ... Foundations' attitudes have long encouraged nonprofit organisations to focus on mission and to regard organisational capacity as worthwhile in principle, but a distracting burden in practice.

They reported that foundations had been studying venture capital (VC) firms, and identified six venture capital practices that were relevant to foundations:

- Risk management
  - Accepting that only a few projects will be 'moon rockets' and managing the risks of success and failure
- Performance measurement
  - Measuring the health and the development of the organisation in terms of staff, revenue and basic operating systems
  - (Note how different this sounds from performance measurement based on project outcomes, or grants spent)
- Closeness of the relationship
  - Venture capitalists offer their investees 'a range of noncash, value-added assistance' including coaching of senior management, hiring of professional staff, and advice over the best forms of finance
  - By contrast 'most foundations never take a seat on a nonprofit board or act as mentors' because they 'believe that such involvement would be intrusive'
- Amount of funding
  - Foundations make lots of small grants, 'undercapitalising everything [they] do' while venture capitalists make few, substantial investments
- Length of the relationship
  - Noting that only 5.2% of 35,000 grants made by foundations in key US states were for more than one year, Letts and her colleagues criticised the brevity of foundation-non-profit relationships and contrast this with the five to seven years typical in venture capital. Foundations, they said, fear that longer grants would make non-profits overly dependent on them
- Exit
  - Where VC firms plan an eventual sale to other investors, foundations do not do the equivalent with non-profits. This leaves the non-profits spending too much time searching for funds to cover their programmes.

They proposed a range of responses that foundations (and by implication philanthropists) could apply to their grant portfolio, including practical organisational support and investment in organisation building, experiments with alternative forms of grant making such as longer term support, and the development of business plans focusing on the long-term sustainability of non-profits.

These ideas have evolved, but are still recognisable from that 1997 paper. In venture philanthropy, the philanthropist does apply many of the techniques relevant to venture capital investment. She involves herself, her colleagues and people in her network in the management of the entity, coaching, encouraging and networking in order to strengthen and develop the structure of the non-profit.

Venture philanthropists engage closely with their non-profit partners. "What I have learned is that you have to do this 'hands-on' with social entrepreneurs", says Ramón Bernat. "You have to be involved." The point is repeated by Theresa Lloyd. "They [the self-made wealthy] see themselves as akin to shareholders or partners and therefore feel they have a right and a responsibility to see what is going on." "In some cases they are amazed that this is such a strange idea. They look at the way an organisation is dealing with a problem and ask 'how does the organisation know that this is the best way of addressing the problem?', 'can one intervene further upstream?', 'how does the organisation learn?'" This can lead to frustration, as Sophie Vossenaar explains, when philanthropists want to do more than just give; "The co-founder of Net4Kids [Loek van den Boog] went to a leading UN agency to offer to help but they could only think in terms of a donation. He wanted to get involved."

Lisa Hehenberger notes the same sense amongst venture philanthropists.

> 'What the VPs told us is that they were really very frustrated with donating. They couldn't see the results, there was no transparency. They realised they could use their professional experience to do some good: money, skills and networks. I think that was the original motivation [for VP]. VPs saw that people working in the sector had skills, but that you could develop hybrid practices, linking financial expertise [and these social sector skills].'

A venture philanthropist looks for measures of impact, and then makes sure that this information is published (see Part five of this book).

She is creative in her financing of the entity, mixing grants, loans and possibly an equity-like investment, and considering not just how much but when organisations need funding. She will invest strategically in a number of entities after a significant selection and due diligence process, and she accepts that some will fail, and only very few achieve their full potential. She supports the organisation over a period – perhaps not the seven years that Letts and colleagues (1997) note amongst VCs, but certainly longer than the one or two years of a foundation grant. And she plans for an exit. This is one of the trickiest moments in the venture philanthropist's relationship with a non-profit because, unlike the world of VC, there is no equivalent in the non-profit world to the kind of money-making exit that a VC might take, for example through a flotation on the stock exchange.

Venture philanthropy in Europe, now

The Annual Survey produced by the European Venture Philanthropy Association gives the latest picture of the sector. Their 2013/14 survey shows that EVPA members allocated €825 million to venture philanthropy and social impact investment (VP/SI) in fiscal 2013, a 28% increase on the previous year. Most of the funding was in the form of grants (57%, by value) but debt instruments (20%), equity or quasi-equity (15%) and guarantees were also used. Alongside the money came strategic consulting and support (81% of VP funds), coaching and mentoring (77%), access to networks (76%), financial management support (65%), fundraising or revenue strategies (61%) and governance (56% of VP funds). An increasing number of VP funds are looking to recycle capital, with 41% of funds, the largest category, saying that they aim for a mix of social return with financial return. These organisations want to be able to inject capital into a social entity, and then either get their money back or generate some positive return on the capital.

Venture philanthropy funds in Europe

The membership of the European Venture Philanthropy Association (EVPA) reflects the broad interest in venture philanthropy in Europe.

There are family philanthropies such as LGT Impact Ventures (www. lgtvp.com) created in 2007 by the Princely family of Liechtenstein, and led by H.S.H. Prince Max von und zu Liechtenstein. The fund uses a venture capital approach, including management know-how, access to networks and finance to support organisations outside Europe with scalable solutions to social and environmental challenges – organisations such as Mothers2Mothers (www.m2m.org/) in South Africa, which hires HIV-positive mothers to educate and support new HIV-positive mums.

There are social investment firms such as PhiTrust (www. phitrustpartenaires.com). Founded in 2005, the company supports businesses and non-profits that have a positive benefit for society. Their investment portfolio includes finance, property, environment and agriculture, with an investment in La Laiterie du Berger, for example – a social enterprise in Senegal that is professionalising the production of milk by small farmers in the country.

A number of large foundations have joined EVPA – well-known examples include Bertelsmann Stiftung and BMW Stiftung Herbert Quandt from Germany, Ikea Foundation in the Netherlands, Esmée Fairbairn Foundation in the UK, or Fondazione CRT in Italy. A number of banks – ABN AMRO Private Banking is an example – are members too.

Many of the members of EVPA have evolved rapidly, reflecting the changing interests in philanthropy amongst HNWI investors in Europe. Noaber Foundation in the Netherlands, for example, constructed originally as a three-part unit with a venture capital investment firm, a social enterprise investor and a foundation, has evolved into a spun-out network including funds that focus on specific populations and themes (Eleven Flowers Fund on youth and health, Ambitus Foundation on music therapy), or methods (Vita Valley, and the Owls Foundation, with their focus on innovation and knowledge transfer in healthcare). Noaber has invested in a range of projects including software to improve patient and hospital management, as well as health initiatives.

EVPA members are following through on their promises, using a range of financial tools to help them achieve their objectives, including loans (MDLF – Media Development Loan Fund – which makes loans at more or less commercial rates to radio stations and newspapers in countries where the media is banned or censored) and Programme Related Investments (PRI – Fondazione Cariplo, see below).

Influence

Some philanthropists in Europe have adopted elements of venture philanthropy without buying the whole package. A member of a wealthy Dutch family, philanthropist and social investor who was interviewed for this book said that his family "had a lot of inspiration from Brenninkmeijers. We talked to them in 2007–8 and they were applying social impact ideas and venture type philanthropy. They wanted to see efficiency measures, innovation." That insight, coming at a time when there was a generational change of wealth through an inheritance, encouraged the family to reflect on their philanthropy. "The Brenninkmeijer conversation was maybe the watershed moment. It resonated a lot with my family." But this was not a miraculous conversion. "It was quite obvious, but it took a while for the obviousness to become clear. We lacked the vocabulary and the analytical framework to understand the change."

This influence comes despite the limited size of the venture philanthropy sector. Its €825 million in venture philanthropy and social impact investment is easily surpassed by the grant-making foundations of just one European country: the 300 largest charitable foundations in the UK granted £2.4 billion in 2013/14 (Pharoah, Jenkins and Goddard, 2015).

Impact

The growing importance of measuring impact is illustrated by the finding that 50% of EVPA's 2013/14 survey respondents are 'almost always' using impact measurement (up from 47% in 2011) and 35% 'sometimes' (up from 25% in 2011).

The debate on impact has continued to be a central part of venture philanthropy, whether amongst full VP funds or amongst foundations applying parts of the VP model. Dr Lisa Hehenberger says that "of all of EVPA's publications, the impact measurement publication has been by far the most popular. People are really interested in measuring impact." But David Carrington is concerned that "impact is becoming a funder obsession", and a diversion: "what is the impact of our funding? It is an unanswerable question because funding is only one element" in the changes wrought by an organisation or project. "You can end up with a situation where the foundation knows that the grant is neither big enough, nor long-term enough to achieve the social change, and that it is littered with conditions that convey the message that 'we don't trust you'." David is harking back to the very criticism of short-termism that inspired the birth of the venture philanthropy movement (Letts, Ryan and Grossman, 1997).

Is impact investment removing funds from philanthropy?

Venture philanthropy exists in a space with few hard definitions. It is, as David Carrington and others have noted, part of a spectrum of investments that runs from disinterested charitable giving to outright profit-first investing. Venture philanthropy lies somewhere near the middle, with social impact investing just to its right, nearer the profit-first end of the scale.

Impact investing is a popular topic in the corridors of Europe's philanthropy and foundation conferences. (Sadly, it is not yet so popular at the fundraising conferences, with the consequence that many non-profits are missing this particular boat.) As Veronica Vecchi and colleagues (2015) note, there are good economic reasons for this. HNWI wealth has increased and the proportion of that wealth invested in alternative assets (impact investment would be classed as 'alternative') is also increasing (up 3.4% from 2013 to 2014). This is money looking for a social home; 92% of HNWI investors regard social impact as important, with those under 40 years of age especially keen on the topic.

Writing in the *Stanford Social Innovation Review*, Michael Etzel, a manager in the Bridgespan Group's Boston office notes that in the USA impact investing is attracting more and more money – most of it, around 55%, from private investment fund managers (Etzel, 2015). Mr Etzel notes that foundations provide only 6% of total impact investment funds, and argues that 'philanthropic impact investment', meaning investments in which funders get some or all of their money back, sometimes with interest, offers many opportunities. 'Philanthropic money can and should concentrate its efforts' on investments that offer anything from 'small losses to modest gains'. This 'is where a large number of financially underserved social enterprises attacking poverty, crime, homelessness, education, green energy, and other issues reside'.

Philanthropists need to make room in their toolkit for the type of impact investing that takes the patient-capital approach best suited for most emerging social enterprises. Evidence from recent research reports shows that philanthropists can expect to be repaid most, if not all, of their investments, making money available for future redeployment. Philanthropists should not, however, expect these investments to generate market-rate returns.

The potential for this form of investment by foundations – variously known as 'Programme Related Investment' (PRI) or 'Mission Related Investment' – is substantial. Take the standard foundation model: put €100 million into safe investments, and use the interest (perhaps €3-€5 million per year) to make grants. Now move to Programme Related Investment and, as well as the €3-€5 million a year in grants you could put €5 or perhaps €10 million from your endowment into investments in social enterprises that are in line with your programme or mission. That is what Fondazione Cariplo has done, putting €500 million, 6% of its total assets as at December 2014 (Anon, 2016a), into 'Mission Connected Investments' such as land for social housing (see www.fondazionecariplo.it/it/la-fondazione/patrimonio/gestione-e-rating-etico-degli-investimenti.html). Total grants in 2014 were €159 million, equivalent to just under one-third of the amount invested in PRI. (Bear in mind that these two figures are not directly comparable; investments form part of the long-term assets of an entity, while grants are spent money.) Interest in PRI is growing – Dr Lisa Hehenberger says that she has spoken (2015) "to a foundation in Spain that wants to do 100% Mission Related Investment. I think that will happen – there is the drive there to do more with the money." But she warns that "for that to happen, impact investment has to be solid," with legal and commercial structures in place, and a market in which to buy and sell.

The concern is that philanthropists will focus on impact investment, or financially borderline 'philanthropic impact investment', at the cost of other forms of philanthropy. It's the cake argument again: people are concerned that impact investment will take an increasingly large slice of a fixed financial cake, rather than increase the cake with a new layer of sponge and cream called 'impact investment'.

We have no data either way, in Europe. And the question may be superfluous. I asked interviewees who are involved in this area to comment and the majority felt that impact investment was complementary to other forms of philanthropy – the bigger cake argument. "Our impact investing is not at the expense of philanthropy" said a Dutch philanthropist and social investor. "We are not reducing the amount we give. These are assets we used to hand over to an investment manager." But he conceded that there could be leakage from philanthropy to impact investment: "this is a real concern". An Italian philanthropist, declining an invitation to be interviewed for this book, said: "I work in the impact investing area and ... I am not involved in the pure philanthropy space." This sounds like a mental map that has clearly differentiated philanthropy from impact investment. Referring to foundations and their Programme Related Investments, Karen Wilson agrees: "I don't think they are cannibalising their philanthropy budget to use in impact investment."

David Carrington emphasises the same point, calling it a "bifurcation" of investments:

> 'For me the bifurcation is a negative consequence of the traditional orthodoxy (preached especially by investment managers) that money is either used for investments made solely to achieve financial returns or is given away for social/public benefit. Social Investment is a challenge to such a traditional bifurcation as it is about setting out deliberately to achieve a blended return of both financial and social returns.'

Others also see a continuum between giving and investing. Ramón Bernat says that, for him:

> 'the frontier between social impact investment and philanthropy is less clear each day. Almost 100% of investments (of any type) can be explained as social impact investments – for example by creating employment. For me, social impact means helping entrepreneurs, change makers, "to make things happen." [He says this last phrase in English.] It is to do with the values of the person.'

Hitting Goliath

Venture philanthropy is Michelangelo's David, poised and ready to throw the stone at the traditional non-profit Goliath. Venture philanthropists, dedicated, inventive, critical, energetic people with money, are on a path that is changing traditional philanthropy in Europe. They are not the only force creating change, but they are an important one.

The government likes philanthropy

PART THREE

The government likes philanthropy

EIGHT

Government acts

Introduction

This section argues that governments have encouraged high-value philanthropy in Europe. But why? And why now?

Across Europe, governments are promoting philanthropy. They are doing this through tax and fiscal changes that favour private giving and by statutory changes that free up the creation or management of non-profit entities. Governments are also forcing philanthropy out into the open with laws on transparency, based in part on fears that it will be misused. Transparency is at the heart of this book, because increasing transparency allows us, finally, to see what is happening in philanthropy in Europe.

But it is not all good. There are government moves against the third sector, 'gagging' legislation and a Europe-wide austerity programme cutting the social services that many non-profits aim to deliver.

This section will review what governments are doing especially where this is relevant to high-value philanthropy, and will try to establish why they are intervening, and whether any of it works.

Your government likes philanthropy

Whether you live in Aberdeen or Vienna (or anywhere in between) you are likely to live in a place where the government is promoting and supporting philanthropy by offering new structures, better tax relief, or money.

Foundations of government

Governments in many countries in Europe have legislated for the creation of a raft of new vehicles for philanthropy. These include new forms of foundation, social enterprises and adapted forms of finance such as bonds. France, the most spectacular and complex example, has created eight separate types of foundation. Germany has also legislated for new foundation types (Anon, 2015c) – for example the 2013 'Gesetz zur Stärkung des Ehrenamtes' (Law to Strengthen Volunteer Work) that created Limited Term Foundations. These temporary foundations, which must exist for a minimum of ten years, can use their entire assets for their foundation mission. Some of this legislation is simply a very necessary modernisation of the law; for example, Belgium produced a new law on foundations in 2002. The previous law had been in place since 1921 (Mernier and Xhauflair, 2014).

According to Marie-Stéphane Maradeix, the creation of the 'fonds de dotation' (roughly, endowed foundations) was "the most important step since the 2003 law [that brought in fiscal relief for giving]". In 2011 there were 852 fonds de dotation. By January 2015 there were more than 2,000, according to the French Finance Ministry (www.economie.gouv.fr/daj/fonds-dotation).

Governments have also pushed organisations into, and sometimes out of, the non-profit sector. Italy saw a dramatic example of government intervention amongst its savings banks and 'Banks of the Mount' (Banche del Monte) with the Amato law (number 218, 30 July 1990) which separated the credit function of the savings banks from their philanthropic work, the former being housed in commercial for-profit banks and the latter in foundations. Marco Demarie says that "this was a real breakthrough in terms of financing the third sector. But the reasons for it were not philanthropic. It was the almost unintended effect of a change to make the Italian banking sector more palatable to the EU, although the result was that ancient traditions of local philanthropy were revived." There are currently 88 foundations in Italy created out of banks, according to the association that represents them, ACRI (www.acri.it).

Governments sometimes exclude organisations from benefiting from charitable, or public utility, status (either of which normally means that donations can be tax deductible). Private schools in England have been the subject of a constant tussle between the Charity Commission, the courts and Parliament. Similarly, some campaigning organisations live on the frontiers of charity law in England; Greenpeace, for example, is not allowed to register as a charity because of its political campaigning activity. So it has established the Greenpeace Environmental Trust as a separate registered charity (registration number 284934) to carry out activities that are not regarded as political, including scientific research, investigations and promoting sustainable development.

Ironically in all this wave of government creativity the one structure that foundations in Europe have been demanding for many years – a European Foundation Statute – has been denied to them. This project was promoted over 15 years by three large foundations (Bertelsmann Foundation, ZEIT-Stiftung Ebelin und Gerd Bucerius and Compagnia di San Paolo) and the European Foundation Centre (Hopt, von Hippel and Anheier, 2009) as a pan-European, or at least pan-European Union, structure that would enjoy equivalent rights and benefits in all EU member states. It was the subject of continued lobbying of the European Parliament and Commission but a November 2014 meeting of representatives of the 28 EU states failed to reach agreement on the Statute, which was then dropped from the 2015 legislative programme and may take some years to reappear.

Money for money

As Beth Breeze and Theresa Lloyd point out in *Richer Lives*, governments have engaged in campaigns such as the UK's Giving Campaign, which ran from 2001 to 2004 to 'encourage a culture of giving' and to 'increase the number of donors and amount donated' (Anon, 2004), principally by promoting the Gift Aid tax-effective giving scheme. The Campaign persuaded the *Sunday Times* to include charitable giving within its annual Rich List, and published research on new financial vehicles for giving. It encouraged four banks, including HSBC, to incorporate philanthropy in their client advisory services. During the Campaign period, more charities made claims for tax repayment under Gift Aid, and there was an increase in cash terms from £420 million in 2001/2 to £590 million in 2003/4, a 40% increase in tax repayments to charities on Gift Aid donations over the three-year period of the campaign (figures from www.gov.uk/government/uploads/system/uploads/attachment_data/file/532381/Table_10_3.pdf).

Two years later, the UK government made another foray into the philanthropy space, this time offering a pot of £200 million for a matched fund for universities in England (and a similar programme in Wales). The programme was designed to encourage the growth of professionalism in fundraising in universities. In its 'Review of Philanthropy in UK Higher Education' report in 2012, More Partnership noted that:

> at the end of financial year 2006–7, 131 institutions reported £513 million in total funds raised from 132,000 donors. Five years later, 152 institutions reported £693 million from more than 204,000 donors. That means 16% more institutions, reporting an overall rise of 35% in funds raised, and 54% more donors (Anon, 2012b)

There were matched funding schemes for culture in 2011 and international development in 2012 and in 2015 the £17.5 million 'Catalyst:Evolve' programme of the Arts Council which offered match funding for new philanthropic initiatives and capacity building and training programmes.

Granted, or not?

"When we look at the funding of the public good, we can see that our government is retreating", says Edwin Venema. "They find it harder to fund the public good from our taxes, so here in the Netherlands we have seen enormous cutbacks for museums and cultural organisations. These institutions are forced to go to private market; private funding of the public good is necessary." In France "55% of associations depend on subsidies", says Dr Arthur Gautier, Executive Director and Researcher at the ESSEC Philanthropy Chair in Paris. "There is a sense of urgency. Social and environmental issues are more pressing and there are less public subsidies."

Barbara de Colombe, Executive Director of the foundation that supports leading French business school HEC, agrees.

> We see that government cannot continue to play its historic role. We have a huge national debt, so the state cannot continue with everything. More and more people realise

we [in higher education in France] need to work together with philanthropists to make sure we are still competitive, and provide the right level of public education. Private resources will play a more and more important role in sectors such as higher education because we need investment and the state can't do it all anymore.'

A philanthropist with a family foundation in France told me that "foundations are having to fill in where government cannot. Now, the government is coming and knocking on our foundation doors."

Are governments cutting back on funding for the social sector, and freeing up the sector, in the hope that philanthropy will fill the gap? Marie-Stéphane Maradeix feels that she can see the signs. "There is a very significant detachment of the state", she says, noting that for the first time in 2012 state grant-aid support for the non-profit sector fell below 50% of the sector's income. Most of the rest is service agreements. "Philanthropists are aware of this", says Marie-Stéphane Maradeix, but few want to step into a gap created by the state.

These comments reflect widespread concern that governments are cutting back on support to the non-profit sector.

Is this true?

Surprisingly, data on overall government spend on the third sector is hard to find. But here is the UK's National Council for Voluntary Organisations (NCVO): 'Statutory support of the voluntary sector had increased in real terms, from £8 billion in 2000-01 to £13.9 billion in 2009-10' (www.ncvo.org.uk/policy-and-research/funding/what-the-research-tells-us). That is a 74% increase in real terms over a decade – hardly 'cutting back'. NCVO estimates that in 2015/16 the sector lost £1.2 billion per annum compared to the 2010/11 figures, as the result of cuts in public expenditure (http://data.ncvo.org.uk/a/almanac13/almanac/voluntary-sector/income-in-focus/how-are-public-sector-spending-cuts-affecting-the-voluntary-sector/). Deduct this estimated downfall in income from the £13.9 billion and you still get a 59% increase in state funding for non-profits between 2000/01 and 2015/16.

In Spain, even in the depths of a significant economic crisis, state funding for the third sector increased. The data is partial – it refers to around 600 organisations in the social sector – but it shows that state funding increased from €10.3 billion in 2008 to €10.5 billion in 2010, an increase of 1.6% in cash terms over the two years (Anon, 2012c). But the pattern is one that appears to be steady – in the 2008 edition of the report, cited in a comparison between 2010 and 2008, 46.4% of the 775 social sector entities in that study reported that public sector finance had increased and 32.6% said it had stayed the same. Only 21% said that it had, for them, decreased (Anon, 2012d).

In the Netherlands, the Central Bureau for Fundraising (www.cbf.nl) gathers data from 1,450 member organisations. Its detailed fundraising and income figures show that government grants increased from €1.3 billion in 2011 to €1.59 billion in 2014, a 21.5% increase in cash terms, or a 17% increase in real terms.

I discussed the gap between the perception that governments are cutting back and these hard data that indicate the opposite with Professor René Bekkers, Director of the Centre for Philanthropic Studies at VU University Amsterdam, and Dr Pamala Wiepking, Department of Business–Society Management, Rotterdam School of Management at the Erasmus University Rotterdam. Professor Bekkers made the point that government cuts to services in general (for example, cuts in social services) may have created more demand than the non-profits, even non-profits with bigger budgets, can meet. "Cuts in government budgets have been made in areas in which third sector organisations are active. This changes and sometimes increases the demand for services from these organisations."

Dr Wiepking commented that some:

> 'philanthropists look at this from their individual perspective and their opinion about the withdrawing government is based not on facts, but on personal observations and media preferences.
>
> Despite the fact that, overall, governments may be increasing public spending, they may decrease public spending in certain areas, such as is the case in the Netherlands for culture and arts. If philanthropists focus on areas that do receive lower levels of government funding, their observation can be correct.
>
> And depending on which media the philanthropists consume, they might get the impression from that media that government is cutting back on public spending. The public debate in the media in the Netherlands and UK

certainly has been that government funding is decreasing, especially following the UK government's "Compact" (see www.compactvoice.org.uk/sites/default/files/the_compact.pdf). In the Netherlands we have a similar initiative, which we call "participatiesamenleving", the participatory society.

The picture is complicated across Europe, with problems of definition. The difference between a grant and a contract for services can be very tiny, but may mean that funds are counted in different ways. But even allowing for these differences in definition, and the questions of allocation of resources and of perception raised by Bekkers and Wiepking, the data appears counterfactual; people in the sector say that they are experiencing cuts, yet the data seems to show steady or even increased funding. As in so many areas of philanthropy, we need more data, and much more research.

Transparency, by law

Governments are changing the laws on transparency for a host of reasons, including concerns over money laundering and corruption.

European foundations do not have glass pockets. For years they have enjoyed discretion and privacy. When around 2001 I contacted the lawyer then managing the office of Stichting Ingka Foundation (the Netherlands-registered foundation that owns part of the Ikea furniture group) I was told that the foundation was registered in the Netherlands "because we do not have to publish anything" including annual reports and accounts.

This subject, which is a particular interest of this book because of its potential impact on high-value philanthropy, is the focus of Part four on Transparency.

Tax

Governments are encouraging private finance for foundations and associations by making gifts tax efficient. When in 2010 the government of Andorra introduced the first corporation tax (Andorra has been famous as a European tax haven) it ensured that non-profit foundations, associations, religious groups, universities and, of course, political parties were exempt (Bisbal Galbany et al, 2013). The government did this, according to one commentary, as part of the 'internationalisation and modernisation of the [tax] system' (Oliver Arbós and Contreras, 2012). As we will see in Chapter Nine, the drive toward a more 'modern' system – meaning, in this context, one that encourages philanthropy – can be seen elsewhere in Europe.

Sweden introduced its laws on giving a year later (2011), creating for the first time a deduction for lifetime philanthropic giving – legacies to foundations were already free of tax (Surmatz, 2014). Individual donors giving to foundations and other non-profit organisations active in certain areas can deduct 25% of their gift up to a maximum of 1,500 SEK. Part of the pressure for this modernisation of the law came from the European Court of Justice rulings in the Stauffer and Persche cases (see box, 'Across the Border, with Stauffer and Persche').

France, the UK, Germany, Spain, the Netherlands, Italy and Switzerland have all seen their own modernisation of tax relief for giving, with the emphasis on making giving cheaper.

The European Foundation Centre publishes up-to-date information on the tax relief available to donors. Summarising a 2015 report (Anon, 2015e) and focusing on the larger economies in Europe we can see three systems in place: countries such as Finland and some of the former Soviet bloc countries that offer no tax incentives at all, those that allow deductions up to a cash limit, or a limit linked to income, and those that offer deductions of a proportion of the donation. As at mid-2015 the situation in Europe was:

- No tax incentives
  ○ Finland
- Donations deductible up to a low threshold (under €2,000)
  ○ Denmark, Norway
- A proportion of the donation amount can be deducted
  ○ Portugal (25% of the value of the donation can be deducted from income tax)
  ○ Sweden (up to 25% of the value of the donation can be deducted)
  ○ Spain (between 30% and 75% of the value of the donation can be deducted)
  ○ UK (the pre-tax value of the donation can be deducted from taxable income, and the non-profit can claim the income tax deemed to be deducted from the donation)

- Donations deductible up to approximately 10% of income
  ○ Austria, Belgium, Greece, Italy, Liechtenstein, Netherlands, Poland (6% of income)
- Donations deductible up to approximately 20% of income
  ○ Germany, Luxembourg, Switzerland
- Donations deductible up to higher proportions of income
  ○ Ireland, up to 30% of income
  ○ France, up to 66% of income.

The list above is a significant simplification of a complex map. Bear in mind, for example, that individual regions within countries can offer differing tax regimes for donors: Catalonia (Spain) and the regions of Belgium are examples.

These allowances change frequently so expect to find, by the time you read this, differences between the outline shown above and the latest situation as reported by the European Foundation Centre. They are also very open to gaming, especially if a philanthropist has assets or income from a number of countries. A brand-name international charity, for example, formerly accepted donations from an Austrian donor via his Swiss-registered foundation in order that he could enjoy the better tax relief Switzerland then offered.

Le fiscalité Français

Giving in France is cheap. A donor to a foundation in France gets a tax reduction worth 66% of the gift, with an upper limit equivalent to 20% of net taxable income. A gift of €1,000 thus costs the donor just €340. We are not going to enter the intricacies of the French tax system here, but the Fondation de France provides a useful calculator at http://isf.fondationdefrance.org/calculatrice.

For an individual who is paying the wealth tax (Impôt de Solidarité sur la Fortune, ISF) there are also reductions. ISF is payable by individuals holding assets of €1.3m or more (as at 1st January 2016, see http://www.impots.gouv.fr/portal/dgi/public/particuliers. impot?pageId=part_isf&espId=1&impot=ISF&sfid=50), with a cumulative scale starting at 0.5% for the lowest wealth bracket and rising to 1.5% on the highest. For certain foundations (the list is defined by the 'TEPA' law of August 2007, full text at https://www.legifrance. gouv.fr/affichTexte.do?cidTexte=JORFTEXT000000278649&cate

gorieLien=id), ISF tax payers can reduce their tax liability by up to 75% of their gift, to a maximum deduction of €50,000. So a taxpayer with a €3,000 ISF liability who makes a gift of €4,000 can eliminate her ISF – because 75% of €4,000 is €3,000. In other words, the ISF tax payer can make a €4,000 gift for a total cost of just €1,000. This is of course very attractive to high-value philanthropists, who are likely to be subject to ISF.

The changes in fiscal deductions brought in by the French government in 2007 were important, according to Marie-Stéphane Maradeix, who was then Development Director for the École Polytechnique. "I could see, when I worked at the École Polytechnique, that people were very clearly taking advantage of the campaign on ISF to make their gift."

Across the border, with Stauffer and Persche

In a series of cases starting in 2006, the European Court of Justice opened up the frontiers of Europe to giving. The best known of these cases are the Stauffer case in 2006 and the 2009 Persche case, but there were also judgments for Missionswerk, Laboratoires Fournier and the European Commission vs. Austria. These are expertly summarised by Thomas von Hippel (2014).

The Centro de Musicologia Walter Stauffer is an Italian-registered foundation that awards scholarships to young people from Switzerland. The foundation owns a building in Germany from which it obtains rental income. German tax law exempts foundations (technically, 'public benefit organisations') registered in Germany from corporate income tax for this kind of rental income, but foreign public benefit organisations do not enjoy the exemption. The case tested the question of whether this German rule infringes fundamental European freedoms.

The European Court of Justice ruled that rental income is protected under free movement of capital. They found that 'a restriction on tax incentives cannot be justified on the grounds that the organisation concerned has its registered seat in another Member State' (von Hippel, 2014). In other words, the tax relief offered to an Italian foundation earning rental income in Germany should be the same as that offered to a comparable German foundation.

The Persche case, and the later Missionwerk case which was about a legacy, were more clearly about donations across frontiers. In the former case, a German resident (Mr Persche) donated bed and bath linen, walking frames and other equipment to a Portuguese charity, the Centro Popular de Lagoa. Under German tax law, in-kind donations like this are treated as tax-deductible, so Mr Persche requested a deduction in his personal income tax declaration for 2003. The tax authorities refused his request.

When, six years later (Mr Persche was clearly a very determined individual), the case reached the European Court of Justice the court ruled that donations including in-kind donations are protected under the free movement of capital.

It should be emphasised that it was not only the German authorities that were found to be at fault. The tax authorities of Belgium and Austria also had judgments against them in the Court for similar cases.

From these cases, the European Court of Justice 'developed a general non-discrimination principle as regards tax law in the area of public-benefit activities' (von Hippel, 2014), ruling that member states can decide whether or not to provide tax privileges for public benefit organisations, but that if they do, they cannot exclude foreign-based organisations and their donors from tax privileges if they fulfil all of the requirements of the national public benefit tax law, apart from having their headquarters in another EU member state. The Court ruled that governments could not require organisations to carry out their philanthropic activities only in the state in which they get a tax privilege; in other words, a French taxpayer living in Lyon who wishes to make a gift to her *alma mater* in Italy should get the same tax treatment as her neighbour who donates to Insead. The Court introduced the idea of a 'comparability test' to identify whether or not a foreign, EU-based organisation met the requirements of a national tax law.

The European Foundation Centre's Transnational Giving Europe (TGE) programme notes that as the direct result of these two cases 'most Member States have adapted their laws' to allow a donor in EU Member State A to make a donation to a charity in Member State B, and to claim the same tax relief as they would get if they donated to a local organisation (Surmatz, 2014). TGE was created by leading foundations prior to the Stauffer and Persche cases, to allow individuals, foundations and companies to transmit donations tax efficiently from one EU state to another. In theory, TGE should have been made redundant by the European Court of Justice rulings. But a long-standing member of TGE told me privately that there was continued demand for their services because governments had made it administratively difficult to claim tax deductions for cross-border gifts. The 'comparability test' introduced by the Court was being used by some tax authorities as a barrier, requiring tiresome and unnecessary paperwork on the part of the donor and the non-profit. As a result, and despite the fee – it is modest – charged by TGE, individuals and foundations were using the programme rather than face the bureaucracy of their national tax authority.

Governments, gaming

When governments permit charitable lotteries to develop they often create substantial grant-making entities – high-value philanthropy, of a sort. At present there are charity lotteries in the UK, Ireland, Sweden, the Netherlands, Germany, Spain and Denmark (Association of Charity Lotteries in the EU, www.acleu.eu). France has the 'loto' managed by La Française des jeux (FDJ), a company that is 72% owned by the state; its 2015 income of €13.7 billion was paid out to winners (66%), distributors (6.2%) and to the government (www.groupefdj.com/fr/groupe/activite/finance/).

Novamedia in the Netherlands illustrates just how substantial the market is. At the time of writing Novamedia ran lotteries in three countries – the Netherlands, Sweden and the UK. In the Netherlands, the company runs three lotteries through the Holding Nationale Goede Doelen Loterijen NV, of which the National Postcode Lottery is the oldest and largest. The company claims that since December 2014 Novamedia and its combined lotteries are the third largest grant-maker in the world (www.novamedia.nl/web/Who-we-are/Organisation-Novamedia.htm) after the Bill & Melinda Gates Foundation (USA) and the Wellcome Trust (UK). The total grants made by the three Dutch lotteries in 2015 were €443 million (www.novamedia.nl/web/Who-we-are/Figures.htm). In 2015 the Swedish Postcode Lottery gave €115.8 million to charities, including its own two foundations, the Svenska Postkod Stiftelsen and the Postkodelotteriets Kultur Stiftelse (www.novamedia.nl/web/Charity-lotteries/Sweden/Swedish-Postcode-Lottery-Nieuw.htm). The combined total – €559 million – would place it just behind the UK's Wellcome Trust, which made grants of £674 million (€805 million) (Anon 2015i). Thanks to this, the Postcode Lottery has become a significant source of income for non-profits in the Netherlands. 'The share of lotteries in the total private income of charities has increased in the period 2007-11 from 9% to 12%', according to Sigrid van Aken, COO of Novamedia in the Netherlands (Zeekant, 2015).

The structure of the Dutch lotteries illustrates how governments have legislated for new non-profit entities (www.postcodeloterij. nl/organisatie/governance-holding.htm). The Stichting Aandelen Nationale Goede Doelen Loterijn foundation owns 100% of Holding Nationale Goede Doelen Loterijen NV, which in turn owns the rights to the three Dutch lotteries (Nationale Postcode Loterij, Vrienden Loterij and BankGiro Loterij). These rights are licensed to Novamedia BV. This company is 100% owned by Novamedia Holding BV, which in turn is 81% owned by Stichting Novamedia Fundatie (a foundation), with the remainder being owned by Cella Media BV (a for-profit company). The structure mixes for-profit with non-profit – a combination that would have felt uncomfortable to many in Europe just a few years ago but which now appears increasingly normal.

Grant making by the lottery's related foundations can be innovative. Stichting Doen (www.doen.nl) funds a range of activities to create a green, socially inclusive society. It has invested in social enterprises in the Netherlands and abroad for more than 20 years, and was one of the earliest of the impact investors. Its investments are typically in start-ups that are in line with the foundation's interests or via investment funds abroad.

Charity lotteries illustrate a number of points about how philanthropy is changing in Europe.

- They have created a substantial flow of assets into the non-profit sector; whether these are new assets or whether this is a zero-sum game is not clear.
- They have created some of the largest foundations in Europe, amongst which are foundations with innovative grant programmes that challenge convention.

- They have created structures that mix philanthropy and business, non-profit and for-profit.

There are concerns about Europe's lotteries. Some of these are moral or religious concerns about gambling, some are health issues linked to addictions to gaming, and some critics have pointed out that lottery tickets are bought predominately by people on low incomes, so this can be seen as a hidden tax on the poor. Despite these concerns, lotteries are apparently popular, and a growing source of grants to many of Europe's non-profits.

Government grudges

Politicians might say that they love a little charity, but that does not mean that they only do good. Too often, politicians also harm the sector.

The most dramatic of these harms has been the recent period of government cuts to social services, education and health. Blamed by the politicians on the banking crisis that started in 2008, but visibly in line with a longer term interest in neoliberal policies, these cuts have undone, and continue to undo, much of the good work of the non-profit sector. Whenever we hear a politician in Europe talking up philanthropy, or the 'big society', we should bear in mind that this may be the same person who voted for cuts in government services to the poor.

Politicians' duality, or possibly duplicity, was highlighted during 2015, when the Westminster government, reacting to press reports about an elderly volunteer in Bristol who had taken her own life, began a series of policy initiatives designed to control fundraising. These controls were not targeted at high-value philanthropy, but the sense amongst philanthropists that there was something rotten in the UK non-profit sector was supported by incendiary press articles about fundraising bad practice.

The impact of this campaign against charities has been felt in the morale of fundraising teams across the UK. Fundraising is the supreme act of belief in the goodness of humanity, of continuing to ask despite the many who say 'no'. Fundraisers' morale hangs on a thread, and the summer of discontent engendered by the press and the Westminster government has left many feeling lost and unloved. Governments intervene in the delicate balance of philanthropy at their peril.

The controls on fundraising by the Westminster government seem to be part of a pattern in the relationship between the state and the non-profit sector. The Transparency of Lobbying, Non-Party Campaigning and Trade Union Administration Act of 2014 (www.legislation.gov. uk/ukpga/2014/4/contents/enacted/data.htm), known in the sector as the 'gagging act', was criticised by charities working together as the Commission on Civil Society and Democratic Engagement, which claimed that it would make them cautious of criticising government in order to avoid legal challenges and reputational damage. A 2016 clause in government grant agreements, 'banning grantees from using taxpayers funds to lobby government' (www.gov.uk/government/ news/government-announces-new-clause-to-be-inserted-into-grant-agreements), underlined this shift toward silencing the non-profit sector.

We are in a period of flux in the relations between philanthropy and the state, and Theresa Lloyd says that "the rolling back of the state" means that people are asking "whose job is it to pay for public benefits; who should pay for culture, for example?" Even the definition of public benefit has become unclear according to her. The weak economies of Europe, and the widespread neoliberal thinking amongst politicians, mean that governments are unwilling to provide further public benefits from the public purse. A case in point is tax relief for giving; Marco Demarie says that, at least in Italy, "our public debt is too great to allow the government to increase tax relief for giving".

Philanthropy cannot fill the gaps left by states' withdrawal from health, culture or environment – there is no conceivable way that donated money could replace the universality of a taxation system (even allowing for those who avoid or evade). Philanthropy is not helped by governments playing nice cop and bad cop simultaneously, saying that they encourage philanthropy but then clamping down on organisations attempting to benefit from it.

NINE

Why government acts

Introduction

In the last chapter we looked at how governments have encouraged high-value philanthropy in Europe. In this chapter we ask why, why now, and does any of it work?

Why are governments supporting philanthropy?

Seen from across the Atlantic, or sometimes from across the Channel, Europe can appear homogenous: stable democracies offering rights to citizens, more or less capitalist economies and, to focus on the subject matter of this book, active civil society organisations supported by a mix of state and philanthropic partners.

But of course there are differences, and for high-value philanthropy these differences can be pronounced. We can identify four models of civil society in Europe.

From the Angles, to Scandinavia

The four European models of civil society are nicely outlined in *Philanthropy in Europe* (MacDonald and Tayart de Borms, 2008, p 8).

The model familiar to many readers is the Anglo-Saxon Model of the UK and USA, where civil society organisations (CSOs) 'are viewed as being a counterweight to the state'. In this model there is a 'strong culture of volunteerism, and foundations support civil society and fund issues that governments do not'.

In the Rhine Model (Belgium, Germany, Netherlands), CSOs are contracted by the state to deliver services in areas such as health and education. They depend on government funding and, as a consequence, the 'fiscal and legal climate does not strongly favour donations and gifts', and the growth of foundations has been slow and late.

In the Latin/Mediterranean Model it is traditionally the state that is responsible for delivering social services, with the church doing 'charity' work. 'The state is a strong economic actor and ... CSOs face a challenge in being accepted as independent and autonomous. There is an effort to control organisations and associations politically.' This can occur in various ways – the state insists on formal government representation on the boards of Italian banking foundations and certain foundations in France, for example.

> Gifts and donations are not encouraged by the fiscal system and volunteerism is viewed as a threat to the job market. Foundations have difficulty ... supporting and funding what government does not ... because when they move into what is perceived as political territory, they are challenged by politicians who question their mandate.

By contrast, volunteering and personal initiative are seen as positive in the Scandinavian Model. Here CSOs often identify a need which is later filled by government, with which they have a strong relationship. But 'gifts and donations are not strongly promoted in the fiscal system'.

The authors remind us that 'these models are of course evolving and changing, as are our societies'. We can see particularly strong evolution, and some convergence, in tax relief for donations, for example. But the differences are still discernible, and help us understand the basis on which governments act, or do not, to promote philanthropy.

To understand the tensions in these models I spoke to Dr Arthur Gautier in Paris. He has studied the evolution of parliamentary debate on philanthropy:

> 'There have been some really lively debates in France. In the 1980s and 1990s the Communist Party was opposed to tax breaks for philanthropy because of the potential private influence on the public good. The Socialist Party was really split with some wanting tax breaks, some not. All the right-wing or centrist parties were pushing for the tax breaks. Now the left has faltered and the Communist

Party has lost many votes. Many people from left and right take a more pragmatic approach and say that we need philanthropy.'

But he warns that the situation could change again. "So far tax breaks have been protected, but there are concerns that under a new conservative government they might be in danger."

L'évolution des mentalités

Announcing plans in the French Senate for a new law that would give more generous tax relief for donors, Jean-Jacques Aillagon, then Minister of Culture and Communication said: "Cela suppose aussi une évolution des mentalités de nos concitoyens, afin qu'ils soient mieux mobilisés sur les objectifs du mécénat" (It [the reform] also implies a change in the mind-set of our co-citizens, so that they feel more engaged with charitable objectives) (Allaignon, 2003).

This sentence is at the heart of government action on philanthropy, and it begs the counter-question: can governments change the mind-set (or 'evolve the mentalities') of philanthropists?

In France, at least according to the Observatoire de la Fondation de France, the answer is 'yes'. The Observatoire's 2008 report describing the 'growing interest of the French State for philanthropy' and the 11 laws that were passed between 1987 and 2008 on structures and tax for philanthropy says that 'it is without doubt [these] reforms in the interventions of the State in the social sector which have provided the starting point for the little revolution that we are engaged in' (Thibaut, 2008).

The debate led by Jean-Jacques Aillagon in the French Senate on 13 April 2003 was prior to the introduction of law number 2003-709 of 1 August 2003. The debate and associated documents are summarised in the Senate's website (for the full text of the debate see www.senat.fr/seances/s200305/s20030513/s20030513001.html#int39). Aillagon said that the new law was an "important programme of measures in favour of giving, of foundations and of associations, which aligns with the public interest. It deals with a true reform of the law and of taxation [that will] encourage and facilitate the development of giving and of foundations in our country". He talked about modernisation of the tax regime as it relates to philanthropy, a repeated theme in debates on fiscal relief for donations (the 2008 act that created endowed foundations in France would be called 'the Law for the Modernisation of the Economy'). In the 2003 debate Aillagon said that "France is undoubtedly suffering from a considerable delay in this area [fiscal relief for donations] in respect of other countries of Europe and of the USA".

So here we have a second reason for fiscal reform – modernisation. The promotion of philanthropy through the tax system is seen, or at least is justified to the electorate, in terms of modernisation.

For Aillagon, "public [that is, state] activities and individual generosity are ... converging streams ... leading to the global development of our country".

France had heard this idea of converging public and private interests before, in the Assembly, when in 1987 Edouard Balladur introduced a law on the development of giving ('mécénat') by saying that in a wide variety of sectors – culture, research, humanitarian aid, environment and education – 'the initiatives of individuals and of businesses can usefully complement the actions of the State and of regional government. It would be useful to encourage them by defining an appropriate [that is, more generous] fiscal and legal framework' (Aillagon, 2003).

The vision of civil society and the state converging sounds like a good idea, and it must be helpful for politicians to put themselves on the side of the good guys in CSOs. But it may be a long way from what is actually happening, as CSOs criticise the state for its policies, especially its austerity programmes.

There were also political motives for bringing forward the 2003 legislation. The French Senate was debating these popular tax reliefs at the same time, as Senator Yann Gaillard pointed out (www.senat. fr/seances/s200305/s20030513/s20030513001.html#int39), as they were "in a difficult period when people only talk about cuts". I will come back to this point of political populism when we look briefly at the introduction of fiscal benefits for donors in the USA.

Why governments give tax relief to donors

So why do governments support philanthropy through tax relief and other measures? Is there, as one author claims, 'a profound shift in the relationship among [sic] the state, commercial marketplace, and civil society' (Johnson, 2010)? Theresa Lloyd says that "we are in a debate about the role of the state. The confusion between state and charity means trustees have never had to make the case for private philanthropy."

Is this change driven by 'neoliberal ideologies' as some claim? Or is it just honest, heart-warming politicians being charitable?

According to Steve Rathgeb Smith and Kirsten Grønbjerg (2006) there are three models to explain the interest that governments have in non-profits: 'Demand and Supply', 'Civil Society/Social Movement' and 'Regime or Neoinstitutional'.

Demand and supply

The Demand and Supply model refers to the failure of for-profit markets or governments to supply all of our needs. Neither business nor state is very effective at meeting our needs for religious belief, nor particularly good at supplying our need for the arts and culture, for example. This can be described as a transaction – where non-profits supply services for which there is demand that the government does not meet.

Demand and supply – *if they didn't pay for it we would have to*

"The government looks at philanthropy as a way to replace what they can't do any longer", says Marco Demarie. Some charities provide services (education, housing, health) also provided by government. When charities take on the service, they relieve the government from that expenditure. Donors giving to those charities are thus paying for public services. If they did not donate, the services would have to be provided by the government at full cost. In this context, as Ineke Koele (2007, p 64) argues in *International Taxation of Philanthropy*, the tax deduction 'may be regarded as a tax expenditure by the government. The same result could be achieved by granting direct subsidies to the same organisation.' Demand and supply could be behind the widespread European definition of 'public utility'. Associations in a number of European states that win approval from the government as 'public utility' organisations can offer fiscal benefits similar to those offered by foundations.

Demand and supply – spillover benefits

The vaccination programmes of Médecins sans Frontières (MSF, www.msf.org) provide direct benefits to the individual, but also help others by preventing the spread of contagious diseases. This is a 'spillover benefit', otherwise known as a 'positive externality', where benefits accrue to people who are not the original consumers of the good. A subsidy, in the form of a tax deduction for donors to charities, encourages charities to provide goods with spillover benefits.

The high level of poverty in Scotland – 940,000 people in 'relative poverty' after housing costs (Anon, 2016b) – means that there is substantial demand for foodbanks, a demand that neither the Westminster government nor the for-profit food retailers are willing to meet. Various non-profits – registered charities whose donors get tax relief for their gifts – fill the gap. The Trussell Trust is one of the most active. Alongside its distribution of food packages to needy families, the Trust offers educational and training programmes for its clients on topics ranging from nutrition to state benefits and employment. These programmes create a spillover benefit: the parent in the nutrition class will feed his children better, and the person in the class on job seeking might win the job that brings the family out of extreme poverty.

So governments give tax relief to donors in part to reduce costs. Without the subsidy of the tax relief it would fall to the state to meet the demand for services. By giving this relief and relying on the humanitarians in the non-profits, they create additional spillover benefits – a useful multiplier.

There is competition between the state and civil society in the supply of services; across most of Europe education, health, culture, heritage and environmental protection, and emergency services are offered by both government and non-profit organisations. This can raise concerns that government might 'crowd out' non-profit initiatives; for example, where the government supplies widespread free hospital care it may dissuade private philanthropic organisations from doing so. We reviewed the debate on 'crowding out' in Chapter Four.

Civil and social movements

Alexis de Tocqueville (1805–1859) 'argued that America's democracy rested on its extensive network of voluntary organisations' (Rathgeb

Smith and Gronbjerg, 2006, p 229). This is the basis of the Civil Society and Social Movements model for government-non-profit relations. 'From a civil society perspective, the non-profit sector is regarded as the embodiment of certain values that are crucial to democracy and good government.' The non-profits create a value in society – 'social capital' – made from the tissue of participation, cooperation and collaboration that voluntary organisations help to weave. Participation promotes transparency and accountability in government (think about pressure groups and campaigns) and thus improves the quality of government services. The existence of a wide range of organisations, supported by a large number of philanthropists, gives the citizen choices that she might not have under a state monopoly. And participation in voluntary organisations may lead people to participate more widely in public life – Scotland's Youth Parliament (www.syp.org.uk) is an example. Even the rights organisations – traditionally pitted against government – create value for society by demanding new and better services: safe hostels for women victims of domestic violence, for example.

The Civil Society and Social Movements model locates government support for non-profits, and by extension for philanthropy, as support for the values and attributes of a democratic society. This is not a model that explains why governments make grants (they don't, generally, to organisations that might campaign against them) nor why governments offer tax relief. But it does help us understand why many governments allow organisations with a strong social change ideology to register as foundations (and enjoy tax relief on donations); the Heinrich Böll Stiftung (www.boell.de/) in Germany, linked to the Green Party there, is an example, as are liberal or socialist think tanks such as the Konrad Adenauer Stiftung (www.kas.de) or the Fondation Jean Jaurès (https:// jean-jaures.org/). David Carrington (2009) argues that 'philanthropy is political' and notes that some of 'the most effective philanthropic efforts will challenge orthodoxies, will irritate or anger governments or established institutions'. These challenges are not all left to right, and Carrington notes that 'the development of "neo-con" political policies in the USA, for example, was nurtured and supported over more than a decade by strategically targeted philanthropic funds'.

Civil society and social movements – friends on the outside

There is also the view that government support for civil society can create a body of knowledge that will survive political changes. Ineke Koele (2007, p 63) notes that 'it may often be advantageous for government to support non-profit entities which provide continuing expertise and are not directly subjected to political (i.e. electoral) influence'. Government support for universities may be an example: many European universities are managed by private foundations and increasing numbers of the public universities have established private foundations through which to channel philanthropic funding. Koele links this reasoning with 'Interdependence Theory', the idea that the non-profit sector depends on government support, and that 'in order to substantiate its political power, governments may wish to receive support from the people working in the non-profit sector' and from beneficiaries. This is stretching the optimism of politicians to its limits; it would be hard to argue that tax relief for donations is a major vote winner (compared to jobs, health and social services, for example), while on the other hand it is equally hard to imagine the employees of, say, Greenpeace France voting for the kind of liberal (conservative) politician who would typically favour tax relief for philanthropy.

Regimes and institutions

The Regime and Neoinstitutional Perspectives model emphasises that the relationship between government and non-profits can be an uncomfortable one – witness the barriers against international non-profits created by the Russian state, or the abuse of non-profits for personal gain in regimes such as Spain where transparency is lacking. The model is based on the idea that the way in which a government provides for its needy people dictates the government–non-profit relationship. Thus the Scandinavian countries, with their powerful state welfare systems, create different relationships than those in the US. The governing regime also reflects those in power, and the authors remind us that 'class power shapes the allocation of state resources, which in turn further reinforce class power' (Rathgeb Smith and Gronbjerg, 2006, p 234). Philanthropy is constructed by some authors as reinforcing class structures – the rich and powerful giving to the poor and weak in order to remind the latter that the former are indeed in charge.

These arguments move from theory to practice when we look at tax relief. We can see echoes of the four models in reviewing why governments give tax relief to donors. To do that, let us start with the spiritual home of tax relief for charity, the USA.

US deductions and reasoning

US Federal income tax charitable gift deduction was first introduced by the War Revenue Act of 1917, to sweeten the bitter pill of rate increases in the federal income tax, brought in to fund the US involvement in World War I. Legislators 'feared that the increases would reduce individuals' income "surplus" from which they supported charity. It was thought that a decrease in private support would create an increased need for public support and even higher tax rates, so the deduction was offered as a compromise' (Simmons, 2013). The idea that a tax deduction would encourage more giving is at the heart of US policy today. As the Joint Committee on Taxation reported to the House Committee on Ways and Means, 11 February 2013 'empirical studies generally support the proposition that taxpayers respond to tax incentives when making giving decisions. In other words, taxpayers increase donations as the after-tax cost of giving decreases, and they decrease donations as the after-tax cost of giving increases.'

The 1917 tax deduction was also supported by legislators who thought that it was an effective way to distribute public money directly to charities, meaning less government interference. Many legislators believed charities could deliver social services better than the government, and that it should be individuals rather than the government who decide which non-profits to support. Finally, some legislators argued that money donated to charity should not be considered income at all, and thus should not be taxed.

These arguments were repeated in 2013 evidence to the House Committee of Ways and Means, when the US Joint Committee on Taxation argued that there are ethical and economic reasons for tax deductions for charitable contributions. I have summarised the reasoning below, and one can see the parallels with the four models discussed above.

Crowding out

If the altruistic contribution by a donor to a charity results in a decrease in the donor's wealth, then it should not be taxed under a comprehensive income tax system. This argument allows the converse, acknowledged by the Joint Committee; if people experience a 'warm glow' from giving, then they are benefiting...and in this case they should not be allowed a deduction. How the tax authorities were proposing to measure the warmth of the glow is not explained, but this sounds awfully like the 'crowding out' debate we saw in Chapter Four.

Civil society and social movements

The Joint Committee argues that deductions create a level playing field, allowing a neutral choice between providing a service either by a government agency or by a private charity. On this basis, the preferential tax treatment of philanthropy is not simply an economic action; it is an affirmation of a government policy to encourage, through taxation, the activities of non-profit organisations that are beneficial to society.

Demand and supply – subsidising public goods

'In the absence of subsidies, the private market provides fewer public goods than is optimal.' When an art collector donates part of her collection to a public art gallery, she is making a private contribution to a public good. Without a subsidy in the form of a tax deduction for the art collector she might give less, or not give at all. Where neither the free market nor the government produces all the goods and services we need, non-profits fill the gap. Different tax regimes encourage non-profits to carry out non-commercial activities that do not generate any, or sufficient, profit (Weisbrod and Cordes, 1998).

This argument allows the Joint Committee to warn that where there is not genuine, widespread, public benefit, the tax deduction may not be warranted. They argue that 'donations to a college may benefit select students and faculty at a college ... If the larger public is unable to share in the benefit of the charity's activities [then these] donations are private contributions to private goods and there is no economic rationale for a charitable contribution deduction.' Note the 'economic rationale'. It is an 'economic rationale', not a political rationale. Just listen to the political clamour when governments threaten to remove the charitable status from private schools and thus, potentially, threaten donors' tax deductions.

In summary, tax relief in the USA is promoted by legislators in order to:

- save future state expenditure, by ensuring continued private contributions to non-profits
- allow the public to choose charities directly, rather than have them selected and funded by the state
- meet an ethical belief that donations are not income, because they reduce an individual's wealth
- avoid taxing something from which an individual gains no benefit (so long as she does not experience that 'warm glow')
- subsidise the creation of goods from which the public benefits, such as art collections
- and, in 1917, to make an unpopular tax rise acceptable to the voting public.

Your government likes philanthropy

Your government likes philanthropy and so does mine. There are indeed, as Culture and Communication Minister Allaignon said, converging streams of interests between state and civil society.

We have demand and supply across Europe – demands for social services that governments cannot or will not meet, and a voluntary sector willing to supply providing that the donors will too. Governments – witness the evidence to the US Senate – believe that more generous fiscal treatment of donations will encourage donors to give more, so they meet the growing demand by opening up fiscal support for giving. They might be wrong, or at least partially wrong if the evidence on the take-up of tax relief in the Netherlands (see below) is an indicator, but mere evidence is hardly enough to counter the common sense of politicians.

We also have a range of moral and belief-based arguments on the value of civil society to democracy. These are genuine expressions of beliefs, but also wonderfully vote-winning, giving something for (almost) nothing.

These factors have come together now, in Europe, to create a strongly positive political environment for philanthropy across left-wing, right-wing and centrist regimes on the continent. But it is a delicate balance, requiring both parties to participate. "There is a dilemma in this", says Ulrik Kampmann in Denmark. "If the public sector cuts back, should we take it over? We can only solve this problem together. When the public sector gets cut we say we will not fill in the gaps."

Does it work?

Will these changes in the ways that governments relate to philanthropy end up changing the way we think? Governments clearly hope so. But there is an important distinction between values and behaviours here; a philanthropist in France might prefer to support, say, modern dance but she is encouraged by tax relief to support science. The results of research in neuroscience in which people are asked to obey rules that conflict with their own preferences indicate that 'rules do not change values, just behaviours', in the words of Etienne Koechlin at the École Normale Supérieure, Paris (Spinney, 2015), who has carried out empirical studies in this area. New rules from governments might change the way we give, but not the values which drive that giving.

In the field of tax relief for donations, the evidence is mixed. We saw in Chapter Eight that a UK government programme to boost claims for Gift Aid tax relief increased the value of claims by 40% over three years. But evidence from the Netherlands shows that only a small proportion of the public takes up tax deductions. Less than 5% of the Dutch population deducted donations from tax in 2005. This reluctance is not because tax relief is new – it was introduced in 1914 as a regulation to 'prevent double taxation of maintenance payments to support relatives' (Bekkers and Mariani, 2009), with the formal charitable gift deduction being created in 1952. Bekkers and Mariani review the history of the tax deduction and attempt to establish whether it actually stimulates donations; they see some effects, but find that other factors are more important – specifically, whether donors were going to reduce or increase their giving anyway. They find that few people use the deduction: in 2007 just under half (49%) of Dutch households reported total donations over the threshold amount of €60 that would allow a deduction, but less than 5% of the Dutch population claimed the deduction. In a finding that should send a chill down the spine of fundraisers and tax advisers alike, Bekkers and Mariani show that 'in 2005, literally none of the households in the IPS [data set] with gross incomes exceeding €1.2 million used the deduction. Apparently, the charitable deduction has not found its way to the most wealthy in the Netherlands.' In other words, the argument used by US policy makers, that tax relief would encourage donations, seems to be on shakier ground in Europe.

There is another effect of fiscal relief however. As Odile de Laurens and Sabine Rozier pointed out in a 2012 report for the Fondation de France, 'for potential philanthropists, [fiscal reliefs] are a sort of official stamp, a public legitimisation of philanthropy'. Bekkers and Mariani agree, saying that tax deduction or other indirect subsidies 'may send a positive signal to private donors that charitable organizations are worthy of support'. This official stamp of approval, used by foundations across Europe and also by those associations that achieve 'public utility' status, is thought to be useful for fundraising. As far as I am aware, however, its supposed positive benefits have never been tested.

Governments, tax and philanthropy

Philanthropists need government, and vice versa. Breeze and Lloyd (2013, p 42) quote one of their wealthy UK interviewees as saying: "Philanthropy alone cannot end poverty, nor end environmental destruction, nor alone build a cultural sector. In all of these areas it needs a state partner either to tax wealth and support the poor, or to legislate against polluters, or to take the arts to the public."

This is not because governments will do the job of philanthropy. Nor can philanthropy move the sums of money that governments can. The gap between the amounts given in philanthropy and the amounts taken in personal tax is enormous. For example the total amount donated to charity by UK adults in 2014 was £10.6 billion according to the estimates of the Charities Aid Foundation (Anon, 2015l). Meanwhile the OECD calculation of UK total government income from personal income taxes in the same year was £160.6 billion – 16 times the income from donations. In France the picture was even more extreme.

Estimated total declared giving there in 2011 was €2.1 billion whilst the total government income from personal income taxes in 2011 was €150.4 billion, more than 70 times charitable giving, and this despite a year-on-year rise of 8.6% in declared donations (Tchernia, 2014, latest statistics available). Note that in the case of France these are donations declared to the authorities for tax relief; the total actually given will be more than the €2.1 billion declared.

Governments – just meddling?

Governments across Europe are attempting to manage philanthropy, but the approaches vary from legislation to self-regulation – the UK's Fundraising Standards Board (www.frsb.org.uk) is an example of the latter. But a recent review found that:

> government oversight of philanthropy, even in countries with extensive institutional philanthropy, is often haphazard and a patchwork of regulatory standards and jurisdictions. Such seemingly random regulation often reflects the 'neither fish nor fowl' nature of philanthropy – it is neither the public domain nor business, the sectors at which law is most frequently directed. (Johnson, 2010)

The review cited for example the situation in Spain, where 'there are 60 supervising authorities and 17 autonomous regions, each with its own set of laws and decrees' with which foundations must comply. The 2015 European Foundation Centre report on the legal framework for foundations in Europe highlights these differences (Anon, 2015e). For example, in the 40 European countries surveyed (including Russia), seven have a legal maximum for the amount that can be spent on administration costs, nine have other non-legal mechanisms for controlling the amounts spent on these costs, and 24 set no maximum.

In one sense we can answer the question at the start of this chapter. We can say why governments are encouraging philanthropy in Europe; to evolve our mentalities, to modernise the relationship between the state and non-profits, to encourage a convergence of interests between the state and civil society, to provide supplies and spillover benefits that neither the state nor the for-profit sector can, and to support the democracy-building potential of the non-profit or civil society sector.

So yes, we can say why they do it. What we cannot say is that there is any really satisfactory evidence to support these theories of change. It all looks good, but as in so many areas in Europe we simply lack the data to be certain.

And that leaves us exposed to other politicians, from the left or the right, who say that they want to dismantle this relationship, and especially tax relief. Without evidence, we risk losing the tax relief on which so many organisations depend.

PART FOUR

Transparency

TEN

Seeing change

This section argues that increasing transparency has led to changes in philanthropy in Europe.

Introduction

Uncovering philanthropy in Europe can be a frustrating process. Especially if you are used to the openness of a sophisticated philanthropic market such as the USA. There, just a little bit of research using a well-known search engine will get you information on the interests, activities and finances of all the leading philanthropic foundations in the country. Charity Navigator (www.charitynavigator.org/) and Charity Watch (www.charitywatch.org/home) provide information on charity efficiency. A bit more research, using a free-to-access data set such as Guidestar (www.guidestar.com) will unveil the annual statutory returns (the 'Form 990') of all of these foundations, with information on the organisation's income, its investments, its grants, its board members and its key paid staff, including their salaries. If you are looking for an individual philanthropist a brief search will tell you that she is a member of the Founder's Circle at her *alma mater* and that this means she has made a gift of at least $500,000. Further searches will reveal information about her various homes and their values, and her business connections.

For years, researchers in Europe lived in the dark ages, unable to find anything – barely even a name – when we searched for philanthropy here. We looked with envy at the wealth of information available to our US counterparts.

In the last few years this balance has started to shift a little. In this section we will look at what is happening in Europe and try to understand the basis for our concern with privacy, or even secrecy. I will review the practical impact on fundraisers, wealth managers and foundations of the changes in publicly available information. We will test the idea that this lack of information may be holding high-value philanthropy back by slowing the development of social norms for giving.

Europe has suffered for its secrecy, and I will look at cases of corruption and the misuse of funds that can be blamed on the lack of transparency.

The section starts by clarifying what we mean by 'transparency' and the ways we can see into organisations.

Different ways of seeing

Greg Michener and Katherine Bersch (2013, p 233) argue that 'transparency dispels opacity, the first refuge of corruption, inefficiency and incompetence'. It is from this idea that Transparency International, the 'global coalition against corruption', springs. But what do we mean by 'transparency'? Michener and Bersch argue that transparency has two constituent and overlapping parts – visibility, the 'degree to which information is complete and easily located', and what they call 'inferability', the 'extent to which it can be used to draw accurate conclusions'. Inferability 'has everything to do with the quality of the information or data' and its disaggregation, verifiability and simplification. Both conditions – visibility and the ability to make inferences from the information – are required for transparency to exist.

This two-part definition is readily applicable to the non-profit sector. For example, while we can say with some certainty that the Ministry of Health, Social Services and Equality in Spain (www.msssi.gob.es/) has complete information on the charitable foundations under its protection, we can say with equal conviction that the information is not easily located, at least by members of the public. Thus the visibility condition is not met.

Equally, where a foundation has a programme in, say, girls' education they may publish lists of the projects they support and the amounts granted to those projects (although even this, in continental Europe, is relatively uncommon) but they leave us unable to infer the impact that the programmes had. We can see the money, but not the change.

Seeing inside

These two axes of transparency – visibility and the ability to make inferences – occur outside and inside organisations. An individual who wants to find out about a foundation wants 'public visibility' – the capacity to see into the organisation from the outside. But she also wants to be able to understand what she sees, whether that is financial, programme, leadership or impact information. This is 'external transparency', combining the two measures of visibility and the ability to make inferences.

Then there is 'internal transparency', which refers to the visibility and clarity of information within an organisation or decision-making process. Non-profits can be internally complex, meaning that a person in one department cannot see what her colleagues are doing in another. Universities are complex because they are big and diverse and it is practically impossible for a fundraiser in a university to know all of the relationships that a philanthropist might have with the institution, or to know about all of the university's activities. This lack of internal transparency limits the ability of the fundraiser to turn information into donations. The big UN agencies and NGOs face this problem, finding it hard to get information from a refugee camp or a disaster zone to their national fundraising teams. Modern technology, and particularly Skype and mobile phones, is making a dramatic difference to this problem. But even relatively small organisations can suffer from this problem when the pressures of work and the relatively weak internal systems mean that, for example, Jane the fundraiser has not spoken to John the social worker for the last six weeks, so has no clear idea of what he is doing.

Internal transparency is especially relevant to high-value philanthropy. Consider a mid-size NGO with a mixed income stream including some government support, grants from half a dozen foundations, two company sponsors and a direct marketing programme that relies on mailings to bring in donations from 25,000 supporters. The NGO wants to develop relationships with high-value philanthropists. This type of fundraising is based on building personal relationships, on meetings in person, on understanding the interests, motivations and the economic capacity of a small number of high-value philanthropists. All of this information is vital to the fundraiser who wants to build a solid, long-term relationship with a donor.

If this sounds odd, replace the word 'fundraiser' with 'account manager', replace 'high-value philanthropist' with 'client' and replace 'NGO' with 'private bank'. The process that a private bank would go through to win a client is virtually identical to that used by the NGO.

In an NGO with a high level of internal transparency, where the fundraiser is in regular contact with senior management, with board and other key stakeholders, there is a good chance that she can develop a successful programme. Conversely such a programme will be nearly impossible in an NGO in which links to programme staff are weak, where the fundraiser is not permitted to work directly with the board ('she is too junior'), or where the hierarchy, or internal barriers, or both, restrict information flows and the capacity to make accurate inferences.

There is an effect that the visibility of philanthropy has on the viewer, and later in this section I will review evidence that this may affect the market price for philanthropy.

Emotional transparency

Uniquely in non-profits, transparency is not just about information. It is about emotion too. The relationship between philanthropist and non-profit is a complex one, but is sometimes characterised as 'head and heart': the donor is giving because she has seen the budget, read the reports, understands the impact of the non-profit. But she is also giving because she has been touched, emotionally, by what they do. She has visited the hospital and met the kids, or she has spent a morning with the homeless men in the shelter, or she has talked to the brother of a man with cancer. Alongside the flow of information and data there is a flow of emotion. The emotion is visible – you can see it on the faces of the children – and we can draw inferences from it, some of them subconscious ('she is in a desperate situation, I can see that').

Fundraisers know that philanthropists need to see and feel, to see data, facts and pictures but also to live the experience, to feel the flow of emotions. Fundraisers working with high-value philanthropists in organisations such as Oxfam organise field visits to meet the beneficiaries in order to create this emotional transparency; the University of Oxford does the same when it organises a dinner for scholarship students and their benefactors.

Looking backwards

There is a lot of pressure on non-profits in Europe to be more transparent. So it is worth pointing out that the transparency that we see in the for-profit world – with public companies publishing quarterly or annual results in their websites, and an enforcement of laws and regulations regarding openness in corporate financial affairs, was not ever thus. As Christopher Napier (2010, p 245) points out in the UK chapter of *A Global History of Accounting, Financial Reporting and Public Policy: Europe*, it was only the tiny handful of joint stock companies such as the East India Company, chartered in 1600, that made available financial records for investors.

> Although the East India Company allowed stockholders to inspect its accounting records periodically, the Board of Governors preserved a high degree of secrecy over its financial affairs and this led to occasional financial scandals and, in reaction to these, public criticism and calls for investigations of the Company's financial position.

It was not until the 19th century with the advent of the railways in the UK, and their requirement for huge investment, that publishing of accounts in a more substantial way began to emerge. The influence of first the stock market, then business taxation, and finally the emergence, in Scotland in 1854 (www.icas.com/regulation/icas-charter-rules-and-regulations), of the accountancy profession encouraged companies to publish their accounts.

Demand for more transparency

Theresa Lloyd says that today "there are role models – people who are willing to stand up and speak [about their philanthropy]. They want to be part of a congenial society." In Italy "there is pressure to change" and to open up more transparency amongst foundations, says Marco Demarie. "People are beginning to talk more publicly about their philanthropy. The media is more interested in that. It's become a matter for public consultation." Sophie Vossenaar, a board member of FIN, the Dutch Foundations Association, says that "transparency has gained traction over the last 10-15 years. Part of it comes from the

Government side – driven by 9/11 and the desire to uncover terrorist funding. There have also been scandals amongst fundraising charities, and government wants transparency to help with that." Both of these reasons for transparency are covered in this chapter.

Ulrik Kampmann, the former Director of Development at Realdania in Denmark, agrees with the need for more public visibility amongst foundations. "Danish foundations are talking about transparency as a way of working. We have changed the legislation, and have to explain how we are doing certain things. Transparency is a game changer, and that is for the better."

Seventy-five percent of respondents to a 2013 survey by GrantCraft reported observing an increased demand for funder transparency over the past five years (Parker, 2014). Respondents said that it was important to move toward greater transparency, and listed the following benefits:

- Less time spent explaining goals and strategies to potential grantees
- Better, more on-target grant applications
- More effective and informed grant-making based on feedback from grantees and other stakeholders
- Stronger and more open relationships with grantees and other non-profit organisations
- Closer relationships with other foundations leading to more collaborative grant-making
- Increased public trust.

In the survey, numerous interviews with funders and an analysis of blog posts and survey responses indicated that 'true transparency comes down to a mind-set, one in which funders believe they are most effective when they approach all aspects of their work by saying "let's publicly share this"'. While transparency can be challenging for many reasons, including limited staff time and potential vulnerability, funders interviewed for the study agreed that sharing what they know and creating space for dialogue was essential to accelerating change.

In a prescient warning written before the 2015 wave of criticism of the UK non-profit sector, Parker reports foundation leaders as saying that 'it is much more risky … to hide behind a veil of secrecy with the possibility that a reporter or watchdog group will publish damaging and incomplete findings'.

Visible companies

The impact of public visibility on giving is more apparent in the business world, where Corporate Social Responsibility programmes have become the norm for public companies in Europe and, increasingly, for larger private or family-owned firms. As Coral Morera Hernández (2015, p 89) points out:

> Corporate giving today is, as well as being a donation, an act of communication that companies use to reach out to society. It helps to build better relationships with [the company's] public, who don't perceive it as conventional publicity but rather as personal satisfaction, either via culture and the arts, or [support for the poor]. Of course the company benefits in terms of image and notoriety – it is not anonymous but then neither were the corporate donors in the olden days; to think otherwise is to allow yourself to be carried away with a certain romanticism ... There is no need to make an exhibition of one's corporate giving because if that were the case it would be a sponsorship, for publicity. But it is right that society knows the donor: 'it is not right to hide a fact that could serve this same community to know which local companies are most concerned for its welfare' [Antoine, 2003, p 126].

It seems reasonable to propose – at least in Europe – that public visibility of Corporate Social Responsibility has encouraged its spread. Organisations such as ADMICAL in France (www.admical.org/), Arts and Business in the UK (http://artsandbusiness.bitc.org.uk/) and Business to Arts in Ireland (www.businesstoarts.ie) have fostered the public face of CSR in culture and, in the case of ADMICAL, in sport, social support, heritage and environment.

Why so private?

When asked about foundations that they are familiar with, more than half (53%) of the German population say that they do not have a clear idea of what they do (Anon, 2015c). This perception is well-founded: in 2000, only 15% of German foundations published their annual report and just 9% used the Internet to do so. The situation in Belgium is similar, with a 2014 report saying that in the 12 years since a 2002 law on foundations they have become more numerous, more professional but that they are 'paradoxically still relatively unknown' (Mernier and Xhauflair, 2014). Colleagues based in the Netherlands report that most of the 163,000 foundations thought to exist there do not publish accounts despite new regulations (see below) designed to encourage them to do so.

Why are they so private? The report on German foundations cites six reasons:

1. Executives 'invoke foundations' independent nature and high level of freedom'
2. The foundations are the funding body, so should be able to determine the level of openness themselves
3. Transparency would add unnecessary bureaucracy
4. There is not a culture of internal communication between founders, the board of trustees, the executives and employees
5. Foundations lack a culture of learning and accepting failure
6. More transparency 'is viewed much more as a risk for the foundation's reputation, which in the absence of a market, is the organization's most valuable currency in a competitive environment'. (Anon, 2015c)

These arguments were refined further in the Netherlands by FIN, the Dutch association of (principally) endowed foundations.

In July 2013, the Dutch Government made an amendment to article 5b of the General Taxes Act of 1994 (https://zoek. officielebekendmakingen.nl/stcrt-2013-20451.html), requiring foundations that are approved for tax relief to publish on the Internet:

• the name of the institution
• its official registration number, Article 12, section A of the Trade Register Act 2007
• its postal or physical address, or phone number, or email address
• the goals of the organisation, according to its own by-laws
• the main features of its current policy
• the board composition, remuneration policy of the institution and the names of the directors

- an up-to-date report on the activity of the institution
- the statement of income and expenditure, with notes, of the institution.

These regulations followed a June 2011 'covenant' signed by the Dutch Prime Minister and the Samenwerkende Brancheorganisaties Filantropie, or Cooperative Association for Philanthropy, an umbrella body including endowed foundations, the churches and fundraising organisations, which agreed to more transparency and better coordination of policies and investments, amongst other issues.

There are some exceptions: organisations where there are concerns about the personal safety of directors or their families do not have to publish their board members' names. Churches or related organisations are only required to publish a statement of income and expenses and an overview of planned spending with an explanation. The same is true where the foundation's main assets are shares in companies, or where the foundation is not actively fundraising.

One of the interviewees for this book, who is the manager of a group of family foundations, explained the background:

> 'If you wanted to get tax relief then the numbers had to be [published] in the Internet. The FIN (the Vereniging van Fondsen in Nederland, Netherlands endowed foundations association, www.verenigingvanfondsen.nl) convinced the Ministry that foundations holding equity only had to publish the profit and loss accounts, not the balance sheet. I'm not sure why FIN made such a fuss. In five or six years we will be where the US foundations are now [in financial transparency]. The Ministry is closing in on the sector, and also on the Church foundations; as of 1 January 2016, Church foundations will also be required to publish profit and loss figures in the internet.'

Note the fine distinction in the foundation association's argument: that while it was acceptable for the public to see their profit and loss figures, they were not prepared to let the public see details of the endowment behind it. The foundation manager suggested that this was because people did not want the public to know where the money was coming from, or the potentially personal details that might reveal about an endowment, a shareholding or real estate investments.

A similar distinction has shown up in Scotland, where the charity regulator, OSCR (www.oscr.org.uk) has decided to 'redact' (remove) 'all personal and sensitive information ... where people can be identified' from charity accounts before they are published in the OSCR website. Trustees' names will not be published and we will not be permitted to know, therefore, who are the people entrusted with charity money in Scotland (Cullen, 2016, referencing www.oscr.org.uk/charities/faqs).

Another interviewee from the Netherlands, on the board of a family foundation and involved with FIN told us that:

> 'at FIN we argued that the law should differentiate between fundraising organisations and endowed foundations. We fought to make sure that the law would not require us to publish home addresses for board members, and to make sure that we did not have to list who we give to and how much. The law says we just have to give top line information. We didn't want people to start discussing with us why you gave to one organisation and not to another.'

The Dutch foundation manager gave a motive for privacy that has been cited elsewhere in Europe: "some people simply don't like transparency; in the Dutch culture of philanthropy the left hand is not supposed to know what the right hand is doing".

Don't let your left hand know what your right hand does

This is a reference, frequently cited in Dutch, French and Italian philanthropy, to the biblical Sermon on the Mount, and especially to the Gospel according to Matthew, Chapter 6, verses 1–4.

1   Be careful that you don't do your charitable giving before men, to be seen by them, or else you have no reward from your Father who is in heaven.

2 Therefore when you do merciful deeds, don't sound a trumpet before yourself, as the hypocrites do in the synagogues and in the streets, that they may get glory from men. Most certainly I tell you, they have received their reward.

3 But when you do merciful deeds, don't let your left hand know what your right hand does,

4 So that your merciful deeds may be in secret, then your Father who sees in secret will reward you openly.

The verses weave together ancient ideas that are still present in Europe. Don't be seen to be doing good 'or else you will have no reward'. The reward offered in the Bible is 'from your Father who is in heaven' but the philanthropist is only offered this reward if the gift is unseen. This is the basis of an inner struggle in some donors between the desire to do good and the religious belief that one must not be rewarded on Earth; the temporal rewards for philanthropy, including the feelings of warmth and satisfaction at doing good, conflict with this religious belief.

The two Dutch interviewees, and the exhortations of Mathew 6:1-4, add three further reasons to explain why public visibility has been so lacking in European philanthropy. We can add these to the six reasons for German foundations' privacy cited above:

7. 'We didn't want people to start discussing with us why you gave to one organisation and not to another'
8. It is not right to be seen to 'do your charitable giving before men, to be seen by them'
9. Don't let your left, public, hand know what your right, charitable hand, is doing.

This is a story in evolution. It seems that a younger generation of philanthropists, or perhaps more accurately a generation of people who have made their wealth in their own lifetimes, are more willing to consider public visibility. Our Dutch foundation manager illustrated this with a tale of two cities:

'I don't normally go to charity gala dinners. But last year I went to two charity dinners, both for the Red Cross. One was in Amsterdam, one in The Hague. Both had a charity auction. In the Amsterdam dinner, where there was a lot of new money, you bid by raising your hand. In The Hague dinner, where people were from families with old [inherited] money, the bids were made by sealed envelopes. New money in the Netherlands has a bit of US style about it.'

Marie-Stéphane Maradeix, former Development Director at the École Polytechnique, says that the idea of publicly stating one's philanthropy is changing in France. "Recognition is also a factor", she says. "When we unveiled the donor list at the École Polytechnique people came up to me and said 'I am not in the best segment [of the list]'." This could be because of the influence of their experience in the USA. "The grandes écoles introduced US methods into France – peer to peer fundraising, grading of donors into levels … It was a good idea. Some of our students had studied in the USA [and so understood the system from there]."

Edwin Venema, Editor in Chief of *De Dikke Blauwe* in the Netherlands, has a similar view:

'Philanthropy is still very Dutch. You don't brag about your giving. It is still very Calvinistic – giving in silence is still a virtue. But there are a couple of new philanthropists who are giving their names to their foundations. We are a very egalitarian society – the real achievers are not very much appreciated. There was no Dutch philanthropist who joined the Bill Gates [Giving] pledge. There is criticism that Dutch philanthropists are not coming forward. But despite that resistance, Dutch philanthropy is becoming more and more visible.'

Public access to annual reports

As data on foundations has become more available, so we have woken up to the size and impact of the sector. Take Spain, for example. Studies published in 2011 and 2014 showed that the sector is larger, and further reaching, than had previously been thought (Rubio Guerrero and Sosvilla Rivero, 2014). Thanks to the 2014 study, which reviews data from 2008 to 2012, we know that the foundation sector manages €7.4 billion in assets, and enjoys €7.3 billion in income, 84% of it (all figures from 2012) coming from the private sector. Foundations spend €7.9 billion annually with most going to culture and recreation (39%) and education and research (22%). By counting attendees at foundation-sponsored cultural events, scholarship pupils and other beneficiaries, the researchers calculate that foundations touch the lives of 29.7 million people – equivalent to 60% of the population of Spain. The sector is highly visible in a country in which the third largest bank by market capitalisation is owned by a foundation.

But visibility, as we saw above, is just one part of the duality of transparency. We also need to be able to understand what philanthropic organisations are doing. For this we need access to their annual report and accounts. As we have seen in the Dutch case, these are not yet widely available in Europe. As a 2015 review shows (Anon, 2015e), there is no requirement to make public the annual reports of foundations in:

- Austria
- Croatia
- Cyprus
- Denmark (for non-commercial foundations)
- Germany
- Italy
- Liechtenstein
- Switzerland.

Thus four of the largest markets for foundations in Europe (Denmark, Germany, Italy and Switzerland), and two more of the most interesting (Austria and Liechtenstein) do not require their foundations to make their accounts available to the public.

There are all sorts of subtleties here, as we have seen with the Dutch situation. In some countries, the laws on reporting are simply ignored. Spain has a 2014 law on transparency, access to public information and good governance (Ley 19/2014, de 29 de diciembre, de transparencia, acceso a la información pública y buen gobierno). This law established a 'transparency portal' in which foundations that received a 'significant' (the word is not defined) income from state grants would publish their annual reports. A review by the author of the relevant section of the Portal (http://transparencia.gob.es/servicios-buscador/contenido/cuentasanuales.htm?id=CuentasAnuales2014&lang=es) in March 2016 showed that just 41 foundations had published their annual reports there. Given that there are 8,734 active foundations in Spain and that 28.5% of them – around 2,400 – are receiving government grants (Rubio Guerrero and Sosvilla Rivero, 2014), it is clear that the transparency law is being widely disregarded.

Transparency and the tax deal

As the result of a 2016 controversy over the tiny amounts of tax that Google, or more accurately its parent Alphabet, paid in the UK, there have been concerns that the traditionally strong willingness in the UK to conform to tax rules (known as 'tax morale') might be compromised (see, for example, Ford, 2016). One way of countering that loss of trust, says Ford, would be to force companies to publish their tax returns, as happens in Denmark and Norway. Transparency here might restore confidence in the tax setting process. In a concluding sentence that might equally be applied to philanthropy, Ford says: 'When it comes to tax morale, a little fiscal voyeurism might do a surprising amount of good.'

As we saw with the legislation on endowed foundations and their annual accounts, we can say something similar about fiscal voyeurism in philanthropy. There is a trade-off between transparency and tax exemption. 'Foundations are under pressure from governments to be more transparent about their work ... Lawmakers ... assert that if foundations are benefitting from tax-exempt status, they are obligated to make their work and operations open and available to anyone who asks', according to Susan Parker (2014).

Transparency – not all good

Transparency is a popular topic amongst European philanthropists and their NGO partners. There is much talk – at conferences, in training sessions and amongst researchers – about the need for greater transparency in the sector. At the 'Who Owns the Transparency Agenda?' event in 2015 at the European Foundation Centre (www.efc.

be/event/interact-who-owns-the-transparency-agenda/), transparency was described as 'a long-held commitment within the non-profit sector ... part of its DNA and an issue that [is] firmly on the horizon for the future'. Transparency is seen as good for the sector, because it promotes greater professionalism and creates a form of self-regulation.

But transparency has also caused problems for the sector. The Financial Action Task Force (www.fatf-gafi.org/), established in 1989, is a policy-making body that sets anti-terrorist financing and anti-money laundering standards. FATF uses transparency as 'a means to tackle global money laundering and terrorist financing' (www.efc. be/event/interact-who-owns-the-transparency-agenda/). The result has been that governments have imposed restrictions on civil society organisations, justifying these by claiming that they help to prevent terrorist financing. Judith Sargentini, a Dutch GroenLinks ('Green Left') Party MEP who specialises in digital freedom, found various cases where FATF regulations 'have prevented civil society action. For example in the Netherlands an Islamic charity fundraising for the support of Palestinian orphans has been unable to find a bank willing to transfer their money to Palestine' because the action was perceived by the bank as a risk. Vinit Rishi, Director of Administration at the Oak Foundation, describes the problems that the foundation had in making payments to Oxfam and the International Committee of the Red Cross and Red Crescent for a 'Syria Appeal': 'the bank says [that it cannot make these payments] because it's complying with the recommendations of the Financial Action Task Force', writes Mr Rishi (2016), before pointing out that both Oxfam and ICRC are 'already regulated, duly registered, filing documents annually and doing so publicly'.

When we can't see inside – corruption

The lack of transparency – visibility for a non-profit's finances and activities – is still the cause of significant problems in the sector in Europe. There is an underlying – but hard to measure – sense that non-profits might not be doing the 'right thing' with donors' money and the criticism that working methods are unprofessional. Conversely, forcing open the doors of non-profits helps people to understand how they work. Cases of corruption in European non-profits have also shifted public opinion on philanthropy. According to René Bekkers and Pamala Wiepking (2015), 'the Dutch public has become much more educated about philanthropy' thanks to scandals about apparently overpaid senior staff and the corrupt use of donations.

"Distrust is an element", says Arnout Mertens. "Here in Rome we have had Vatileaks and the 2014 case of the Franciscan order and missing funds [in which the press claimed that millions of euros were missing from the Order of Friars Minor]. You only need one case to ruin the work of 100 organisations doing good."

These scandals that have hit the sector in most countries across Europe, including the UK (concerns over fundraising practice, evolving into a series of enquiries and newspaper revelations during 2015), the Netherlands (public outrage at the salaries paid to CEOs of leading non-profits) and Spain.

Transparencia – a nóos around the king's neck

The Spanish case has all the ingredients of the best tabloid story. The royal family, a princess, a well-known sportsman, politicians – and millions of euros. At the heart of this story is the fact that most foundations in Spain do not publish annual accounts, and that many have weak structures of governance.

The story starts in 1999, when Iñaki Urdangarín was a student at ESADE, the business school in Barcelona, under Professor Diego Torres. Urdangarín was studying for an MBA to complement his outstanding sporting career – from the age of 18 (1986) he had been a professional handball player with FC Barcelona Handbol, and had participated in the 1992, 1996 and 2000 Olympics. At the 1996 games in Atlanta he met Princess Cristina, daughter of the then King of Spain, and the couple married in 1997. He retired from professional sport in 2000.

Back in 1999, Professor Torres had established a foundation, Instituto Nóos (the 'Nóos' in the name refers to the Greek word for mind or intellect). The foundation was inactive until in 2003 Urdangarín was appointed as its President. During that period Diego Torres involved various members of his family in the entity, including his wife as treasurer and two of her brothers as board members. Instituto Nóos was one of a large number of entities – foundations and companies – created by Torres. These shared the same address and just one employee. The Instituto Nóos had a board but Urdangarín and Torres were the people who 'led the group as bosses, holding absolute control and decision-making power over it', according to the Spanish tax authorities quoted by the *Diario de Navarra* (2014).

Instituto Nóos, whose logo described the business as 'Strategic Studies of Sponsorship and Patronage', sought contracts with regional and national governments to identify opportunities to combine sports events with sponsorship. They won a €3.7 million contract from the Valencian Autonomous Government and Town Council to run a conference on the advantages for cities of large-scale sports events. But it was their relationship with the government of the Balearic Islands that was to expose the foundation to public, and then judicial, attack.

In 2003 the then President of the Balearic Islands invited Urdangarín to his office to negotiate a contract. The introduction had been made by José Lluis Ballester, the islands' sports minister and, by happy coincidence, a close friend of the royal family, who spent part of each summer on the islands. Ballester was a yachtsman and had frequently sailed with Prince Felipe and his sisters Cristina and Elena. The Balearic President signed a €1.1 million contract with Urdangárin's Instituto Nóos without requiring any of the normal procedures for competitive bids.

There then followed a period from 2004 to 2006 of substantial contracts for the foundation, followed by payments from the foundation to one or other of the web of companies created by Torres and Urdangárin in Spain and in Belize (El Páis, 2012).

In 2006 the bubble burst, with the first questions in the Balearic Islands parliament on the topic. In June that year the King requested via an intermediary that Urdangárin disassociate himself from the Instituto Nóos. The scandal started to spread and various cases against Urdangárin, against his wife the Princess Cristina and against the President of the Balearic Islands were opened by prosecuting judges (Brunet and Gilabert, 2016).

The case – with its perfect chemistry of royalty, politics and bad charity – attracted acres of media coverage, with a media scrum at each of the hearings. It came at the same time as a fraud in another foundation, the Fundació Orfeó Català-Palau de la Música, in which there was a similarly rich mixture of politics, bad charity and the emblematic Modernist building of the Palau de la Música in Barcelona.

The Instituto Nóos case is illustrative of bad governance. A board made up of family members, and a web of associated companies including at least one registered in the tax haven of Belize, all helped to ensure that this was a foundation that was destined to go off the ethical rails. It is also illustrative of the lack of transparency in the non-profit sector in Spain – both in the lack of any financial information about the foundation and in the ways in which it worked with the Balearic Islands government. These problems are absolutely not limited to Spain and its royal family. They occur across Europe. The USA is not exempt, and Deborah Archambeault, Sarah Webber and Janet Greenlee (2015) have compiled a database of 115 incidents of fraud occurring in US non-profit organisations in recent years.

Why we can't see inside – the Italian case

Talking to the fundraisers at the annual Italian Festival del Fundraising, one hears at least one of the reasons for the lack of transparency in Italian organisations:

"Donors won't let us use their name."

"They don't want to meet other donors."

And, the most damning: "They don't want the authorities to know – it's a question of tax."

Fundraisers at leading NGOs told the author that they were attracting donations from philanthropists, including a number of gifts in the €40,000–€100,000 range and at least one of millions of euros. But they were unable to persuade their donors to share their names or their stories, to talk about their gift or to have their name put on the new building or project.

Why is this happening? There seem to be two main reasons. First, traditional Catholic Italian culture discourages public displays of philanthropy. At the 2015 Festival, Chiara Bianci of the LUISS (Libera Università Internazionale degli Studi Sociali Guido Carli) university in Rome said that this is the Catholic interpretation of the 'Sermon on the Mount' (see above).

There is also another more temporal reason for anonymity. In a country in which tax avoidance, if not evasion, is widespread, people of wealth are concerned that if they make a large gift public, they risk having to pay more tax. The tax authorities are reported by fundraisers to be using estimations of wealth based amongst other things on any reported charitable gifts. So reports of a large gift to a charity could result in an even larger tax bill. Donors frequently ask to make gifts in cash in order to avoid any formal link with the charity.

Ironically this means that the left hand of the state is not coordinated with its right. Because at the same time as the tax office is using donations to crack down on people of wealth, it is offering attractive tax relief to people who give to certain causes. Tax relief for gifts in Italy can reach 100%, for gifts to emergency relief agencies including the Red Cross and UNHCR (United Nations High Commissioner for Refugees). Universities also attract substantial tax discounts. But these are ineffective if fear of being found out stops donors making gifts in the first place.

In Italy this creates a vicious circle. Many donors do not talk, publicly, about their philanthropy. So their peers do not hear about the gifts. They lack the 'social information' (see below) that will help them decide how much to give, so while one wealthy individual can think that her €10,000 gift is substantial, another will believe that his €1,000 is very generous. This situation is not universal – there are donors such as Luciano Balbo of Fondazione Oltre who declares himself a donor on the foundation website. But Mr Balbo is unusual.

To compound the difficulties of building relationships between non-profits and philanthropists, the foundation sector in Italy is still largely invisible. A handful of very large foundations built from the old social savings banks are reporting their finances and their good works. But there are likely to be many thousands of foundations in Italy, and this long tail of family and religious organisations is effectively invisible. Only the tax authorities know who they are and what they have in assets and income, but there is no sign that the government is going to release this information any time soon.

At some point in the lifetime of this book the situation in Italy will change. You will know this has happened when you can select a regional government's foundation register (try the Padua Province register at www.provincia.pd.it/index.php?page=registro-provinciale-delle-libere-forme-associative for example), find a foundation, and see its financial and governance information. That is not, at the current time, possible.

Why we can't see inside – France

A 2008 report from the Fondation de France stated that French foundations were 'few and generally little known to the public' (Anon, 2008). Describing foundations as 'prestigious but too confidential', the report said that the foundation sector had allowed itself to be assimilated into the wider non-profit sector and had not felt the need to broadcast information.

> Foundations … have not felt the need to group together, to study their own sector or to make comparisons between themselves. This specifically French attitude has without doubt evolved as the result of the tradition of discretion and individualism associated with wealth in our country.

The situation almost a decade later has changed and there is now more transparency than there was in 2008, but the tradition of discretion remains strong, and France does not, yet, enjoy the kind of open-door access to information on foundations, and the people behind them, that we can see in the USA.

Why we can't see inside – the view from next door

Sometimes it helps to take a look from the other side of the fence.

Seen from Europe, philanthropy in the Arabic-speaking world presents a very cloudy picture. It can appear hidden, almost secretive, or alternatively wildly flamboyant. Philanthropy can seem to be an obligation, a tithe, and thus more like a tax than a gift. Philanthropy in the Gulf States is led by the royal families, so it can look more like government spending.

There are many challenges in this region identified by researchers and people working in the sector. There is a significant issue of transparency, meaning that it is impossible to find even the most basic data on the philanthropic sector. Foundations do not publish their accounts – even Dubai Cares (with US$1 billion in assets), so modern in so many other respects, does not publish audited accounts on its website (or anywhere else). So we have no clear idea of the value of the foundation's endowment or of its income or spend. The many thousands of endowed foundations in the region are also a closed book, with almost universal lack of reporting.

Regulation of the sector is confusing and open to interpretation. Fundraising, for example, is prohibited in many countries of the Gulf with only the Red Crescent and certain licensed local organisations permitted to raise funds publicly. And yet the UN agencies and INGOs (international non-governmental organisations) manage to raise funds in the region using a variety of methods, including the Internet, that avoid requests that are too obvious.

There are useful summaries of what is actually happening in the Arabic-speaking world – such as the reports and research of the John D. Gerhart Center at the American University of Cairo (http://schools. aucegypt.edu/research/gerhart/Pages/default.aspx), or the work of the Arab Foundations Forum (see Farouky, 2016, for a recent example). But as a starting point it is worth noting that 'the idea of philanthropic giving is deeply rooted in tradition and closely linked to the Arabic concept of *takaful*, or social solidarity' (Ibrahim and Sherif, 2008, p 3).

A structure, the *waqf* (plural *awqaf*) or endowed foundation, emerged early in the Muslim era as a safe deposit for charitable assets, particularly property. The *awqaf* carried out the same range of activities as you would see in the early definitions of charity in Europe – providing for the poor, widows, orphans, the sick, travellers and scholars, or providing a public good such as a water supply.

Although it is not a perfect parallel to the use of the word in English, alms are also given in Muslim societies. *Zakat* is a form of giving which is based on a percentage of accumulated wealth. *Zakat* is one of the five pillars of Islam, 'a practice that is seen as both a spiritual and a social obligation' (Ibrahim and Sherif, 2008, p 3). It comes in various forms – there is giving in kind and giving in cash – and the donations are collected at the hundreds of thousands of mosques across the region, each with its own *zakat* fund.

Zakat is an ancient method of giving, and it can be organised in ancient ways. As Dr Youcef Benyza (2015) explained in a paper given at the regional conference on philanthropy, Takaful 2015, *zakat* funds in Algeria are organised hierarchically with the mosques passing the funds up to a regional *Zakat* organisation which in turn reports to a Ministry of *Zakat*. Funds are distributed by the regional *Zakat* organisation to poor people identified by social services. The processing of the funds is not audited, and the rules of governance are opaque – with the result that the Algerian press regularly report scandals of misappropriated funds. But the funds' organisers argue that *zakat* funds are sacred and that once a monetary gift has entered the fund it is no longer the property of humankind, no longer in the temporal realm. They make this case in order to defend the absence of audits or controls.

From the European side of the fence it all looks very questionable. But we can see many of these characteristics here, too.

Try, for example, to find the religious foundations of southern Europe. Millions of Catholics go to Mass each Sunday and contribute to the Church collection. Tens of thousands leave donations to the Church in their will. Where are these funds? In registered Catholic foundations – which do not report their accounts in the public domain. Indeed it is hard enough to ascertain whether they exist at all. Why? Is it because in Europe, too, alms are regarded as sacred and beyond the reach of man, or his auditors?

Similarly, the lines between state and private sector philanthropy can be blurred. Italian savings bank foundations include many local politicians on their boards. Political parties in Spain have closely associated foundations, such as Fundación para el Análisis y los Estudios Sociales, linked to the Partido Popular. Lotteries – the source of large-scale funding for non-profits in the Netherlands and the UK, for example – are closely linked to the governments that create them.

Europe and the Arabic-speaking world have built their modern philanthropy on ancient traditions and deeply held beliefs: the Greek 'philanthropy' and the Arabic '*sadaqa*'. Both cultures developed vehicles for doing good: alms and *zakat*, foundations and *awqaf*. Both are adapting these traditions to meet the modern world. But both have one foot stuck in the sands of history. As a result they share the same problems of lack of transparency, outdated governance, poor quality legislation and weak supervision.

The philanthropic sands of the Arabic-speaking world are moving fast: venture philanthropy is taking hold in the region (Emirates Foundation, www.emiratesfoundation.ae, is an example), and, as Naila Farouky (2016) points out, there is a focus on social enterprise development and other tools. The *awqaf* could evolve quickly – they must hold many millions, or possibly billions, of dollars of assets – and there is talk of '*e-waqf*' for online giving. *Zakat* is already electronic – during Ramadan 2013, UNHCR was the first UN agency to run an online *zakat* appeal, raising an average of $696 per donor (Chahim and Carnie, 2015).

If the rulers and governments of the region can find a way of regulating the sector and enforcing transparency it is conceivable that the region will do what it has done in so many other areas, and leapfrog the years of development we have gone through in Europe to create a fully modern philanthropic sector with a wide range of ways of doing good.

ELEVEN

Transparency in practice

Transparency and organisational culture

Work with non-profits in Europe for any length of time and you will realise that they are no different from other types of organisation or community. There is as wide a range of styles of internal organisation amongst non-profits as there is amongst companies, or clubs, or neighbourhood associations, or possibly even families. Each of these ways of organising has an impact on internal transparency, the extent to which people within the organisation are aware of the work, the knowledge, the skills or the connections of others.

Internal transparency is often best seen from the outside. The philanthropist who approaches an organisation with an offer of help may be met by a well-informed, tightly coordinated team of people who can provide her with the information she needs. But she might equally be met by a junior fundraiser who has no real idea of what her colleagues are doing, and no power to convene those colleagues to find out.

The types of organisational culture envisaged by Kim Cameron and Robert Quinn occur across the non-profit sector in Europe, and will serve to illustrate the ways in which organisations handle internal transparency. They propose four models of organisational cultures (Cameron and Quinn, 2011, p 22–4):

- The Clan Culture: 'A friendly place to work...like an extended family'
- The Adhocracy Culture: 'A dynamic, entrepreneurial and creative place to work [where] ... people take risks'

- The Hierarchy Culture: 'A very formalised and structured place to work' governed by procedures
- The Market Culture: 'A results-oriented organisation. The major concern is getting the job done'.

This is emphatically not a book about organisational culture so we will not be debating here the pros and cons of different ways of modelling organisations. We simply use Cameron and Quin's typology as a structure in which to place examples of non-profit organisations in Europe and to illustrate the points about internal transparency.

Clan Charity

Clan organisations are places of 'sensitivity to customers and concern for people', say Cameron and Quin, where the leaders 'are considered to be mentors and, maybe even, parent figures'. This should make them ideal organisations to build strong and lasting relationships with high-value philanthropists. Some do. A small organisation that we shall call Clan Charity works like this. It is one of Europe's many hospital clown charities, bringing humour and theatre to children and adults in hospitals in a thriving city. The organisation's entrepreneurial founder – we will call her Rosie – attracts huge loyalty from her colleagues, and commitment and devotion to the cause are high. Rosie is the public face of the charity, the person to whom everyone turns when they want a decision, the person who sets the moral tone for the organisation and its chief fundraiser. It is Rosie who has the relationships with the handful of wealthy families who provide around half of the organisation's annual income.

The organisation publishes its accounts in its website, where it also reports on its activities. Internally, staff at the organisation are well informed (this is a small organisation with most people working in one large open plan office). Donors receive regular reports about activities they are supporting, and turn to Rosie if they want to know more.

The transparency does not extend as far as sharing information about key donors. Rosie keeps those cards close to her chest – not from jealousy but simply because that is how it has always been ('tradition' is one of the features of Cameron and Quin's Clan Culture organisations).

The advantages and disadvantages of a clan culture are obvious from this description. Clan Charity depends on Rosie. So long as she continues to give great service to her philanthropist customers the organisation will continue to enjoy great donor loyalty. But if Rosie stops doing that because she gets distracted by a new project or leaves the organisation, the team would have to make a new start.

The Hierarchy Foundation

This organisation works with people who have been the victims of wars, which means, inevitably and tragically, that it works principally with women. It has the standard construction of an NGO, with a head office in Europe and field offices in the Global South, and again following the standard model it works with partner organisations in the South to deliver services to the war survivors who are its target beneficiary population. Donors, to date, have been almost exclusively governments but the organisation has recently started to consider working with private philanthropists and foundations.

The organisation is small, but as the result of elements of its structure and history it is highly formalised, with rules, protocols and procedures which the management spend a lot of time debating.

The organisation publishes biannual reports on its programmes on its website, but does not publish full audited accounts. Donor governments get detailed reports about the projects that they are funding.

The Director does most of the organisation's fundraising and he has a clear view – good internal communications – of what is happening in the field. But this information does not move around easily within the organisation and so delegating fundraising to other members of staff has proved difficult; the potential junior fundraisers don't know enough about what the organisation is doing to enable them to make a strong case to a donor. The procedures and protocols are also slowing down private sector fundraising, because the organisation requires a rigorous reputational analysis for any donor who wishes to give more than €5,000.

Hierarchical organisations occur throughout the non-profit sector just as they do in the for-profit world. Their protocols and procedures help to ensure efficiency where they are working in an established funding environment which is also highly procedural; thus they are especially to be found amongst organisations that are largely or wholly funded by governments. Philanthropists and private sector funders can find them very frustrating: Why does it take four weeks to get a report from that project in India? Why can't we just phone up and arrange a meeting? Why can't I associate my name with your work on cancer? These experiences, where an energetic, enthusiastic philanthropist from a business background who wants immediate results meets the internal rigidities of a hierarchical organisation, create dissatisfaction with the non-profit sector, and may be one of the factors that are driving philanthropists to set up their own foundations.

The Adhocracy Association

The author's first fundraising role was in an adhocracy organisation fundraising for medical research into a muscle-wasting disease that kills children. The organisation had a charismatic, energetic Director who took all the key decisions, who could swing the organisation round onto a new strategic track in minutes, and who was a brilliant fundraiser. Backed by a wealthy and equally entrepreneurial Chair, Paul had developed new products (the organisation put together the first charity team for the London Marathon in 1982), new ways of working including an in-house print and production unit, and new corporate relationships. He took risks and mostly they paid off.

Paul delegated to key staff including communications, corporate fundraising, trusts and foundations, events and community fundraising. There was a regional team of community fundraisers, running a UK-wide network of around 400 local branches.

Most donors had relationships with these staff rather than with the Director and there was, for the time (the early 1980s), a relatively transparent relationship with donors, who would meet the families of kids with the disorder, would participate in events and would receive bulletins and reports. The element that frustrated some donors and where there was neither visibility nor the ability to infer information was the organisation's strategy. The dynamic, responsive, entrepreneurial and creative side of the organisation was perfectly capable of devising a new strategy or product over a pint of beer in the Dog and Duck, and then to apply it the next morning.

Adhocracies are like fast-growing, entrepreneurial companies. They are not for the conservative, steady-as-she-goes investor. In the investment market these companies are marked out for 'sophisticated investors'. No such definition exists for philanthropic investors, and 'non-sophisticated' donors – regular, ordinary donors – are often attracted to this type of organisation because of the colour, energy and vitality that they project. Sometimes that ends in disillusion, sometimes (as in the case described here) in growth and success; the medical research funded by this organisation has succeeded in substantially extending the life expectancy, and increasing the life quality, of the young boys who have the disorder.

The Market Leader

The Market Leader is a global organisation working with refugees and others displaced by wars. After years of relying on funding from governments it began, timidly at first and then, with the recruitment in 2009 of a focused, competitive, results-oriented Director of International Fundraising, to develop a worldwide private fundraising programme. The programme included the whole range of fundraising tools from street-level 'face-to-face' donor recruitment to a substantial, well-resourced programme to recruit 'major donors' from amongst high-value philanthropists.

The Market Leader is externally transparent but internally there has been an issue over getting project information to fundraisers, and thus to donors. At the level of consumer fundraising this is not so relevant; asking a donor for £15 and saying that this 'Could provide a refugee family in Jordan with winter clothes to help them fight the cold' is an open offer showing an example of how a donor's gift will be spent. Donors are expected to understand that their gift may be used for that or other purposes. But in the world of high-value philanthropy this project information is highly relevant. Here, many donors want to know that the £150,000, or the £1.5 million that they are giving is going to a specific activity or project. And it is here that the issues of internal transparency have caused some problems. Reporting on a project means that a fundraiser must contact a field office and get photographs, up-to-date information and news. For the field office this is bothersome, time-consuming and a distraction from their (tough) daily work. If the donor is, say, the Dutch government and the donation is, say, US$100 million then the field office will accommodate the request. But if a week later they receive a similar request for an individual donor whose gift is US$150,000 then they might understandably be more reluctant. This tension in transparency is not at all exclusive to the Market Leader. It occurs across the swathe of large, government-funded organisations as they move toward private sector funding, where a donor of a tenth, or a hundredth of the size of a government grant wants as much or more attention, data and reports.

Internal transparency varies widely across non-profits in Europe, and this has an impact on each organisation's ability to work with high-value philanthropists. Clan, Adhocracy, Hierarchy or Market cultures mean advantages and disadvantages, risks and returns for philanthropists.

How transparency changes philanthropy

Theresa Lloyd says that philanthropists "are far more willing to stick their heads above the parapet now" than just ten years ago. Could it be that increasing visibility of philanthropy in Europe is having a positive effect on giving? If one person of wealth hears that another gave €10,000 to the school appeal, does she respond by making a gift of a similar value? Pamala Wiepking thinks so; "Leadership gifts have an effect. You need to see other people give before you give yourself", she says.

Participants in a UK survey of high-income households (£100,000 and over per annum) 'reported that they would consider what others would be donating and what people would be expecting of them' (Booth, Leary and Vallance, 2015). An interviewee (male, age over 45, income £200,000-500,000) is quoted as saying that 'if I sponsor someone at work then I have to be aware that I earn more than almost everyone else; that has to be reflected'.

Dr René Bekkers (2012) agrees in part with this idea. He says that there is 'overwhelming evidence' for social influences in giving, and particularly the influence of other high-value donors. Bekkers uses geographic proximity – people living in the same municipality – and looks at what happens to donations in the year after a change in giving patterns in a municipality. He hypothesises that 'information on the proportion of people donating affects donor behaviour, but not information on the amount donated by others'. While he finds that 'the tax records [in the Netherlands] show that amounts donated by high level donors are strongly sensitive to ... changes in giving by other high level donors in the area', he suggests that the sensitivity affects the proportion of people giving, not (so much) the value of the gift. Focusing on high-value donors he finds that 'increases in the proportion of donors in a municipality are strongly associated with increases in the amount donated one year later' – a 1% increase in the proportion of donors is associated with a 7% increase in the amount donated – but that increases in the average amount given in a municipality are not strongly related to changes in the amounts given in the subsequent year – a €1,000 increase in the amount donated by peers is reflected in just €43 in extra donations in the following year.

Social information and high-value philanthropy

Nevertheless, work by Shang and Croson (2009, see box below) suggests that the level of a gift, especially where the 'right' level is unclear or ambiguous, is influenced by social information. In other words, the information that one donor gave €10,000 may be just enough to encourage another donor to give at the same level. The effect seems to depend to some degree on ambiguity, which is the perfect description for high-value philanthropy in Europe: if I were a rich man, should I donate €1,000? €10,000? €100,000? €1 million? It appears that people of wealth in Europe do not know what level of gift is expected of them; they lack the 'social information' that would guide them.

Social information and giving

Jen Shang and Rachel Croson (2009, p 1426–35) demonstrated in 2009 that social information has an impact on how much people give. They conducted a field experiment using public radio in the USA because 'each individual has an incentive to free ride, [to] listen to the station and not contribute to its continued functioning. However, the community as a whole is better off when the [radio] station is funded.' US public radio also meets an 'ambiguity condition' which states that if there were a clear guideline on what to do then social information on what other people are doing would not influence the individual's decision. This idea is simply illustrated with an example: if we know that the entry price for a museum is €10 then that is what we pay; we don't pay more just because we see that someone in front of us pays with a €20 bill and tells the museum to keep the change. In public radio, by contrast, donors 'have relatively little idea of what the "right" contribution might be'.

Shang and Croson collaborated with a public radio station on the US East Coast that has three on-air funding drives per year, where DJs (disk jockeys, or presenters) ask for donations and suggest multiple contribution levels, with a gift at each level ($50, $60, $75, $120 and so on up to $2,500 – a total of 11 levels of contribution). Previous research had shown that most donors cannot correctly recall how much they had contributed in the past, and this, combined with the 'multiplicity (and range) of recommended contribution levels ... mean that potential donors have relatively little idea of what the "right" contribution might be'.

During the fundraising drive, DJs encouraged listeners to phone in. During the calls, the caller was asked 'How much would you like to pledge today?' and then some of the callers were told 'We had another member, they contributed $75/$180/$300'.

The results show that 'social information can positively influence contributions'. There were 'significantly higher contributions' when donors were told: 'We had another member, they contributed $300.' The effect was to increase average contribution from $106.72 to $119.70. The effect was 'robust for new members but is never significant for renewing members', and the authors suggest that this is because there is greater ambiguity for new donors – they don't know what level of gift is expected of them, and when a radio station staffer says that someone else gave $300, this pushes their level of giving toward that target. The authors also found, a year after the study, that 'new donors who were provided [with] social information were around twice as likely to contribute again one year later ... and when they contributed, [to give] more'.

I asked Jen Shang, who is Professor of Philanthropic Psychology and Research Director of the Hartsook Centre for Sustainable Philanthropy at Plymouth University, about her work on social information.

> 'People rely more heavily on others' behaviour when they are not sure what behaviour is accurate in a given situation. This is particularly the case for those who have never undertaken the behaviour, i.e. they cannot anchor their current behaviour on their past behaviour. Social information doesn't have to be money. It can also be about

the kind of impact that one aims to achieve and how one wants to achieve it. Peer influence on those dimensions can be as important as peer influence on the amount of giving. Similarly, social information does not have to be what others actually do. It can also be what people ideally like to do. It doesn't have to be what people did in the past, it could also be what people plan to do in the future.'

The lack of social information on high-value philanthropy, the privacy of giving, is one of the defining differences between Europe and the USA. A European philanthropist told this author during 2015 that the ambiguity was about the amount, not the gift in itself.

'In Europe we won't go out and say "I've given a million." That is not done. My father, the fifth generation in a wealthy family, was a philanthropist. He had a lot of credibility. When someone has credibility and says we need to support an issue, then people do. He said "Only mean spirited people give anonymously, but you don't say what you give." That is where we are very different from the USA.'

Social information in France – the case of HEC

Public visibility has had an influence on the means by which people give, according to Marie-Stéphane Maradeix. "Transparency has allowed new money to discover venture philanthropy, new philanthropy, the leaders in philanthropy. Transparency has made donors visible. One can see the structures – foundations – and their accounts."

Barbara de Colombe is the Executive Director of Fondation HEC. The foundation was created in 1972 by the alumni association of the eponymous business school, and aims to support the development of the school with bursaries, research funding, resources for teaching, and scholarships for visiting professors. HEC's first fundraising campaign, 2008-2013, raised €112 million from 7,500 individual donors, alongside companies and foundations. It is building a permanent endowment for the school, currently standing at €50 million, and in 2014 received donations of €12.8 million, of which 64% came from individual alumni and 36% from business partners (http://www.fondationhec.fr/, figures from Annual Report for financial year ending 31 December 2014). The school has 152 'Grands Donateurs' who give €150,000 or more, out of more than 9,000 individual donors.

She says, of transparency:

> 'In France the culture is that success and money are taboo. We have had to find new ways to give recognition to philanthropy, and this has "de-complexed" giving a bit. We wanted to give the right light to philanthropy. Not too much. Not a copy and paste from the American way.'

The HEC Campaign had 152 major donors who gave between €150,000 and €10 million. Barbara de Colombe told me that, at the start:

> 'the majority did not want to have their name on the [donor recognition] board on the main campus. We said it was not to congratulate yourself. It is because it shows to students that they are there thanks to inter-generational philanthropy, and to show the diversity of people who support the School. We explain that one gift may encourage two or three other gifts. They understand that.'

She went on to explain:

> 'We give recognition, but not too much. We have 15 classrooms named after donors of €1 million or more. Their name, with a brief biography, is on a panel next to the door. They give a brief presentation when we name the classroom. They understand that it is not to give publicity for them. In the end, out of all our donors – there are around 9,000 – only two, maybe three, wanted to be anonymous.'

This, for some outside France, will appear a subtle play of words. Donor recognition, 'but not too much'. Explaining to a donor that the recognition is not self-congratulatory, that it has a wider impact, bringing in new donors, showing current students that they are there in part thanks to the efforts of previous generations – these carefully worded arguments have broken down the barriers to donor recognition and allowed HEC to publish their donors' names online and on-campus.

Barbara commented that these forms of donor recognition are spreading in France. She noted that the École Polytechnique (www. polytechnique.edu) publicly announced in June 2015 a €5 million donation – he had previously given €2 million – from alumnus Patrick Drahi, the president of telecoms group Altice (http://etudiant.lefigaro. fr/les-news/actu/detail/article/patrick-drahi-premier-mecene-de-polytechnique-16149/), to build the 'Drahi-X Novation Center', a business and entrepreneurial faculty, named after the donor.

This is not wholly new to France. Visit the Musée du Louvre in Paris and you will find (in the Apollon Circle) the names of 'Principal Donors' engraved in gold in the marble walls (http://louvre-passion. over-blog.com/article-votre-nom-grave-dans-le-marbre-116450424. html). These include the Greek government (1829), J. Pierpoint Morgan (1911), Baronne Edmond de Rothschild (1936) and of course the 2005 gift of Prince Alwaleed Bin Talal Bin Abdulaziz Al Saud. The gift of €17 million from the Alwaleed Bin Talal Foundation was the largest private gift to the Louvre's Islamic Arts Hall (www.louvre. fr/sites/default/files/medias/medias_fichiers/fichiers/pdf/louvre-press-release-budget-and.pdf). It is worth noting that from Barbara de Colombe's point of view, this gift was a turning point, catalysing the introduction by the French state in August 2008 of endowed foundations, 'fonds de dotation'.

Donors in France have been visible – in the sense that their names have been listed in public at least at the Louvre – since the early nineteenth century. The 'Revue philanthropique' was published in France from 1897 to 1934 (there had been predecessors since at least 1816), so there was public visibility of giving in France more than 100 years ago (Seghers, 2009). And yet the majority of Barbara de Colombe's donor audience did not, at first, want their names inscribed on the HEC donor recognition board.

This enigma runs throughout continental European philanthropy. For an outsider it appears to be a trick, to the cynic it appears to be false modesty. But it is neither of these things. It is a delightfully subtle play of words and position, a sort of French flirtation with philanthropy, where the two lovers dance together at a masked ball and only after much persuasion (Barbara de Colombe is very persuasive) do they come out as donor and recipient.

There is a further subtlety here, inherent in the word 'public'. Martine Godefroid, Managing Director of Factary Europe, suggests that it is not 'public' visibility, but visibility amongst a group of peers that counts. "I think that reporting has influenced [philanthropy] a bit but it is not necessarily public domain information. The fact that people start to talk about their philanthropy in their private networks and circles is also key. That is where they learn about others' donations." She makes the point that the 'public' in 'public visibility' does not have to mean the general public; learning at a private dinner in L'Arpège that your friend has donated might be enough to inspire you to give, too.

Transparency, the professionals' approach

From the world of venture philanthropy, Dr Lisa Hehenberger has an explanation of what is behind the new transparency. It has to do with the growing professionalism of the sector, and the elusive hunt for impact.

'The whole [venture philanthropy] space is moving toward more transparency, toward concrete results and trying to measure them. Transparency is different in different countries. In the US and UK there is much more transparency. In continental Europe, only a minority of the big foundations are publishing accounts and impact reports. In the venture philanthropy space the publishing of impacts and accounts is a must. Impact measurement is pushing us toward transparency.'

Wolfgang Hafenmayer agrees with Dr Hehenberger that the growing professionalisation of the sector is encouraging transparency.

'Professionals want to be transparent. They want to learn from each other. The professionals want to learn from each other's mistakes. Their main intention is to improve impact, not to win market share. People are doing more thanks to transparency. But more than transparency, it is role models that the media talks about. [People such as] Gates, Zuckerberg have a greater influence than transparency. The world still works on role models. Peer pressure, the more people in your peer group who do something then the more you feel you should.'

Karen Wilson says that thanks to public visibility, "social impact has become cool [fashionable, the right thing to do]. This is led by younger entrepreneurs. It's not like the old model, like the Rockefellers, where you used to wait until you were retired, or dead, before you did your philanthropy."

Peak transparency?

In Lester Salamon's epic *New Frontiers of Philanthropy*, Rick Cohen points out that by 2009 US 'corporate-originated charitable funds' held US$9.56 billion in donor-advised funds, more than the entire community foundation movement in the US. A 'corporate-originated charitable fund' is a legal charity, a foundation, managed by a for-profit company on behalf of its clients. The biggest of these funds in the USA are Fidelity Investments Charitable Gift Fund, Schwab Charitable Fund and Vanguard Charitable. The latest filings available from these foundations (the 'Form 990' of the Department of the Treasury Internal Revenue Service) show the spectacular growth in this sector. By June 2015 the three largest funds alone had net assets of more than US$28 billion;

Fidelity Investments Charitable Gift Fund, EIN (registration number) 11-0303001, year ending 30 June 2015, US$15.3 billion

Schwab Charitable Fund, EIN 31-1640316, 30 June 2015, US$7.5 billion

Vanguard Charitable Endowment Program, EIN 23-2888152, 30 June 2015, US$5.2 billion

To update and confirm Rick Cohen's analysis, the data from 2014 shows that the total assets held in donor-advised funds amongst the 608 community foundations in the USA was US$27.5 billion, less than the total held by the three largest corporate-originated equivalents (Anon, 2015f).

The funds provide a wall of confidentiality for their clients, so that an individual or a firm can make a donation to a non-profit without revealing their identity. Fidelity emphasises this point in its website (www.fidelitycharitable.org/giving-strategies/give/making-transition-from-private-foundation.shtml):

> 'Donors concerned about privacy might also want to opt out of a private foundation,' says Victoria B. Bjorklund, a lawyer with Simpson Thacher & Bartlett in New York. The foundation's yearly tax filing, IRS Form 990-PF, is a public record that shows assets, gifts, grants, and the names and addresses of trustees, directors, and officers. ... Donors who give through a public charity with a donor-advised fund can keep a lower profile – or remain anonymous, if they wish. All the grant recipient will know is that the donation came from an individual donor-advised fund of the sponsoring charity. This might appeal to people who don't want credit for their generosity, are trying not to call attention to their wealth, or wish to avoid solicitations from other charities.

The private banks of Europe have been jumping enthusiastically onto the same bandwagon. A number of these banks, such as UBS, Rabobank, or Coutts, have created charitable foundations for their HNWI clients. Clients can make donations to the bank foundation, which in turn passes on the donations to NGOs, universities and cultural organisations. They often do so anonymously, and sometimes in very large amounts; I know of a €1 million donation made anonymously like this to a leading children's organisation in 2015. By giving via the bank, the wealthy client can ensure anonymity.

Does that sound fine? Yes, in some respects. The idea of the anonymous donor has a long and honourable history. But imagine that an NGO has a policy of not accepting donations from people who are heavily invested in arms manufacturers. It receives a large, anonymous donation via a bank foundation. Who was the donor? The bank says that this is a client in good standing. But was she the boss of an arms company? Of a tobacco firm? Of the mafia? Due diligence is impossible in these circumstances.

If the banks in Europe are as efficient at selling the idea of corporate-originated charitable funds as their American counterparts, then these foundations, and this anonymity, will continue to grow. We may have just reached peak philanthropic transparency in Europe.

The European vision of transparency

Transparency is more than just visibility. We have to be able to understand what we see if it is to be of any value to us. Non-profits in Europe have not been good at transparency – neither at basic visibility nor at 'inferability' – but that is changing now. Governments and the new professional staff in organised philanthropy are pushing open the doors to show the public what we do. Some of this is too late; many high-value philanthropists have already lost faith in Europe's established non-profits and set up their own foundations in order to manage their giving themselves. We will have to wait to see whether future philanthropists learn to trust non-profits now that they can (mostly) see inside.

PART FIVE

Enter the professionals

TWELVE

Working for change

This section argues that professionals have entered the sector and have changed the way we do high-value philanthropy in Europe.

Introduction

It's a job. Not a vocation, or a calling, or something you do in your spare time. Whether that refers to raising funds or granting them, the role has changed from unpaid to paid, from volunteer to staff, from 'amateur' to 'professional'. This change has occurred all across Europe with local variations but with a clear trend toward more professionalism.

Professionals, defined

What do we mean by a more professional non-profit sector? Professional is used as the reverse of 'amateur' to mean a person engaged in an activity as a main paid occupation. It is used to refer to people who 'belong to a profession' or who have 'qualified in a profession'. And that is approximately the sequence that we have seen across Europe in the fundraising area of the non-profit sector: first the volunteers (or 'amateurs') were replaced by paid fundraisers, and then those people joined a profession in the sense that they themselves created professional bodies and associations such as the Association Française des Fundraisers (www.fundraisers.fr/), and finally we have seen the emergence of qualifications in fundraising across Europe such as the Postgraduate Certificate in Fundraising (www.il3.ub.edu/ca/postgrau/postgrau-captacio-fons-fundraising.html) at the University of Barcelona (on which this author teaches) and the Master in Fundraising (www.master-fundraising.it) at the University of Bologna, Italy.

On the other side, foundations have taken on staff, philanthropic advisers are emerging across Europe and an increasing number of banks have philanthropy teams. In this section we will meet some of these people and learn about their work.

Foundation professionals

Foundations are getting more professional; the numbers of people employed by foundations is rising. Figures from the foundation sector in Spain (see Table 12.1) illustrate this trend, showing a 29.5% increase over the five years 2008–2012 (Rubio Guerrero and Sosvilla Rivero, 2014) – and this during a severe economic downturn in the country.

Table 12.1 Foundation employees in Spain, 2008–2012

Year	Average number of paid staff
2008	27.55
2009	30.95
2010	38.19
2011	36.14
2012	35.68

Source: Rubio Guerrero (2014).

The growth in professional staff is attributed, in a 2014 report on foundations in Germany, to the growing number of living founders who look for entrepreneurial professional management 'that is focused on achieving goals and impact, and forms the basis for the skills and expertise profile of the foundation management of the future' (Anon, 2015c).

It was not ever thus. Helmut Anheier reported in 2001 that:

> the majority of German foundations ... employ no staff at all: nine out of ten foundations are run and managed by volunteers only. In Scandinavia, we would find similar results: all but a few of Denmark's 14,000 foundations have paid employment at all, and only eight of the over 2,500 Finnish foundations have more than 10 full-time staff. (Anheier, 2001, p 10)

The numbers of people employed in foundations in France has grown with the growth in the sector. In 2005 there were an estimated 55,462 foundation employees, plus 11,001 individuals made available to foundations by their employer (in the case of corporate foundations) or by other third parties such as universities or associations (Anon, 2008). By 2013 there were 84,100 foundation employees (Anon, 2015a), a remarkable 52% increase in eight years. There is a similar picture in Belgium, although 'whilst foundations are professionalising more and more, as at 31st December 2012 only 13.5% of Belgian foundations are employers (i.e. 140 foundations out of a total of 1,036)' (Mernier and Xhauflair, 2014). These foundations employed 7,250 full-time equivalent staff. Most of these staff worked in public scientific research foundations including universities and research centres.

We should not confuse these figures for the whole foundation sector with the professionalisation of private, operating or grant-making foundations. In Belgium, just 172 full-time equivalents worked amongst private foundations, which 'make very little use of salaried staff', say Amélie Mernier and Virginie Xhauflair (2014). Arthur Gautier reminded me that "the largest private foundation [in France] is the Fondation Bettencourt Schueller (www.fondationbs.org), and they only have 15 staff".

Have these professionals improved the efficiency of foundations? There is very little data that shows a measurable outcome for the growing numbers of professionals in the European foundation sector. In part this is because the heterogeneity of the sector makes any kind of comparison meaningless; one really cannot compare the output of a day's work by a professional programmes officer in the Bertelsmann Stiftung with the day's work of a professional fundraiser in Fundació Oxfam Intermón. Both are professionals, both are working for foundations, but they might as well be on different planets.

The new staff are bringing new ideas into the foundation sector. Marie-Stéphane Maradeix has worked on both sides of the sector, with the grant-making Fondation Daniel et Nina Carasso, and previously as Director of Development (a fundraising role) with the École Polytechnique (2007-2011), after working in a similar role at ESSEC Business School (2002-2007). Maradeix underlines the growing professionalism of the sector: "At the Fondation Daniel et Nina Carasso I am trying to build a new generation foundation – we call it a 'Fondation 3.0' – that is strategic, based on the theory of change and working with new tools such as capacity building, social impact measurement, impact investing, advocacy and others."

> 'Philanthropy is modest [in value]. One has to be an agitator, to encourage innovation. One has to have a will to respond to the needs of the planet, strategically. At the foundation we put in place strategic objectives, and then we aim to work with the best experts. Marina [Carasso] says "here is the challenge – how are we going to meet it?"'

The philanthropy advisers

"The world of professional [philanthropy] advice is growing hugely", says Theresa Lloyd. They are working as independent philanthropy advisers, working within banks, in consultancies, and in non-profit organisations. According to one UK report, 'in recent years, philanthropy advice has become an area of professional services approaching a tipping point' (Anon, 2015g). The report suggested that two in every five HNWIs in the UK had taken some form of philanthropy advice and that those who did gave almost twice as much to good causes as those who did not ($£15,676$, against $£8,788$) in the year before the survey. A very similar ratio was seen in a 2014 survey in the US, where people of wealth 'who consulted with an advisor gave a higher total amount ($96,878) than those who did not consult an advisor ($47,531)' (Simmons, 2014, p 4). The subjects of such advice included the tax benefits of giving, understanding need and selecting social causes, and measuring impact.

"Philanthropy is being sold like a luxury product", says Marie-Stéphane Maradeix. "Banks understand the commercial potential of engaging in their clients' philanthropy." In Switzerland, for example, UBS, Lombard Odier, Credit Suisse and HSBC are amongst the banks with professional philanthropy advisers on their staff. Philanthropy specialists such as LGT Venture Philanthropy and WISE employ them, as do organisations such as the Edmond de Rothschild Foundations.

"ABN AMRO MeesPeerson (www.abnamro.nl/nl/privatebanking/index.html) established a philanthropy desk a couple of years ago for their wealthy clients", comments Edwin Venema, Editor in Chief of *De Dikke Blauwe* in the Netherlands.

'Rabobank has done the same, as have private banks; the banks are jumping on the bandwagon in the last couple of years. In the case of ABN Amro, it is the bank with the largest number of wealthy clients. Their research last year showed that their wealthy clients were making average donations of €11,000.'

The same picture is occurring all across Europe and the UK crop includes Coutts, J.P. Morgan Private Bank, Charities Aid Foundation and, an unusual example, Tyne & Wear Community Foundation.

Why are the banks entering this market?

A banker in the 2013 CAF/Scorpio research illustrates how discussions about giving deepen a relationship with a client: 'When you start talking to someone about their philanthropy, you learn what gets them up in the morning; how they want to change the world; what makes them angry; and what they want for their children' (Anon, 2015g).

'In the UK, boutique philanthropy advisory services really started with New Philanthropy Capital, founded in 2002 by former Goldman Sachs employees Peter Wheeler and Gavin Davies', writes Charlotte Eagar in a 2014 article for the Financial Times' luxury market magazine *How to Spend It*. 'They turned their sharp financial eyes to inspecting suitable charities to benefit from their and their one-time colleagues' munificence' (Eagar, 2014). The number of philanthropy advisory services is growing in the UK and Eagar attributes this to two linked changes. First, the 'seismic shift of UK wealth from inherited money to the self-made', which created an 'enormous change in philanthropy in Britain over the past decade' as inheritors who held their wealth in trust for future generations gave way to self-made wealth. As a result, 'London became the global capital of the cash-rich, time-poor. With their newly embraced US culture of huge pay packets and endless working hours, the new rich also embraced the US culture of philanthropy.' These cash-rich, time-poor clients access research, well-managed field trips and networking meetings on philanthropy by paying the new breed of philanthropic adviser to help them. The fees are substantial, with Prospero World, a London-based adviser cited by Eagar as charging £12,000 per annum for its 'Gold' membership, which includes advisory services, access to research and invitations to participate in field trips. Prism the Gift Fund (www.prismthegiftfund.

co.uk/) is reported to charge 2-5% of incoming funds, or a quarterly fee starting at £750.

The issue of charging for services has long been contentious in this field and may have slowed the development of philanthropic advisory services in Europe. "The banks came in there thinking that they would provide an extra service that they can charge for", says a philanthropist living in France, who spoke off the record for this book. In the CAF/Scorpio report cited above (Anon, 2015g) based on a 2013 survey, '73% of wealthy individuals – said it should be a low-cost or no-cost service'. But this may be changing. 'There's an interesting movement in the market that's picking up quite significantly, which is people paying for support around insights so that they can become experts', said Jake Hayman in a 2014 *Financial Times* article (Murray, 2015). Hayman is co-founder and chief executive of the Social Investment Consultancy, a consultancy that provides advisory services to individuals and foundations committing sums between £250,000 and £25 million.

Clients expect high levels of service – Geneva Global's Kenny Washington is reported as saying, 'We give the same level of advice as you would expect if you were making an investment' (Eagar, 2014), while Jake Hayman says: 'What we're running is essentially a mini-MBA or PhD course in social change' (Murray, 2015). Theresa Lloyd emphasises the personal characteristics of a good adviser: "What philanthropists want from wealth managers is that they have a sense of shared values."

The interest amongst HNWI investors in philanthropy and social impact investment has arrived at the same moment as the banks' realisation that these are areas in which they could provide new services to new clients. "The two processes have coincided", says a member of a wealthy Dutch family who was interviewed for this book. "We bank with Bank X. They are developing philanthropy services, which is useful." But not all HNWI clients are keen to use their services. "I think it's a lot of whitewashing", says one French philanthropist. "I question the capacity of a bank to think about the philanthropy sector in a way that would satisfy a philanthropist. I'm not sure there's a lot behind it."

While there is no data – yet – on the growing number of professional philanthropy advisers, there is evidence that individual firms are growing in value. For example, Prism the Gift Fund, the donor advised fund and donor advisory consultancy set up by Anne Josse and Gideon

Lyons of HNWI investment firm Regent Capital, reported income of
£16.5 million for year ending 30 June 2014 (www.charitycommission.
gov.uk), up from £5 million in 2011/12 and from just £247,609 in
2009/10.

The sector is developing the second stage of professionalism
outlined in the introduction – professional associations. Step (www.
step.org), the professional organisation for family asset managers, has
a 'Philanthropy Advisors Special Interest Group' led by a committee
of 12 people. Philanthropy Impact (www.philanthropy-impact.org) is
encouraging more professionals into the sector with tools and training.
The International Association of Advisors in Philanthropy (www.
advisorsinphilanthropy.org), however, does not yet live up to the
first word of its title; its membership list is largely based in the USA,
and includes no one in the UK or Switzerland, the key philanthropy
advisory markets in Europe.

Good advice?

But there are concerns that the advisers are not yet equipped to advise.
Some will admit privately that they know little about the non-profit
sector and rely on personal networks (rather than on objective criteria)
to filter organisations. "There is a demand from family offices to
do social investment, but they don't know who, don't know how",
says Miquel de Paladella, the CEO and co-founder of UpSocial in
Barcelona.

The Dutch philanthropist cited earlier is concerned that the
investment services on offer are limited, and that the banks have not
really grasped the value, and potential, of impact measurement:

> 'I expect these asset managers to be more than just a broker.
> When you buy in to their flagship [investment] fund they
> do best of class within each sector. I am waiting for the
> moment where that logic flips to an impact logic. Not
> best of class in financial returns, but best in impact. It will
> have to happen. At the moment there is little traction for
> the idea; the banks are regulated so it is difficult.'

The philanthropy hunters

The growth in the numbers of professional fundraisers – philanthropy hunters – has been spectacular in Europe.

As the profession has grown, so it has specialised. There are fundraisers who specialise in direct marketing, mass consumer fundraising. There are those who specialise in relationships with companies for Corporate Social Responsibility (CSR) and sponsorship programmes. Some work on EU and government grant-aid programmes. There are some – fewer in number – who focus on fundraising from foundations and grant-making trusts. And there are fundraisers specialising in 'major donors' – relationships with high-value supporters. "There is not a big charity [in the Netherlands] that does not have a major donor fundraiser on their payroll, and I can't count the number of seminars, and books on major donor fundraising", says Edwin Venema in the Netherlands. The fundraisers are having an effect, says Dr Arthur Gautier in Paris; they are "one of the primary causes" of change in philanthropy.

Fundraising teams are supported by other professionals – people who specialise in social media marketing, in communications, in data and analysis. In high-value philanthropy one relatively new profession is especially relevant: prospect researchers. These are the true philanthropy hunters, professionals who specialise in researching, identifying and evaluating potential high-value supporters. Some of the techniques used by prospect researchers are summarised in Chapter Sixteen.

There are those, such as Theresa Lloyd, who argue that while the number of professional fundraisers has increased, the level of professionalism has not. "Most major donor fundraising is amateur in the extreme and, as we found in research for our book [Breeze and Lloyd, 2013] many major donors think that", she says, citing cases where senior high-level philanthropists are given young, inexperienced fundraisers as their key contact. This feels like a critique of a new, young profession, and we can expect that Europe will build a corpus of senior, experienced fundraisers specialising in high-value philanthropy. We have a long way to go, but we will get there in the end.

A personal story

I was the 118th person to join the Institute of Fundraising, the UK's association of professional fundraisers, when I signed up in June 1986. I am a lucky member of the first cohort of people in Europe who have had the privilege of spending a working life in fundraising.

I had started in fundraising in 1980. I had never heard of the profession before I saw the advert from the charity. My boss at the then Muscular Dystrophy Group (www.musculardystrophyuk.org/) was a former J Walter Thompson (JWT) executive, Paul Walker. When I joined, Paul's second in command, the head of fundraising, was Fran Willison, who had also come in from JWT. Paul and Fran were part of a revolution that was happening in the UK non-profit sector in the 1970s and 1980s.

My perception as a 23-year-old fundraiser was that many charities were run by retired or semi-retired, often ex-military, men. The Muscular Dystrophy Group had broken away from the pack by recruiting a Director and a Head of Fundraising from an advertising agency. The organisation had moved from a passive charity to an active fundraiser. This professionalism was happening across the sector in the UK with a raft of new people who went on to become today's fundraising gurus, including Ken Burnett, Bernard Ross and the late, great, Tony Elischer.

New professionals were entering the non-profit sector at a moment in which the perception of social need was changing, again. Until the 1980s, Muscular Dystrophy Group appeals had been based on the helpless crippled child, whose total disability was portrayed in press advertisements and in nearly life-size models of a child in a wheelchair holding out its hand. It was 'charity' for 'cripples'. But people with disabilities were beginning to assert their rights. Alf (later Lord) Morris, Labour Party MP for Wythenshawe, had pushed through the UK's first disability rights bill in 1970 (the Chronically Sick and Disabled Persons Act). We, the new professionals in charities working with people with disabilities, were charged with updating the images and messages of fundraising. The same changes were happening in the international development NGOs, which were formulating policies on how to represent hunger and need in the Global South without patronising their beneficiaries.

Why professionalism?

There are good reasons for employing professional fundraisers: modernisation and efficiency, improved customer service and communications, understanding risk and managing knowledge are all motives for more professionalism, especially in high-value philanthropy.

Modernisation and efficiency

I was not the 118th fundraiser in Britain. There have been fundraisers for hundreds of years. In the late 19th and early 20th century there was a 'subscription Collector' at Glasgow Convalescent Home (Cronin, 2011), who was 'central to its financial viability' and whose work resulted in an increase in subscriptions and donations from £958 to £2,231 in the period 1867-1936. This was part of a growing professionalisation of the mutual part of the non-profit sector that had been taking place, according to Alison Penn (2011), since the eighteenth century. 'Efficiency and objective-oriented activity' encouraged organisations to build larger organisational structures, and to 'modernise' away from their social values toward commercial ones.

We can see the same combination of modernisation and efficiency across Europe now, in the second decade of the 21st century. Universities, for example, have professionalised their alumni relations departments as a first step toward building professional development departments that combine alumni relations with fundraising.

The pressure to professionalise was increased in the early 20th century in part because of the increasing share of funding (for welfare, at least) offered by the state. There was government pressure to amalgamate organisations in order to reduce the complexity of the sector; sometimes governments did this by inviting only one organisation to join a national Advisory Board and thus to get close to power. That is what the British government did for the National Institutes of the Blind, to encourage the development of one umbrella organisation, which smaller local organisations would join.

The pressure also comes from donors, who like organisations to be efficient. More than two-thirds (68%) of the respondents to a 2014 Indiana University/Bank of America study referred to the efficiency of the organisation – in other words its capacity to effect change in proportion to its income – as a deciding factor (Simmons, 2014).

Customer service

To be slow, or late, or muddled in your response to a high-value philanthropist is, most likely, to ensure that she never gives again. This is why customer service is so paramount to private bankers and wealth managers and, increasingly, to non-profits. There is increasing competition for the philanthropic attention of people of wealth, with both private bankers and non-profits creating donor-advised charitable funds for their clients.

Competing with the resources of a well-endowed private bank sounds like a nightmare for a non-profit. And yet many are doing well; SOS Kinderdorper in the Netherlands, for example, is now managing 11 donor-advised charitable funds for philanthropic clients, and I describe the example of Fondation Caritas in Chapter fourteen. What these and other non-profits are learning is that these customer relationships have to be strategically managed. Not just 'managed', but managed according to a structured programme, a 'Service Matrix' that links the customer service to the value that the customer brings to the non-profit. Non-profits are introducing quality control methods too; the Chief Executive of one brand-name non-profit in the Netherlands calls each of the biggest donors individually each December to ask them how well his organisation has handled their needs this year.

Communication

Review research into the reasoning of philanthropists, and the need for professionals becomes obvious. The 2014 Indiana University/Bank of America study cited above gathered data by interview to establish motivations (Simmons, 2014). The principal motivation, identified by just under three quarters (74%) of individuals interviewed was 'being moved at how a gift can make a difference.' This response combines two ideas; it implies that the person sees evidence that her gift made a difference – and 'being moved' by an emotional or empathetic link with the cause. These elements can occur spontaneously in philanthropy – going out of your way to help an infirm person across a busy road combines both – but to achieve any sort of scale, or to be philanthropic at a distance, requires the presence of a professional fundraiser, who should be able to communicate the emotional element of the appeal with its impact: heart and head.

At the most basic level a professional can communicate the values, mission and work of the organisation to a potential donor. This happens more than one might imagine. Fundraisers from Oxfam and Greenpeace have told this author, independently, that donors at their high-value donor social events in Europe arrive with very inaccurate views of the organisation that is hosting the event: an Oxfam fundraiser said that some people came to the event 'thinking that we only dig wells'.

Understanding risk

Philanthropy is fraught with risk. Mostly, this is because the donor is giving against a future promise: 'we will build the school if you give us the money.' Amongst fundraisers it is widely believed (although, as far as I know never tested) that asking for a donation toward something that has happened ('we built the school; would you now donate?') is not effective.

Philanthropy is also risky because of the long supply chain, which starts with the donor and passes through the NGO to a partner who may be thousands of kilometres away. Managing that long chain is hard. Harder because the NGO or its partner may be working in a situation where there could be physical danger (remember the Médecins Sans Frontières staff killed in hospitals in the Levant), political risks (think of NGO partners working in the Sudan) or physical risks (earthquakes in Nepal).

After demonstrating that people take a different view of risk in their philanthropy than they do with their investments, Sargeant, Eisenstein and Kottasz (2015) argue that the role of fundraisers could be to help philanthropists 'realise how their (sometimes irrelevant) past experience influences their risk assessment in philanthropy, so they may adjust properly and arrive at a more "accurate" assessment of the risk at hand'. They suggest that philanthropists could be encouraged to take 'rational small steps out of their comfort zone', with each step representing a slightly higher level of risk. They argue that the area of risk and return is nuanced near the edges, where return (impact) is highly likely (in other words a philanthropist can be nearly certain that the school she is donating to will in fact be built) or highly unlikely (where a project has consistently failed, but organisation X's new method might just succeed).

In these areas near the boundaries of probability, where they are nearly certain that an outcome will be achieved or where it looks nearly impossible, philanthropists are more likely to give. A senior UK hedge fund manager who had donated more than £1 million to a hospital in Burkina Faso said to this author early in 2016: "Yes the country is landlocked, poor and under siege, but that is exactly why I am there."

Sargeant, Eisenstein and Kottasz note that the perception of return against risk is coloured by philanthropists' focus on social impact, discounting the important area of personal benefit and return; the 'return' they see is less than the total return from the project, so the risk seems proportionately higher. Their research showed (2015, p 14) that people who:

> considered personal gains found much more depth and personal value in their philanthropy, typically reflecting on the meaning of their life as articulated through their giving, the intellectual stimulation of trying to solve difficult and often intractable social problems, and/or the sustained enjoyment derived from developing their competence to contribute to social change.

Knowledge management

Oxford Thinking, the campaign for Oxford University, has raised £2.3 billion through more than 74,000 gifts from philanthropists including André Hoffmann, who donated £3.3 million to endow a chair in Developmental Medicine, and Leonard Blavatnik, whose £75 million helped to create the Blavatnik School of Government. In a significant fundraising campaign there may be hundreds of potential high-level donors or partners, with a team of account managers actively managing the relationships between the non-profit and the potential supporter.

This creates a need for strong knowledge management, to identify potential partners, to maintain and develop a relationship with them across a large, complex organisation, to introduce them to the right project, programme or activity, and to report back to them on progress, once their donation has been banked. There are the legal requirements of Europe's data protection and privacy legislation to consider too, all adding to the complexity of managing knowledge well.

This complexity is another of the reasons why non-profits are employing more professional staff. The profession of fundraiser is specialising, with experts in foundation fundraising, in corporate relations, in 'major gifts' and in prospect research (see Chapter Sixteen).

Where professionals don't reach – the board

Non-profit board members in Europe are generally not selected for their fundraising potential. It is a common complaint wherever professional fundraisers meet – at the bar of the annual International Fundraising Congress in Noordwijkerhout, for example – "my board is useless".

Many organisations have structures that require them to elect a specific type of board. So, for example, the Trust Fund for Victims, the organisation that works with the victims of war crimes identified by the International Criminal Court in The Hague, has a board selected from amongst representatives of the countries which signed the Rome Statute that established the Court. Some of the international organisations that occupy Brussels, London and Geneva have similarly elected boards. Elected boards can produce good results in high-value philanthropy, but this is rare. They are chosen for other reasons, they may not see fundraising as part of their role (or may be suspicious of the whole idea) and they are elected for all sorts of good reasons, but not, generally, for their personal wealth or high-level connections. Colleagues from the USA find this hard to believe. Boards in Europe seem anachronistic to the 'give, get, or get off' culture which tends to characterise US boards, although Edwin Venema says that he sees this changing in the Netherlands, where "it is becoming more and more clear that people are invited onto the board on the basis of give or get" but this shift is going to take time to spread around the rest of Europe.

Board members themselves are frequently reluctant to join in fundraising activities. Theresa Lloyd told me about one anonymous board chair who said to her: "'fundraising is so vulgar and embarrassing.' He dropped names like gold-edged confetti … but he never once introduced me – a fellow board member – [to one of his friends]."

There is sometimes a striking difference in attitudes between the board and the fundraising team, with the former suspicious of the latter. This may reflect different generations' understandings of philanthropy – board members being 'Inheritors of Philanthropy' while their normally much younger fundraising colleagues are 'Field Militants' in the segmentation used by the study cited in Chapter Four (de Laurens and Rozier, 2012). This picture is shifting in Europe but we are still a long way from boards that are fully focused on philanthropy.

What is so different about fundraising from high-value philanthropists?

'Major donor' fundraising is not new to Europe. Princes, priests and professors have been at it for centuries. Conferences on 'major donors', books on 'major donors' and consultants in 'major donor fundraising' are relatively commonplace in Europe now. Just a few years ago they were rare.

This author has argued for many years that the phrase 'major donor' is a misnomer because it appears to promote a purely financial measure of giving. While for a small minority of high-value gifts the money is the only value that the organisation gains from the relationship, for the majority of such gifts the person behind the money is in fact the most valuable part of the donation. If she is capable of a high-value gift she is likely to have substantial wealth, and if she has that then she is likely to be well connected, influential, potentially notorious (in the positive or negative senses of the word) and have skills and experiences that are of substantial value to the organisation.

Sensible organisations build more-than-the-money partnerships with such donors, because they have the power to move an organisation towards its strategic goals. Take the example of the Lumos Foundation created by Harry Potter author J.K. Rowling. The objective of the foundation is to 'help the millions of children in institutions worldwide regain their right to a family' (www.wearelumos.org). The foundation wants to change the pattern of orphan childcare especially in the former Soviet bloc countries of Eastern Europe by promoting the return of children to their communities. Ms Rowling's name and notoriety, her connections and her financial muscle (she donated the royalties from one of her books) have encouraged governments in Eastern Europe to change policies, moving children out of institutions (and preventing newly orphaned children from ever entering them). The impact she has had goes far beyond the money; the foundation calculates that it has shifted government spending from institutional childcare to care in the community in an amount equivalent to more than ten times

Rowling's donated royalties. This is a strategic outcome, influenced by high-value philanthropy; for this reason we call people with influence and wealth 'strategic partners'.

The professional fundraiser charged with managing a relationship with a strategic partner has a very different role from that of other fundraisers in her team. A fundraiser responsible for direct marketing (face-to-face, direct mail, email) for example has one type of unwritten contract with his donors: give us the money (for our educational project), and we will do the work (of building the schools and training the teachers). He can operate relatively independently of the programme activities of the non-profit, drawing on stories and data from his programme colleagues, but not bound to them. He can work effectively in a steep organisational pyramid where his role, to put it in the bluntest terminology, is to bring in the money.

By contrast, the fundraiser working with strategic donors has altogether another task. Her role, yes, includes bringing in the money (she is a 'fund' raiser after all), but the job will demand much more. Her clients, the strategic donors, are likely to demand much more information than the consumer donors. They are likely to want to meet senior staff and board members. These factors alone would mean that the position of this fundraiser has to be different from that of her colleagues; she needs access to the board, for example, and the political power within the organisation to request board members' presence at key meetings.

But there is more. At least some of these strategic donors will want to understand the social or environmental problem that the organisation is trying to solve, and to use their power, connection and influence to help find a solution. They may want to participate in the organisation's decision taking; as long ago as 2006 Rob John was writing about a German venture philanthropy fund that 'BonVenture will normally secure a place on the investee's board, or if not will have access to the board and its papers' (John, 2006). The philanthropist, in Theresa Lloyd's view, "wants to meet the chief executive or programme director. Having relationships managed by a very nice young person is not enough. People with significant philanthropic investment potential want to meet those who are responsible for delivering the mission."

To meet the needs of these donors, the professional fundraiser must take on a new role. She becomes the strategic donor's representative in the organisation, helping the donor to understand the organisation and to make the most of its potential, and helping the organisation win the greatest strategic advantage from its relationship with the donor.

There are a few professional fundraisers in Europe who have achieved this type of position – some of the interviewees for this book have reached this point – but for too many their place in the hierarchy and their lack of political weight in the organisation mean that they cannot make the most of their strategic donors. They are professionals, but they lack the organisational support needed to work.

Criticism of professionalism

Professionalism in the non-profit sector has its critics. Catherine Shoard, writing about local philanthropy in *The Guardian Weekly* says that 'the efficiency with which we must all now organise ourselves has led to a management-creep into all areas of our lives. Including kindness' (Shoard, 2016).

In *New Frontiers of Philanthropy* (Salamon, 2014) there is a thoughtful piece by Dr Maximilian Martin giving the global perspective on philanthropy (inevitably, much of the rest of the book is focused on the USA). Dr Martin argues that social capital markets are inefficiently relationship-driven, not value-driven. He cites Meehan, Kilmer and O'Flanagan, who in 2004 wrote:

> In the for-profit capital market, companies spend between $2 and $4 raising capital (for example, legal, marketing, and administrative expenses) – for every $100 they raise. In the social capital market, however, non-profits spend between $10 and $24 for every $100 they earn through fundraising (for example, obtaining donor lists, sending direct mail, or making phone calls). Non-profit chief executives, meanwhile, spent between 30% and 60% of their time pursuing donations with such 'soft costs' unevenly accounted for in fundraising costs.

Dr Martin signals the limits of 'relationship fundraising', noting that 'non-profit leaders typically spend vast amounts of time on fundraising rather than on the continuous improvement of the work of the organizations they lead'. He creates the phrase 'synthesized social businesses' to suggest that we should move from a world of tiny fragmented organisations, each with its own fundraising programme and its own team of professionals, to one in which we build larger business ventures with a social purpose. 'A philanthropic foundation could acquire [control over] ... a company with the mission to make the good or service available to as many people as possible around the world.'

Have we been effective?

Yes, there has been a revolution in fundraising – it has become a profession, matured as a profession and it has grown. But no, in one important sense it has not made a difference. As Professor Adrian Sargeant never tires of telling us:

> In the UK, charitable giving is estimated to be around one per cent of gross domestic product and while there are annual variations, this figure has proved remarkably static over time. Despite the best efforts of governments, philanthropists and a generation of fundraisers, the needle hasn't moved much on giving since data were first recorded. (Sargeant and Shang, 2011, p 5)

"Fundraising has diversified a lot", says Marie-Stéphane Maradeix, CEO (Déléguée générale) of the Fondation Daniel et Nina Carasso. "It is much more professional than it was. But I do not know if more askers has meant more giving." The significant change has been the growing focus, since 2007 and the 'TEPA' laws (Law of 21 August 2007 in favour of work, employment and purchasing power), on high-value philanthropy. "Major donors are seen as the most important players" in fundraising in France. Here, growing professionalism has an impact; "it makes a difference that there is now a professional account manager for the major donors".

Like the UK, the Netherlands has seen little movement in overall giving thanks to more professional fundraisers. "Giving in the Netherland by the average household is a static market", says Edwin Venema. "It is becoming more and more difficult to attract the attention of the average giver because competition in the market is growing."

This is one of many explanations for the failure of fundraisers to substantially grow income. Some blame the donors who have failed to respond, others blame the fundraisers. Miquel de Paladella, the CEO and co-founder of UpSocial in Barcelona has forthright views, shared by many in the impact investment and venture philanthropy communities; "For big organisations, fundraising for small donations from the public could have a use-by date. It could end, at some point, or be replaced by more direct forms of support." According to Miquel, "there has been a failure of the third sector to provide value propositions that are good enough for philanthropists. The value propositions are insufficient to solve social problems." As a result, philanthropists are taking it upon themselves to solve social problems, often by establishing their own foundations and social enterprises.

Professionals and high-value philanthropy

Non-profits in Europe are employing an increasing population of professionals. Banks are engaging with philanthropy for their HNWI clients, in part by creating teams of professionals. Non-profits and for-profits want to modernise, to provide better customer service, to communicate more clearly, to help clients understand and embrace risk, and to become more efficient at managing the abundance of knowledge that philanthropy feeds on.

The philanthropists have responded to – and supported – this professionalisation of the sector by demanding more and better client service, and evidence for impact. Some have responded by professionalising their own philanthropy, creating one of the hundreds of new foundations registered in Europe each year.

The arrival of these new professionals represents a significant change in philanthropy in Europe – a change that must be for the better.

PART SIX

Redesigning giving

THIRTEEN

The new forms of philanthropy

This section argues that the new tools for giving are going to change the way we do philanthropy in Europe.

Introduction

There is a profusion of new terminology in philanthropy. We talk about 'impact investing', 'social enterprises', 'Social Impact Bonds', 'soft loans', 'patient capital', 'quasi equity' and 'crowdfunding'. We talk about 'Programme Related Investment' or 'Mission Related Investment' and 'philanthropic banks' (an apparent oxymoron, until one realises that these are foundations acting as 'philanthropic banks').

These and a range of other terms have been created by the new professionals operating in the non-profit space. This is a flowering of new, or substantially recycled, tools for philanthropy designed to meet the needs of the new generation of philanthropists and their advisers. As we saw in Chapter Three many of these tools are not new – social enterprises have been around since at least the 16th century, for example – but the interest in them, the level of activity around them, and above all the amounts of money now being applied to them makes them relevant to the study of high-value philanthropy in Europe.

There is a lot of money in philanthropy. A 2009 report estimated that the European foundation sector was spending around €83 billion annually, more than twice the then total expenditure by US foundations of €41 billion (Hopt, von Hippel and Anheier, 2009). But the growth in the foundation sector may not have been properly financed. A 2014 report quoted a foundation expert as saying that 'the "foundation boom" in recent years primarily led to the founding of "undercapitalized" foundations, whose investment income alone is regularly insufficient to finance long-term, sustained activities' (Anon, 2015c).

So how does a modern philanthropist invest in social or environmental good? In *New Frontiers of Philanthropy*, Lester M. Salamon (2014) identifies a range of new tools such as the corporate-originated charitable funds we saw in Chapter Eleven.

Why have these new tools appeared now? Luther M. Ragin Jr (2014) cites five reasons:

- The shortfall in philanthropic and governmental resources against social needs
- The growing sophistication of professionals in the sector, and the focus on scale and sustainability
- An understanding that some investments can create financial and social/environmental returns
- The need for a 'broader toolbox for social engagement'
- The wider acceptance of market-based solutions for social challenges.

David Carrington cites another, broader, reason for the development of these new tools: "Social investors are curious. They have a gut feeling that it must be possible to effect change in ways other than grants."

These new tools run across a spectrum. The creation of this spectrum has been attributed to various people and organisations – Ragin credits the F.B. Heron Foundation with its creation, but this author saw an earlier version created by Pieter Oostlander, then of the Noaber Foundation and later of Shaerpa. The spectrum was a revolution in its time, because it linked two worlds – 'charity' and 'business' – that were previously considered to be ethically and culturally immiscible. Even today, in Europe, many high-value philanthropists would have difficulty in reconciling these two worlds.

Some organisations work across the entire spectrum, and Pieter Oostlander's financial architecture for Noaber Foundation created three funds in one: a philanthropic, grant-making foundation, an investment fund for social enterprise, and a venture capital fund. The design of the foundation has evolved since then but it retains its spectrum-wide interests from Noaber Philanthropy to Noaber Ventures.

This is not a million miles, though it is 454 years, from the model of the Compagnia di San Paolo (www.compagniadisanpaolo.it). The

Table 13.1 The Spectrum of social Investment

Primary driver is to create *societal value*				'Blended' societal and financial value			Primary driver is to create *financial value*		
	Social purpose organisations (SPOs)						Traditional business		
Charities	Revenue generating social enterprises			Socially driven business					
Grants only: no trading	Trading revenue and grants	Potential sustainable 75% trading revenue	Break even all income from trading	Profitable surplus reinvested	Profit distributing socially driven		CSR Company	Company allocating percentage to charity	Mainstream Market Company
Impact only									Finance first
Grant making		Venture Philanthropy				Social investment			
				Impact first					

Source: EVPA, see http://evpa.eu.com/about-us/about-vp/

Compagnia originated in 1563 when a group of Turin citizens created it as a 'brotherhood' to help the poor and to fight the usury of the money lenders. From this grew the Ufficio Pio (1595) as a charity for the poor. The Compagnia started a pawnbroker, the Monte di Pieta, which became a credit bank, evolving into one of Italy's largest banking groups, Intesa Sanpaolo with a market capitalisation of €58.4 billion. In 1991 the foundation separated from its banking activity. There is a similar story with a still earlier beginning over at the Fondazione Monte dei Paschi di Siena (www.fondazionemps.it), created in 1472.

Foundations in Denmark also work across the spectrum. A 1991 Act on Commercial Foundations (Lov om erhvervsdrivende fonde Nr. 756 of 18 November 1991 (EFL), now consolidated into Act lovbekendtgørelse nr. 559 of 19 May 2010) allowed foundations to hold a controlling interest in a business, and to combine commercial and social activities. Perhaps as a result, foundations own 20% of the largest companies in Denmark. A similar legal provision applies in Germany and there are five foundations which hold the majority of stock in substantial corporations (Robert Bosch GmbH, Bertelsmann AG. Körber AG, Possehl and Co., and Fresenius AG) amongst an estimated 500–1,000 German shareholding foundations (Seghers et al, 2015).

Impact

The growing body of professionals involved in high-value philanthropy are increasingly interested in impact, and its corollary, the transparency that allows us to measure it.

'Impact' is the theme of many, perhaps most, of the conversations that one has with philanthropists. As a wholly non-scientific test, 20 of the people interviewed for this book used the word, some of them many times, during their interviews. It is used in a number of ways, with a range of meanings.

Impact is used to mean 'a measurable change in society or in the environment', normally with the implication that this is a change for the better. It was used by some of the philanthropists interviewed for this book to mean 'a change in the way we do things'. It is linked to the word 'investment' to mean 'an investment that brings both financial change and social or environmental change' with, again, the hoped-for changes being positive.

Why are we hearing so much about impact? Interviews and research for this book suggest at least five reasons for the growing interest in impact:

- Growing professionalism in the philanthropic and non-profit sectors
- A search for sustainability in investments
- The identification of significant social and environmental problems, and opportunities
- The entry of foundations
  - As grant-makers interested in impact
  - As investors interested in impact
- The potential for catalysing system change, by demonstrating impact.

The interest in impact matches closely the five causes of a growing interest in new tools for philanthropy, cited by Ragin (2014) above.

Impact, the professional approach

"Some people say that venture philanthropy started in the 1960s", says Wolfgang Hafenmayer:

> 'but it only really took off in the 2000s when businesspeople came into the sector. They brought their business mindset, that of people who had made a lot of money quickly. The impact investing field emerged here. They focused on organisations that could link making money and doing good.'

This link is present, says Hafenmayer, in all asset classes: "in all of them you could find ways of making a positive impact".

Judith Symonds says that "the younger generation want to be certain to have an impact, and to control where their money goes". A member of a wealthy Dutch family, philanthropist and social investor who was interviewed for this book said that:

> 'social impact is new for our family. It combines two things – doing good, and you can reuse money multiple times. We are an entrepreneurial family so we like the

entrepreneurial logic, the discipline and rigour. With a social impact approach you become co-owner rather than just donor.'

But there are nuances, and this philanthropist is not solely interested in impact; his motivations mix giving with the measures of efficiency that impact offers. "Social impact is a complement to [traditional] donations. We have been an impact-first social investor for a long time."

Impact could be a way of expressing your professional status – "professionalism through impact measurement", as Serge Raicher expresses it.

There are many elements of 'being professional'. "People who are spending money in the public area have an obligation to be accountable", says Ulrik Kampmann. "We have to be very clear on how we are accountable; if you want to do that you have to work on fewer areas, to focus on impact." But this creates a dilemma because:

'a foundation's legitimacy depends on it giving a wide range of support. We have to make impact and we have to have that broadness. Knowing that you can't create impact on a wide range of donations, we have to work with partners in NGOs to be more precise where money is doing good.'

Even then, "we have a large degree of uncertainty. We cannot know all the steps from input to impact".

Funders, fundraisers and staff in the field have "become more professional", says Arnout Mertens, General Director at Salvatorian Fathers and Brothers in Rome. "We are moving away from charity to impact. Governments and agencies are imposing more stringent rules. They rarely fund without a needs assessment. If we don't have a financial [management] manual in place then the project does not get the grant."

He cites some of the difficulties of managing for impact; "We need three quotes for bills of quantity – in places where even basic literacy may be a problem. There are visits from funding organisations, financial audits ... There has been a significant change in funder attitudes over the past two years." Arnout debates the practicality of all of this for projects working in what he describes as "forgotten places" – the lost villages of the Global South. Data gathering, reliable monitoring and long-term impact evaluation are all very hard to achieve when there is no electrical power, no or few literate adults and the constant threat of natural or human disaster.

That view is seconded by Marie-Stéphane Maradeix. She illustrates the difficulties and contradictions inherent in measuring philanthropy:

> 'There is a real demand amongst philanthropists to understand impact. They are used to working with KPIs [Key Performance Indicators]. When the foundation board interviewed me for this job they asked me about KPIs. I said that the foundation was working with complex social and/or cultural issues which were not always measurable in the way that industrial products could be. Moreover, measuring social impact requires a long-term vision not always compatible with short-term projects.'

Investment, sustainability and impact

'Social impact investment is the provision of finance to organisations addressing social needs with the explicit expectation of a measurable social, as well as financial, return' (Wilson, Silva and Ricardson, 2015, p 10). "Impact investing is of great interest. People want projects to have an impact", says a philanthropist living in France who spoke off the record for this book.

Investment with impact – an investment that creates both financial and social or environmental value – is a fast-growing class of assets.

In his book *Building the Impact Economy: Our Future, Yea or Nay,* Maximilian Martin (2016) argues that impact is no longer just a moral or ethical issue. The issue now is sustainability, building a future – 'our future, yea or nay' – where 'zones of prosperity gradually expand and a sustainable economy goes mainstream'. Dr Martin proposes that sustainable firms will focus on creating 'shared value', defined as the creation of 'economic value in a way that also creates value for society by addressing its needs and challenges' (he cites Porter and Kramer, 2011).

Martin points out that the search for impact is being driven by demand as well as by the supply of willing investors and philanthropists.

He cites four 'drivers of sustainable value creation' that can combine social return with financial return. These are:

1. 'Massive pent-up demand at the Bottom of the Pyramid,' the 4+ billion people with incomes below US$1,500 per annum
2. The emerging consumer segment known as 'Lifestyles of Health and Sustainability' or LOHAS, who 'prefer products designed to be environmentally conscious, sustainable, socially responsible, and better both for people and planet'
3. The growth of the green economy – he forecasts that investments in clean energy assets will grow more than threefold between 2010 and 2030
4. Modernisation of the welfare state, toward a 'triple E [of] greater efficiency, greater effectiveness and greater engagement with citizens'. This modernisation is necessary to deal with a changing population (ageing, for example) and with the fact that some governments are spending more on healthcare, education and welfare than they are gaining in taxation.

He maps a route to a future 'ecosystem of impact investment'. Like other thinkers in this field, he starts with philanthropy, noting that 'much of the work to develop the "impact investing industry 1.0" ... has been performed by foundation philanthropy' (Martin, 2016, p 176). Impact, sustainability and philanthropy are thus intimately linked.

Slow growth, more interest?

The growth of impact investment may have been aided by the slow economic growth of recent years. "We are at a point where 3% on a real impact fund sounds good", says Serge Raicher. And that growth looks to be spectacular, as Dr Martin reminds us, citing as an example the 2013 Credit Suisse fund-of-funds to invest in agricultural opportunities in Africa that raised US$500 million. The annual J.P. Morgan/Global Impact Investing Network (GIIN) survey of the sector for 2015 reports a 7% growth in capital committed between 2013 and 2014 and a 13% growth in the number of deals, with survey respondents managing a total of US$60 billion in impact investments (Saltuk et al, 2015).

Impact – good quality investing

"A lot of [what is now called] impact investment used to be called 'development capital' in evolving economies, and that used to mean private equity", says Serge Raicher. He reminds us that the UN Principles for Responsible Investment (www.unpri.org) do not differ a lot from impact investing. "A lot of the impact investing is just reminding us that good, sound, responsible investing has a social impact. A lot of people who come to impact investing have first bought into the idea that sound investment has a strong social element."

UN Principles for Responsible Investment

In 2005 the then UN Secretary-General Kofi Annan invited a group of the world's largest institutional investors – including pension funds such as Stichting Pensioenfonds ABP and the Norwegian Government Pension Fund – to help develop principles for responsible investment. The Principles were launched in 2006 and are now an initiative of the UNEP (United Nations Environment Programme) Finance Initiative and the UN Global Compact. There are currently 1,500 signatories, managing a total of US$62 trillion in assets as at April 2016. The value of assets under management by signatories has grown almost tenfold since 2006 and almost doubled, from US$34 trillion to US$62 trillion, in the three years April 2013 to April 2016 (www.unpri.org/about).

The Six Principles of Responsible Investment are:

1. We will incorporate environmental, social and corporate governance (ESG) issues into investment analysis and decision-making processes
2. We will be active owners and incorporate ESG issues into our ownership policies and practices
3. We will seek appropriate disclosure on ESG issues by the entities in which we invest
4. We will promote acceptance and implementation of the Principles within the investment industry
5. We will work together to enhance our effectiveness in implementing the Principles

6. We will each report on our activities and progress toward implementing the Principles.

The interest in impact and its links to investment have attracted a number of foundations, which are adapting their investment strategies to take impact into account.

Foundations of impact

Foundations in Europe seek impact in their grant making, but they are increasingly also seeking it in their investments. As with so much in philanthropy, there is new and not-so-new in this, but for many foundations this is a radical departure in a sector that has, for years, focused only on the financial, and not on the social returns from its investments. That requirement was laid down in regulations – until 2011, for example, the UK Charity Commission guidance to trustees was to maximise financial returns. In that year the Commission issued new guidelines 'on investments that help the charity to achieve its mission where this has no significant financial detriment (mission related investment)' (Anon, 2011b). This new guidance allowed foundations in the UK to make impact investments. As is often the case, the US had been there before: Martin (2016) reminds us that 'the Ford Foundation pioneered PRI [Programme Related Investment] in 1968'. "In no basic definition of philanthropy does it say that you cannot get anything back", says. Wolfgang Hafenmayer. "Sometimes doing good means being tough and saying 'I want something back'."

Philanthropic foundations can provide the first finance that leads to a social enterprise being created: the grant that funds research, or the zero-cost loan that buys a first vehicle or building for a project. Because foundations are not beholden to shareholders they can afford to take on projects that offer no return, or a loss.

This has evolved into the idea of 'de-risking', where a foundation accepts the highest risk tranche of a loan or investment in order to reduce the risks for other investors, and thus to encourage them to join the loan or investment. Dr Martin cites the example of Fondazione Cariplo in Italy, which created the Fondazione Housing Sociale (FHS) in 2004 to promote the growth of social housing; funding of

€85 million from the mother foundation helped the FHS to start the first ethical real estate fund, which in turn led to government interest and further investment. Without that initial de-risking by Fondazione Cariplo these later investors would not have joined in.

Impact issues

Impact is not an easy topic. It has many disparate definitions; it is hard to measure in the field; it can create a mountain of emails, form-filling and data; and it may engender a sense that investor or donor and investee are not truly partners in solving a problem, that the investee is not truly trusted with the money.

"In the old days", says Arnout Mertens, "the missionary from the congregation would raise funds from friends and family. It was based on trust." Now there is a load of paperwork to complete. This leaves missionaries feeling uneasy: "You have to present projects. There is a psychological distance between what the missionaries are working with and funders. There is the feeling that 'You don't trust us'."

"Impact is the route, but it is not the end of the road", says Marie-Stéphane Maradeix. "One of the problems with impact is that it is a long term measure. Sustainable impact is the goal. One would have to say, OK, let's use a scientific method and measure data over 20 years. 20 years!" She described the difficulties and cost of gathering consistent data over the long term.

We are feeling our way towards impact, but we still do not have a widely accepted measure. There are all sorts of experiments and flavours – the Foundation Center's 'Tools and Resources for Assessing Social Impact' (TRASI) database (http://trasi.foundationcenter.org/) lists more than 150 tools, methods and best practices in assessing impact. The leading consulting firms are becoming engaged – the Boston Consulting Group, for example, applying a clear and scalable methodology in 'Gauging Long-Term Impact in the Social Sector' (Reed et al, 2016), or McKinsey & Company providing a 'Social Impact Assessment portal' (at http://mckinseyonsociety.com/social-impact-assessment/). But the lack of one clear methodology winner is hampering development of this sector.

Impact and system change

The hope of some philanthropists is that the interest in impact will spread out of the philanthropic sector and into government. Serge Raicher cites an example, with Social Impact Bonds: "Social impact bonds are not easy", he admits:

> 'but the mind-set behind them is important. We have gone from a militant-driven social sector to one where there is more heart and head, and more accountability. These notions, of accountability and impact measurement, are starting to enter the civil service. We're talking about accountability beyond the elections, about pay-for-success. That change of mind-set is here to stay.'

FOURTEEN

How to do good

Introduction

A philanthropist in Europe who wishes to do good can do so in a wide variety of ways. This chapter will feature some of the more innovative options, and give examples. (For a more detailed list of options see Salamon, 2014).

How to do good

To do good a philanthropist might:

- Help: Help an elderly neighbour get her weekly shopping
- Volunteer: Help via an institution or organisation, for example volunteering for the Red Cross or Red Crescent
- Donate: Make a cash gift to an institution or organisation, such as a one-off donation to an NGO
- Divert tax: In Italy and Spain, taxpayers can divert a small proportion of their tax (in Italy it is 0.5%, or 'five per thousand') to social causes when they complete their annual tax return
- Covenant: Promise to donate for a minimum number of years (typically four) to an institution or organisation. Confusingly known as a 'donation' in many parts of Europe, this pledge carries legal weight and can override the legal requirement to leave wealth to one's family
- Purchase for good: Purchase goods or services, or use a charity credit card at a premium price, knowing that part of that price is going to a non-profit institution or organisation

- Crowdfund: Pledge via a web platform such as Verkami to support a specific project – the pledge is cashed only if the crowdfund reaches its target
- Micro-lend: Lend money via a web platform such as Kiva to a specific person, typically with a micro-enterprise
- Micro-sponsor: Pledge to give to a cause so long as an individual completes a challenge – for example pledging €1 per kilometre to an NGO, so long as her friend runs the 42.2 kilometres of a marathon
- Join: Become a member by giving a regular cash payment to an institution or organisation, for example by joining as a 'Member of the Tate' or 'Amis du Louvre'
- Join a circle: Join a circle of donors either set up by individuals or created by an institution or organisation, such as the four 'Kringen' or 'Rings' of the Concertgebouw in Amsterdam (www.concertgebouw.nl/steun-ons/particulieren-het-concertgebouw-fonds/vier-kringen). Each Kringen offers specific benefits to members in exchange for a graded scale of financial contributions
- Create a donor-advised fund: Make a commitment to an institution or organisation to donate a certain value of funds (typically €10,000 or more) to create a donor-advised fund such as a subsidiary 'foundation' under the aegis of the Fondation de France or via a community foundation
- Leave a legacy: Leave assets by will in a legacy for an institution or organisation
- Lend to a non-profit: non-profits, especially in housing, are offering bonds to private investors. Golden Lane Housing is an example, see http://www.retailcharitybonds.co.uk/bonds/golden-lane-housing/. Brand and Kohler (2014) describe the mobile payments business Zoona (http://www.ilovezoona.com/), which grew thanks to a loan that converted to equity when the company became profitable – a 'convertible note'
- Invest in, or create, a social enterprise: Invest individually or through a consortium in a social enterprise
- Purchase a part share in a Social Impact Bond: Purchase, through a financial adviser, a part share in a Social Impact Bond such as the £20 million bond programme of Scope in the UK, which finances the expansion of their network of charity shops (www.scope.org.uk/get-involved/donate/philanthropy/social-investment-bond)

- Create a foundation: Endow with funds or other assets a registered public benefit foundation ('charitable trust' in the UK)
- Programme or Mission Related Investment: Direct part or all of her foundation's investable endowment toward Programme Related Investments, meaning investments that are linked to the objectives of the foundation, for example by investing in women-led enterprises

How to do good – the details

Divert tax

Italians completing their annual tax return are given the chance to direct 0.5% of their tax to organisations recognised by the government as being of public benefit. The taxpayer nominates the cause by inserting its code number in the tax return. Italian NGOs take out adverts in the newspapers and billboards on the streets and public spaces countrywide to ensure that everyone knows their code number. Leading non-profits generate significant income from this source, with 41 non-profits earning more than €1 million in 2014 (www1.agenziaentrate.it/elenchi%205x1000%202014/Elenco%20 completo%20dei%20beneficiari.pdf) including three (two cancer organisations and Emergency, www.emergency.it, an NGO working with war victims), earning more than €10 million.

Micro-lend

Can we be philanthropic with loans, not gifts? "I was involved in microcredit between 1993 and 2006 – I ran a microcredit investment fund", said the manager of a group of family foundations in the Netherlands. "My view is that you have to give money when you can't do anything else, and you have to lend money if you can. If I see a young person in Nairobi who has some vocational training and I want to help then I lend money. I don't give it."

This is part of the motivation for the growth of the microcredit business. A number of European organisations are involved in this sector. For example, CARE International UK, which forms part of one of the world's leading aid and development non-profits has developed 'Lendwithcare' (www.lendwithcare.org/info/about_us), a scheme for lending sums as low as £15 to fund small businesses in the Global

South. In collaboration with Akhuwat, a partner in Pakistan, CARE has gone on to develop a Shariah-compliant version of Lendwithcare. There are other large players in the sector – one of the largest being Kiva (www.kiva.org/), a US-registered global micro-loan foundation, with assets of US\$24.8 million as at 31 December 2014.

Impact in practice

There are long historic roots for social impact investment, and one can see its origins in the related but distinct field of socially responsible investments. In the mid-1980s this author used the services of the Ethical Investment Research and Information Services (now Viegeo EIRIS, www.eiris.org/), an advisory group on socially responsible investments. The Divest Invest movement (http://divestinvest.org/), which claims 500 participating organisations and US\$3.4 trillion pledged, is a climate change focused endeavour in the same line. A number of European foundations (http://divestinvest.org/europe/), including the Fondation Daniel et Nina Carasso, the Children's Investment Fund Foundation and Bewegungs Stiftung, have joined the movement.

France has a well-developed, officially backed system of retail social impact investment, created by a 2001 law (www.legifrance.gouv.fr/affichTexte.do?cidTexte=JORFTEXT000000770048) and known as 'finance solidaire' (see www.economie.gouv.fr/facileco/finance-solidaire). This system encourages people and companies to save in a 'solidarity fund' which is in turn invested in social housing (around 37% of invested funds), environment (39%), job creation (18%) and international solidarity (6%). The total invested through these schemes in 2014 was €6.7 billion, up 14% on the previous year and almost three times the amount invested just five years previously.

Across Europe, the number of intermediaries that allow people and foundations to make social impact investments is increasing (Wilson, Silva and Ricardson, 2015). These include social investment funds, social stock exchanges such as London's Social Stock Exchange and La Bolsa Social in Spain (www.bolsasocial.com/), and social impact investment wholesalers such as Big Society Capital.

Social enterprise

When social entrepreneur Ramón Bernat was discussing a project to create employment for people with autism and Asperger's Syndrome he decided to create a private limited liability company (an 'SL' in Catalonia) rather than a foundation. "If you want to speak to SAP or Microsoft as an equal, if you want to speak to their human resources director, as an equal, then you have to have a SL. If it was a foundation they'd say *'pobrecitos'* [poor things.]"

Social enterprise is a booming area for high-value philanthropists. The reasons cited above (Ragin, 2014) are all relevant, with the influence of professional advisers being especially relevant here; for example, in 2015 UBS became the first bank in the UK to offer a social enterprise fund with partner Resonance (Palin, 2015).

Linked to the social enterprise field, a number of high-value philanthropists have created companies, not foundations, to channel their giving: Zennström Philanthropies (www.zennstrom.org), legally 'Zennström Philanthropies Limited', a company limited by guarantee, is an example. The company structure allows the founders more flexibility with their investments – they are not limited to making grants that are definable as 'charitable' – and with careful tax planning need be no less fiscally efficient than a registered foundation.

Social Impact Bonds

David Carrington argues that while SIBs are unlikely to become a dominant form of funding, they may become more democratised: "Social impact bonds are expensive. They are on the margins and that's where I think they will stay. [But] the lack of opportunities for smaller scale investments is changing and I believe it is important that it does – that everyone can get involved in making some of their money achieve a blended return".

In Europe there are active Social Impact Bonds in Belgium and the UK, according to Wilson, Silva and Ricardson (2015). Social Finance (www.socialfinance.org.uk/database/) has launched a global map of SIBs showing, at July 2015, 60 SIBs and US$216 million capital raised. The UK has at least 15 such bonds in existence, covering workforce development, homelessness, childcare, foster care, ageing and adoption as well as the mother of all European SIBs, the Peterborough recidivism project. Big Issue Invest (http://bigissueinvest.com/funds/social-enterprise/) is active in the sector and has recently announced the world's first SIB in mental health and employment, designed to help people with profound mental health issues secure work placements. In Germany, the first Social Impact Bond (SIB), designed to place young people in Augsburg into jobs or vocational training programmes is being tested by the state of Bavaria in collaboration with the Benckiser Stiftung Zukunft and investors including the BHF Bank Foundation, two BMW foundations and Bonventure (Anon, 2015c).

Donor-directed funds – the nearly foundations

Instead of going through all the bureaucratic bother and expense of creating your own foundation, you can create a fund under the umbrella of a larger foundation. Legally your 'foundation' is just a subsidiary fund, but in a number of countries in Europe, notably France, you can call it a 'Foundation' and manage it, to all intents and purposes, as though it were a standalone non-profit.

These entities are called 'donor-directed funds' and they are becoming increasingly popular in Europe.

King Baudouin Foundation has 558 donor-directed funds (Mernier and Xhauflair, 2014) managed from its base in Brussels, Belgium. Up the road in the Netherlands 'Fonds op naam' (donor-directed funds) are increasingly popular. Large foundations manage funds for donors – Prins Bernhard Cultuurfonds (www.cultuurfonds.nl) and Mama Cash (www.mamacash.org) are examples – universities (Wageningen, amongst others), cultural organisations (RCO, the Royal Concertgebouw Orchestra or Concertgebouworkest) and NGOs such as Médecins Sans Frontières, SOS Kinderdorper and Cordaid all have donor-directed funds. The Prins Bernhard Cultuurfonds, for example, will create a fund for a donor with a minimum investment of €50,000 and at least €5,000 available for grants each year. Most settlors choose to donate by covenant (this allows tax-efficient donations without an upper ceiling) over five consecutive years. The Cultuurfonds shows a tax calculation (www.cultuurfonds.nl/geven/cultuurfonds-op-naam/voor-particulieren) using this method of giving: the cost for a highest rate tax payer to set up a €100,000 named fund with five annual instalments is just €9,600 per year.

Just as in the USA, where commercial operators such as Fidelity have entered the 'charity' market (Salamon, 2014), so in Europe there are increasing numbers of banks that offer donor-directed funds to their clients. These include Rabobank, UBS with its Optimus Foundation (www.ubs.com/microsites/optimus-foundation/en/home.html), UBS UK Donor-Advised Foundation and other offerings, the Coutts Institute in London, and Bank Vontobel Charitable Foundation in Switzerland, amongst others.

Fondation Caritas France

"In 2006, for the 60th anniversary of Secours Catholique, we wanted to do something big", says Jean-Marie Destrée, Assistant Director General of Fondation Caritas France. "We had a good fundraising team, it was the start of the boom in Corporate Social Responsibility, we had the good brand of the Association Secours Catholique. But certain companies did not want to associate with a charity that was so clearly religious."

Destrée had encouraged the growth of highly skilled volunteer teams – for example his legacy promotion team included a retired senior banker and a lawyer – and through them he met a businessman who was about to sell his company. Over lunch, the businessman said; "Listen, I share the values of Secours Catholique, but it has an income of €140 million, and my donation will get lost in that great mass of money. Also, I want to be involved, to work closely with whoever manages my donation." "That was when the idea came to me", said Destrée, "to create a foundation that would harbour donor-advised funds. We would help major donors with a service where their donation is not lost in the massive income [of a large charity.] We aimed to create something like a family office."

"People wanted to benefit from the fiscal changes – especially ISF [Impôt de Solidarité sur la Fortune, see Chapter 5]."

At the beginning it was associations that were the key clients, associations that wanted to gain the fiscal benefits of a foundation. But Destrée persisted with the focus on people, and now it is largely families that set up donor-advised funds.

"We did two disruptive things. First, we applied an 'open-source logic'. We would welcome founders whatever their project. [One or two other French non-profits] also offer donor-advised funds but they insist that people and the funds stay within their projects. We were open-source."

Initially, this was difficult to sell internally, at Secours Catholique. "The main difficulties were with the fundraising team who were concerned about numbers, results. We told them that this was a mid-term investment." Which, indeed, is what it turned out to be, and Fondation Caritas France has donated €11.7 million back to Secours Catholique since 2009 (source: Secours Catholique Annual Report, 2015).

> 'Second, we lowered the entry level for creating a foundation. Normally, to set up a foundation in France, people expect you to put up €200,000. For us, that was too high. We said €20,000 per year for three years. In fact when you look at how much people give it is almost €200,000 over five years. We were criticised – people called it "market café" giving.'

But the organisation struck a chord with people at the top of the middle – wealthy families who were not the well-known multimillionaires featured each year in *Challenges* (the French business magazine that publishes an annual rich list). Instead, Fondation Caritas France found that it was working with what Jean-Marie Destrée calls 'middle philanthropy'.

"We invested a lot in meetings, face to face." Much of this time was spent helping would-be philanthropists to shape their philanthropic thinking and strategies, and to build their confidence in the team: "one has to build a circle of confidence", said Destrée. People wanted to learn from each other, so Fondation Caritas "encouraged peer-to-peer sharing amongst philanthropists. For example we recently took eight philanthropists to Cambodia for eight days [to see projects]."

Fondation Caritas France has carried out a study which showed that the Caritas 'brand' represents certain values. "Many of the philanthropists [who have created funds with us] come from the philanthropic, Christian charitable traditions – the idea of helping others. Many are non-practising, but they have their values from their parents or grandparents."

One of the benefits for donors working with Fondation Caritas France is that thanks to Secours Catholique they have a wide network of volunteers across France, and partners and projects abroad. "We can provide the connections on the ground" that philanthropists want, said Jean-Marie Destrée.

The Fondation is still young and it has many of the advantages of a startup, including a flexible structure, quick reactions and independence from the sometimes bureaucratic processes of Secours Catholique. As a consequence, decision-taking is rapid. "Our donors like the collegial management between Pierre Levené, Director General and me [Jean-Marie Destrée, Assistant Director General]. They like the fact that they meet the DG or the Assistant DG."

The strategy has worked. By the end of 2015 the Fondation Caritas France had 78 funds under management, a total of €25 million in assets and a continuing growth rate of 15 to 20 new funds each year – which will make it by the end of 2016 the second largest donor-advised fund in France, after the Fondation de France.

"One has to be very professional. [Our clients] are very demanding and we are working in complex areas of tax deductions, and impact. There is a real need for professionals who have a real sensitivity to the work." But this is "Caring Caritas. It is absolutely different to a bank."

The traditional and still popular route: your own foundation

As we have shown elsewhere, philanthropists all across Europe are creating their own foundations. With a bit of planning, this need not be an arduous or expensive exercise.

The amount of capital required to register a foundation varies hugely across Europe (Anon, 2015e). In Sweden, the Netherlands and the UK, for example, there is no minimum capital requirement for creating a foundation. In Malta and Poland, just over €1,000 is sufficient. But in Germany and Italy a philanthropist would need €50,000 to set up a foundation and in France €1.5 million to create a public benefit foundation (source: Centre Français des Fonds et Fondations, Tableau Comparatif, www.centre-francais-fondations.org). France is at the extreme end of the scale in part because it has designed a menu of eight different foundation types, each with their own entry price.

Sweden and the Netherlands, as well as requiring little capital to start up a foundation, have very light-touch administrations, with no government approval required to establish a foundation.

Having your own foundation offers many benefits to offset the cost. A key motivation is the hands-on opportunities that your own foundation offers. "We really feel a sense of urgency", says a member of a wealthy Dutch family, philanthropist and social investor who was interviewed for this book.

> 'We are flexible; we don't have a big bureaucracy – there are just six of us. We are completely unattached and we don't have the size of a big foundation like a Rockefeller. The big foundations are like a government – procedures have become too dominant. That is totally the wrong way to go. Our added value is that we can do whatever we want – we are nimble.'

Redesigning giving – conclusions

We have never had it so good, as philanthropists and fundraisers. The range of products that we can use – from a simple donation to a complex structured social impact investment – is wider than ever before. More importantly, it is more available than ever before as foundations, banks, non-profits and advisers adapt and package these products to meet the needs of their clients.

This democratisation of innovations in giving is delayed, however, by at least three factors:

- The unresolved question of how to measure impact
- The fiscal and legal framework – for example there is no legal basis for a social enterprise in Spain
- Tradition and conservatism on the part of non-profit boards and management, some of whom have increasingly outdated views of 'charity' and 'fundraising'.

These barriers will gradually be overcome by the same forces that are changing philanthropy in Europe. But we could move faster, be more agile, adapt better, if we were willing to take a few risks.

PART SEVEN

Uncovering philanthropy in Europe

FIFTEEN

The deeper view

This section is designed to help you find your way around the high-value philanthropy sector. The section includes a note on academic research in philanthropy, links to research centres, and a chapter on how prospect researchers are using the new transparency to find and understand philanthropists.

Introduction

Europe is gradually uncovering its philanthropy. For the reasons we have been exposing in this book – government pressure and policy change, shifting attitudes to wealth, growing professionalism in the non-profit sector – we are starting to see the good (and, very occasionally, the bad) of Europeans.

Academic research challenges

Speak to researchers in philanthropy in Europe and you will hear about opportunities and barriers. The opportunities and the barriers sound the same.

- Opportunity: we know so little, really, about why people give in Europe. There is lots more to find!
  - Barrier: we know so little, really, about how much people give, and who gives, in Europe. We have no data on which to base research!
- Opportunity: in continental Europe we can compare and contrast different cultures of philanthropy across a relatively small geographic area

- ◦ Barrier: maybe we can't compare and contrast different cultures of philanthropy in Europe. Maybe they are simply not comparable
- Opportunity: the new interest in philanthropy means that foundations are working to promote philanthropy
  - ◦ Barrier: despite the new interest in philanthropy foundations are not funding (enough) research to understand philanthropy
- Opportunity: there is lots of good research on philanthropy in the USA
  - ◦ Barrier: there is lots of good research on philanthropy in the USA ... but does that really help us understand philanthropy in Europe?

In this sense, research in philanthropy is not that different from research into particle physics, pharmacology or phenomenalism – there are always opportunities and barriers in research whether it is in the sciences or the humanities. But philanthropy, especially high-value philanthropy, seems to have suffered from a lack of research. It has also lost out because of the compartmentalisation of research. As Arthur Gautier and Laurence de Nervaux (2015) point out 'private donations have been the subject of studies [in France] by historians, anthropologists, sociologists, political scientists, economists and management researchers ... [but] the knowledge is spread across these disciplines and it is very difficult to get an overview'. Professor Theo Schuyt (2010) underlines the point by noting that over the period 2000-2008 the word 'philanthropy' appeared just once in the title or subtitle of the articles in eight leading European journals on social policy.

Despite the growing transparency that is the theme of this book, there are still huge lacunae in high-value philanthropy; in most of Europe we don't know how much people give, for example. Because we can't get the data, we do very little research in this area. The CAF World Giving Index provides a ranking and some data (Anon, 2015k), but does not distinguish high-value philanthropy from overall giving. A few commercial firms have filled some gaps – Scorpio Partnership has produced some very useful research and my own firm, Factary, regularly publishes reports and data on high-value philanthropy. But these are drops in the ocean compared to the seas of information available in other markets that also target HNWIs, such as asset management, luxury goods or banking.

The fact that we do less research in Europe than in the USA is typical in many areas other than in philanthropy. It is especially notable in philanthropy, however, where a review of the listings of the International Society for Third Sector Research shows that there are 53 academic centres of third sector research in the USA, and just 11 in the next nearest country by volume of centres, the UK (Carnie, 2016). The remainder of Europe shares just 25 centres. These centres are not all researching philanthropy, but the figures are illustrative of one of the differences – staffing and resources would be another – between research in the USA and Europe.

The European black holes

What are we missing in research into high-value philanthropy in Europe? 'Everything' would not be an unfair response: data, resources, money, background, and our own European models for explaining what we see.

None of this research can happen without funding. Pamala Wiepking, one of Europe's foremost researchers in this field, is pessimistic.

> 'Research in Europe is not heading anywhere until we have funds to do this. Without data we can't operate and we need money for data. I have hit my head to the wall hundreds of times with foundations; I don't think that we talk the same language – the researchers, and the foundations. They don't have enough confidence in us to fund research in this area. We could roll out our Giving in Netherlands panel study across so many countries, but we can't get funding.'

Europe is not completely dark. There are pinpricks of light: data in the Netherlands and the UK, a small but active infrastructure of agencies supplying information, and the European Foundation Centre in Brussels. But let us start with the dark stuff.

We have (almost) no data on high-value philanthropy...

"I really don't know", says Pamala Wiepking in response to my question about changes in philanthropy. "We just do not have the data to measure changes in high value philanthropy across Europe."

Dr Wiepking works in the Netherlands, where data on giving is available thanks to the Giving in the Netherlands survey (www.giving. nl/). While there is solid survey data on giving in general, there is very little data on high-value giving, particularly up at the levels of gift that might be called a 'major gift'. The 'High Net Worth Supplement' to the survey takes as its lower cut-off point households whose income and equity combined is at least €60,000 (Bekkers, Boonstoppel and de Wit, 2013), and although the approximately 1,300 names in the survey are drawn from a 'Millionaire's database', the number of donors giving truly significant sums is tiny.

If Dr Wiepking does not have the data then no one does. With colleagues Femida Handy, Sohyun Park and Valerie Mossel, she has compiled the International Philanthropy Database (IPD), the first international comparative data source to include individual giving levels (amounts donated) to charitable organisations, as well as determinants of giving behaviour such as resources and values. This database is accessible to researchers, who must contact Dr Wiepking first (pwiepking@ rsm.nl). The database includes information from a growing number of countries; at the time of writing the European countries featured included Austria, Finland, France, Germany, Ireland, Netherlands, Norway, Switzerland and the UK. But again, the numbers of donors making significant high-value philanthropic gifts in this dataset is likely to be very small.

We lack information on the effects of high-value philanthropy on organisations in Europe. Bearing in mind that organisations such as hospitals, universities and museums are shifting their thinking from a state-funded model to a mixed public–private model, it would be good to know what effect if any this has on how the organisation functions. There is "very little empirical research on the impact of philanthropy on the recipient organisation", says Dr Arthur Gautier. "Does it cause mission drift? What does it really change?"

...So we do (almost) no research on high-value philanthropy

With no or little data on high-value philanthropy in Europe there is very little that researchers can do to study the topic. The volume of peer-reviewed academic papers on the subject, originating from research in Europe, is tiny. We have to look for our light somewhere else.

Sources of light

There are a number of books on high-value philanthropy that are either wholly or partly focused on Europe.

For a background and history of high-value philanthropy in the UK, Rhodri Davies' *Public Good by Private Means: How Philanthropy Shapes Britain* (2015) is excellent. Using examples from history – including recognisable modern brand names such as Coutts and Cadbury – he shows the evolution of philanthropy and the welfare state, identifying key principles in philanthropy about people, head and heart and risk-taking. And if you enjoy looking back to the future, then read the collected writings on philanthropy of Andrew Carnegie (2006); I have seen his 'Gospel of Wealth' in the hands of a number of venture philanthropists in Europe.

Virgine Seghers' *'La Nouvelle Philanthropie'* (2009) is an essential read if you wish to understand the evolution, and some of the internal contradictions, of the high-value philanthropy scene in France. It is built from interviews with individual philanthropists and advisers, who are photographed and named. That last phrase sounds bland, but in the context of France it is surprising: high-value philanthropy in France had been secretive to the point of anonymity and Seghers' book helped to break the mould. Charles Handy's *The New Philanthropists* (2006) does a similar job, based on interviews with philanthropists, for the UK. The *Handbook of Research on Entrepreneurs' Engagement in Philanthropy* (Meijs et al, 2014) is another in this small collection of books that include interviews with high-value philanthropists – what the authors call 'philanthrepeurs', while Renée Steenbergen's *De Nieuwe Mecenas* (2008) is focused on the arts and culture in the Netherlands, using interviews to illustrate the changing role of individual patrons (*mecenas*).

John Nickson's *Giving is Good for You* (2013) is the story of a personal journey into high-value philanthropy in the UK. It draws on Nickson's professional life as a fundraiser, and his skills as a writer and raconteur, to review the forces present in high-value philanthropy. Caroline Fiennes (2012) explains to high-value philanthropists (and to the rest of us) that *It Ain't What you Give, It's the Way that You Give It*. In a clear exposition (she formerly worked for New Philanthropy Capital) she describes how to be strategic about philanthropy, to track impact and to measure results. Dr Maximillian Martin (2016) heads further into the future with *Building the Impact Economy: Our Future, Yea or Nay*. This is one of those rare books that crosses all the boundaries, linking economics, philanthropy, environment and social change in one clear, if dense, model.

The jewel in the crown, though, is *Richer Lives: Why Rich People Give*, by Dr Beth Breeze and Theresa Lloyd (2013). The book is the report of a second major research study. The first, ten years previously, was written by Theresa Lloyd (2004). For the first time in Europe we had comparable data – two studies conducted ten years apart, with the rigorous academic guidance of Dr Breeze, and with an overlapping sample of individuals – in other words people who were interviewed for both studies. This gives us a clear view of how philanthropy has evolved at least in the UK.

Research agencies

Various commercial research groups take an interest in high-value philanthropy. Caroline Booth and colleagues (2015) reported for Ipsos MORI on charitable giving amongst individuals with incomes of £100,000 or more, for example, and Scorpio Partnership (www. scorpiopartnership.com/) in the UK is a regular source of good-quality research on philanthropy amongst people of wealth. Factary (www. factary.com) publishes regular reports and blog posts on this topic.

New Philanthropy Capital (www.thinknpc.org/) in London was in part established to help high-value philanthropists take informed decisions about their giving. NPC has a special insight into the world of high-value philanthropy illustrated, for example, by their report 'Money for Good UK: Understanding Donor Motivation and Behaviour' (Bagwell et al, 2013).

Foundation centres and associations

Europe's network of foundation centres is one of the success stories in philanthropy on the continent. As they grow in size and resources, so they are beginning to publish research on the sector and its evolution. Leading lights in this field include the European Venture Philanthropy Association (http://evpa.eu.com/), which publishes a wide range of research and reports, the Fondation de France with its associated Observatory (www.fondationdefrance.org/article/etudes-de-lobservatoire), the Spanish Foundation Association (www.fundaciones.es) and FIN, the Vereniging van fondsen (www.verenigingvanfondsen.nl/) Netherlands. The European Foundation Centre has also published some research on the foundation sector, but more commonly seems to collaborate in the research projects of others.

Alliance magazine (www.alliancemagazine.org) covers Europe and the rest of the world and focuses on foundations. For a global perspective it is unequalled, with reports written largely by insiders in the foundation community.

The informal sector

Useful blogs on philanthropy are emerging constantly. At the time of writing this, my European blog list includes:

- 101 Fundraising (http://101fundraising.org/), written by fundraising professionals and including a wide range of viewpoints
- CerPhi (www.cerphi.org/), with regular news updates from the Centre d'Étude et de Recherche sur la Philanthropie
- De Dikke Blauwe (www.dedikkeblauwe.nl/), news on giving and social investment, including high-value philanthropy
- DAFNE (http://dafne-online.eu/), Donors and Foundations Networks in Europe, with news on the foundation sector
- LinkedIn (www.linkedin.com/) with a regularly changing landscape of groups and networks
- New Philanthropy Capital (www.thinknpc.org/blog/) covers news on research relevant to the sector
- Philanthropy Age (www.philanthropyage.org), covering philanthropy in the Arabic-speaking world

- Rogare (www.plymouth.ac.uk/schools/plymouth-business-school/rogare), the challenging thinking and writing of Ian MacQuillin
- UK Fundraising (http://fundraising.co.uk/), Howard Lake's longstanding and active news site on fundraising

SIXTEEN

Find the philanthropists

Philanthropists use research, such as the bespoke research of New Philanthropy Capital in London, to identify suitable partners for their philanthropic objectives.

The research that concerns this chapter goes in the opposite direction: enabling fund-seeking non-profits to research and understand their philanthropic partners. This is a very old occupation. Whether you were a 15th century monarch making enquiries amongst your courtiers to find a wealthy merchant who would sponsor a voyage to the Spice Islands, or a 19th century social reformer hunting for a banker to fund a social housing project, you were carrying out research. In the 20th century this form of research gained a name – 'prospect research' – and a professional status supported by associations in the USA and the UK.

Prospect research was born in the USA in the early 1970s, the result, says Cecilia Hogan (2004), of increasing competition and sophistication in fundraising, and of the availability of relatively cheap desktop computers. These allowed easier, faster, more distributed computing and database management. The increasing competition helped fundraising professionals to realise that some people were better at asking than finding out. If their skills lay in talking and listening and selling, then they should apply those skills face to face with donors, rather than face down in a dusty copy of Marquis' Who's Who. The askers were the fundraisers, while those who found out became 'prospect researchers' whose job it was to find potential donors, or 'prospects'.

The profession spread across the Atlantic and by 1990 there were three (yes, just three) prospect researchers operating in the UK, one each at Cambridge University and the NSPCC (National

Society for the Prevention of Cruelty to Children), and this author. Prospect research went through the same evolution as fundraising. The first association in Europe for professional prospect researchers, Researchers in Fundraising (institute-of-fundraising.org.uk/groups/sig-researchers/), was founded in 1993 as a semi-independent 'Special Interest Group' of the Institute of Fundraising; I was its first Chair. The group has grown substantially, has established professional standards, a training programme and a successful annual conference. Early on it established relationships with its sister in the USA, the Association of Professional Researchers for Advancement[1] (APRA, www.aprahome. org). Today there are 2,100 members of APRA and around 500 affiliates of Researchers in Fundraising in the UK. These two organisations set ethical standards, provide training in research, encourage suppliers to provide the data and analysis that the sector needs, and act as an enormous Brains Trust, swapping techniques and time saving tips in discussion groups online.

There is a significant gap between the numbers of prospect researchers in the UK and in the rest of Europe. I estimate that there are no more than 50, and perhaps no more than 30 full-time prospect researchers in the whole of continental Europe. INSEAD (Institut Européen d'Administration des Affaires), the business school near Paris, was the first continental European organisation to employ a prospect researcher; in 1995 the school built a fundraising team including a full-time prospect researcher for its successful €118 million capital appeal. Other business schools (HEC, École des Hautes Études Commerciales, ESADE, Escola Superior d'Administració i Direcció d'Empreses) have followed but they rarely employ more than one researcher. Museums (Louvre) and orchestras (RCO Netherlands) have prospect researchers, as do leading NGOs such as Médecins Sans Frontières with two, one in the Netherlands and one in Spain, but the numbers are tiny compared to the UK and miniscule compared to the USA.

In part this reflects the later evolution in continental Europe of professional fundraising. It also reflects broader concerns about privacy and personal data. But above all it reflects the still-too-low value placed on the professionalism of fundraisers by the leadership of non-profits in continental Europe. If the chief executives truly valued their professional fundraising staff, they would give them the means to do their jobs efficiently, by providing them with skilled prospect research support.

What's your job?

Prospect researchers carry out various tasks, but their primary role is to help the fund-seeking non-profit to identify and understand its major donors. This means that alongside gathering biographical information about actual and potential supporters, prospect researchers focus on three key elements – the *connection* between the donor and the non-profit, her *motivations* for philanthropy, and her *gift capacity* or potential. Information in these three areas helps the fundraising team to work out how best to approach the philanthropist, to frame a project or programme that will interest her, and to pitch at the right price.

None of this is remotely surprising to people involved in finance in the for-profit sector. It is the type of intelligence that any sensible investment adviser would want before meeting a client for the first time – who is she, how do we know her, what is she interested in, and how much could she invest? But continental European non-profits have been cautious and in some cases resistant to this new division of labour in fundraising, citing concerns about data privacy and budgetary constraints.

Researchers carry out all sorts of tasks linked to gathering knowledge for fundraising. A good researcher working with a team of fundraisers might spend five or six hours a day researching prospect profiles, and the rest of her time reporting to colleagues, managing a contacts database, reviewing publications, or building a pool of prospects for the forthcoming campaign. She or he will be a central part of the fundraising team, gathering and sharing knowledge with her colleagues, knowledge that could eventually result in a successful partnership with a philanthropist.

How transparency has made a difference

Transparency has saved time and increased the probability that the right non-profit will seek out and find the right philanthropist for their work. This is most obvious amongst foundations. Swiss foundations, for example, were a closed book to researchers until the Swiss cantonal business directories came online in 1998[2] and the association of Swiss foundations created its website (www.swissfoundations.ch) in 2001. Before the arrival in 2003 of the Spanish Foundations Association, it was technically possible to research foundations, but the process included making a written request to the Ministry of Health (or whichever Ministry was the 'protectorate' for the foundation you were searching) explaining who you were and why you wanted the information. If this was granted (the author was told, at the time, that the process could take months) then at a time and date specified by the Ministry you could visit its office in Madrid and see a basic registration document for the foundation. That was it. Understandably most people didn't bother. Even today, as its many scandals attest, Spain's foundation sector suffers from a lack of transparency in finance and funding.

Today's transparency in Europe allows researchers to:

- Find foundations and their board members in Switzerland (www. moneyhouse.ch)
- Find out who gave to leading business school fundraising campaigns (try HEC or INSEAD for example)
- Easily find financial information about a company in France (www. societe.com) and identify what it sponsors (www.admical.org)
- Discover a charitable trust in Scotland (www.oscr.org.uk)

Given time, limitless determination, and a travel budget including Geneva, Paris, and Edinburgh, these searches were always possible. But in practice they were unfeasible. Transparency has made them feasible.

Lonely non-profit seeks wealthy, wise partner

So, how should non-profits, and philanthropists, seek each other out? Here is a typical sequence, showing the main techniques and including key sources.

The basics

We could be starting this research from various points, but a common one is when a board member, at the end of a long meeting, mentions to a member of staff that she met 'someone called John Hortaygo' at a social event last week and that Mr Hortaygo had said some very positive things about the NGO's work.

It takes a while to work out – normally by checking the name in a search engine and coming up with blanks, and then going back to the board member to find out more – the proper name of the individual. Names in one European country can look strange to the residents of another, so it is vital to get the spelling (and eventually, the pronunciation) right. The name carries many clues – in Spain for example the surnames give you the starter for a family tree; 'Juan Ortega Torres' has a father whose surname is 'Ortega xxx' and a mother whose surname is 'Torres xxx'. And if he were 'Joan' not 'Juan', or she were 'Maria' and not 'María' or Mònica' and not 'Mónica' (note the accents and see www.guiainfantil.com/servicios/nombres/ noms_homes_dones.htm) you would know that they were Catalan, not Spanish.

More names

Names will come in to a researcher from a variety of other directions. She will be reading and clipping the local business press to identify businesses that appear to be doing well, or people buying and selling companies. She will be talking to her colleagues, finding out who they are meeting and adding interesting names to her database.

She may have carried out an analysis of her database to identify donors with specific family names or addresses. Where a match occurs it is flagged in the non-profit's database. Later, these flagged records are researched further to gather biographical information on the supporter. These methods, developed in the USA and the UK, are now spreading across Europe.

'Analysis' covers a variety of techniques. It can include a check against postcode or address-based information on lifestyle and wealth (Experian's 'MOSAIC' system is an example), with a flag or code added to each record in the non-profit's database. The lifestyle datasets are built from census data, credit card data, and the information that consumers share when they respond to questionnaires or register their purchase of a new product. Designed principally around the needs of the financial sector, they allow marketers to segment their customers into lifestyle groups based on age, estimated income, lifestyle stage and purchasing patterns. Non-profits in Europe use these systems to segment their donor or alumni datasets in order to improve the targeting of their marketing.

Analysis of non-profit databases goes further, of course, and can include selections and segmentations based on donors' behaviour, the requests to which they respond most frequently, or their geographic location. Regional appeals, for example for an important heritage building, frequently focus on a segment of donors living within say 50 kilometres of the site.

The objective in the early stages of the prospect research process is to build a pool of potential supporters. This might be 200 people or 50 foundations or 60 companies or a mixture of the three. The size of the pool is dictated by the needs, size and strategy of the fundraising programme that the researcher is supporting. At this early stage the focus is on volume, finding names rapidly rather than researching them in depth.

With the pool of names in place the researcher will start to gather biographical information about each prospect. Biographical information is becoming easier to find in Europe. There are online editions of *Who's Who* for various European countries – France has www.whoswho.fr while Sutter's publishes online biographical directories for Italy and Spain at www.whoswho.eu for example. Many European professionals are using LinkedIn, and www.viadeo.com (which is currently popular in France) is useful, as are compiled directories of businesspeople such as www.nomination.fr and Belgium and Luxembourg's www.topmanagement.net. The automated biographic compiler sites such as www.zoominfo.com are less useful in Europe because their algorithms appear to be based on English.

Motivation, connection, gift capacity – the big three

Researchers try to understand the individual's motivation – why she gives, who she supports, what she cares about – in order to establish whether there is a common ground between her interests and those of the non-profit. They research the connections between the non-profit and the potential donor – do we have a board member who knows her, did she go to business school with our programmes manager – because they are looking for the links that will enable a first contact, or an introduction. And they assess the potential donor's gift capacity, attempting to estimate the largest gift that she could make in ideal circumstances.

A prospect researcher in Paris, Texas, has, if she has the budget, a wide range of online tools designed for prospect research professionals. Her colleague in Paris, France, does not yet have the luxury of services designed for her. This is, very simply, because she is one of only a handful of prospect researchers in France, and not much more than two handfuls in continental Europe. As a result there is not, yet, sufficient demand to persuade suppliers that it is worthwhile building tools for continental European prospect researchers. So researchers in Europe must build their own picture of motivation, connection and gift capacity, and live with the many knowledge gaps that leaves. More transparency has helped, but it is not yet an easy task.

Motivation

A strong clue to philanthropic interests and *motivation* is to be found amongst foundations; if your potential donor or partner is a board member of a foundation that supports work with autistic children, for example, then it is pretty likely that he is philanthropically interested in that topic. We can now research foundation board members by name in some European countries – www.moneyhouse.ch, for example, allows this type of search for Switzerland, the 'Verzeichnis Deutscher Stiftungen' at www.stiftungen.org for Germany (Anon, 2014b), and Fondsendisk for the Netherlands (Duijts, 2015). In England and Wales the Charity Commission database (http://apps.charitycommission.gov. uk/showcharity/registerofcharities/RegisterHomePage.aspx) allows, at the time of writing, searches based on the charity's name but not on board members' names. OSCR for Scotland is similar. However the Charity Commission's dataset has been made available online, and Open Charities (http://opencharities.org/) allows this type of search.

Connections

The same picture occurs with *connections* research. This is vital in building the approach to a potential partner; if we can determine that she went to university with the husband of our board President then we have a good chance of eventually finding a way to meet her. In most of Europe this is painstaking work – ploughing through company registers and annual reports to find out who sits on the same boards, using a *Who's Who* – www.whoswho.fr will allow this search for example – to find out who went to the same university in the same year, and reviewing news coverage through LexisNexis if you have it or Google if you don't to uncover information about partners in business and social settings. Researching one person's connections can easily take eight hours of labour, so it is something for only the best and biggest prospects.

Luckily, informal research works well in Europe. The people with the money in small countries such as Luxembourg and Scotland all seem to know each other. Even in France the informal networks amongst wealthy philanthropists are strong; networks and circles of donors who are sharing information in the Netherlands, Switzerland and Germany are covered in Chapter Four. In Europe prospect researchers will spend a lot more time than their US sisters interviewing board members, staff and donors to find informal information about connections. 'Peer Reviews', in which a group of four to six people sit together and review a list of 80–150 prospects to identify who has a connection, are especially effective in Europe – in part because the meetings are normally accompanied by a glass of wine, and in part because the networks in Europe are dense and strong.

Gift capacity

Research into *gift capacity* is very limited in Europe. Gift capacity is defined as an estimate of the largest gift that an individual could make to any cause, in ideal circumstances, over five years. The estimate is based principally on wealth and past donations. There is very little available financial information about individuals' wealth and almost none, outside the UK, on their past philanthropy. There are various rich lists, modelled on Forbes' in the USA. These are criticised by the people who feature in the lists themselves as being too conservative in their estimates of wealth, but they are a starting point for a struggling prospect researcher who wants to find out something – anything – about potential supporters. At the time of writing, rich lists are published in:[3]

- Austria: *Trend* magazine (www.trendtop500.at/die-reichsten-oesterreicher) publishes a regular top 100 for wealth in Austria
- Belgium: Ludwig Verduyn, a Flemish journalist, publishes a listing on his website, and has published books listing wealth in Belgium (Verduyn, 2015)
- France: The 500 largest fortunes in France are listed each year by *Challenges* magazine (http://www.challenges.fr)
- Germany: *Manager Magazin* (www.manager-magazin.de) publishes a listing of the 500 wealthiest people in Germany in October each year
- Netherlands: *Quote* magazine (www.quotenet.nl) publishes an annual wealth top 500
- Norway: *Kapital* magazine (www.kapital400.no/) publishes a regular top 400. Note that the government publishes tax returns for people of wealth in this open Scandinavian society
- Poland: *wprost* magazine (http://wprost.pl/) publishes a listing of the 100 wealthiest people in Poland
- Scotland: *The Scotsman* newspaper (www.thescotsman.co.uk/) publishes a regular listing of the 100 top earners in Scotland
- Spain: *El Mundo* publishes the annual 'Las 200 mayores fortunas españolas', edited by José F. Leal, with the paper edition available in December (Leal, 2014)
- Switzerland: *Bilanz* (www.bilanz.ch) publishes an annual top 300 for wealth in Switzerland
- UK: The Sunday Times Rich List (Beresford, 2015), edited until 2016 by Philip Beresford, is the oldest such listing in Europe; the *Guardian* newspaper, the *London Evening Standard* and others occasionally publish sector or regional listings

There have been occasional listings in other countries – Greece for example – but these are either infrequent or have ceased publication.

Bear in mind the many limitations on published rich lists – Philip Beresford, speaking at Researchers in Fundraising annual congress, November 2015, London, said that he believes he is reporting only one in four of the wealthy people who should qualify for inclusion in the Sunday Times Rich List. He said that there were a further 25% whom he knew to be wealthy enough to be included, but could not prove it, and 50% whose wealth was so well hidden that he was unable to identify it. He has also spoken about individuals demanding to be removed from, or included in, the *Sunday Times* listing. Many believe that the rich lists understate the true wealth of individuals; a Swiss private banker told this author that clients of his who were featured in the *Bilanz* list had assets at least double the value shown in the list.

The rich lists cover 100–500 people per country. To find out more about the people outside of these golden circles we use business, and especially business ownership sources. These are published across Europe by companies such as Bureau van Dijk (www.bvdinfo.com) and Dun & Bradstreet (www.dnb.com), and for individual countries by a range of suppliers. The original sources for most of this data are the national registers of businesses, sometimes managed by national Chambers of Commerce. Many of the Chambers of Commerce, such as the Dutch KVK (www.kvk.nl), can be accessed direct. Prospect researchers use information from these registers to identify shareholders and from there estimate individuals' holdings, and their value.

Estimating gift capacity in Europe is much more art – or guesswork – than science. There is a temptation to make gift capacity estimation a formula, typically a percentage, such as between 0.5% and 5% of an individual's identifiable assets. In Europe we know so little about people's assets – in many cases we cannot even identify who owns the shares in a company – that the basic data for the calculation is missing. Further, as we saw in Chapter Four, the social benchmarks for high-value philanthropy in Europe are hidden, so we don't know whether we should be multiplying our missing asset figure by 0.5% or 5%, or even 50%. There is no clear strategy for estimating gift capacity; we might base our sums on previous gifts to the non-profit, except that for most European non-profits there is no track record of high-value philanthropy. Or we might just guess, but guess consistently (for example, assessing the gift capacity of all senior lawyers at the same level). Or we might test, by interviewing a range of potential supporters before we start our fundraising programme to establish likely levels at which they might consider gifts to our programme. This latter method is effective at least in establishing broad levels of potential support.

At this point the researcher has what she needs:

- A name
- Biographical information
- Information, or at least clues, on the individual's *motivation*

- A *connection* or, with luck, a few connections linking the individual and the non-profit
- An estimate of the individual's *gift capacity*

The researcher will use this information to evaluate ('qualify') the potential supporter. Some prospects will be fast-tracked for an approach, others will be held for later. Some will be selected for a specific programme or project. Others may be returned to the researcher for further work, typically where there are concerns about the individual's background or the sources of his wealth; many non-profits now have due diligence processes in place to ensure that potential high-value partners are not likely to damage the reputation of the organisation.

These research methods and this sequence is described above in terms of individuals; the process is similar for research to identify potential foundation or corporate partners. Companies in Europe have many forms including partnerships and cooperatives but the substantial division for the prospect researcher is between public companies, those quoted on the stock exchange, and private companies. Public or quoted companies are required by stock exchange rules to publish timely information on a range of indicators including details of board members, financial details and news that could have an effect on stock prices. Most quoted companies have a Corporate Social Responsibility programme, detailed on their websites. Private companies are harder to research, but across Europe they are required to register with national or regional governments, or with the national chamber of commerce. These registers are mostly in the public domain, and are the basis for compiler sources such as Bureau van Dijk, listed above.

Foundations, as we have seen in earlier chapters of this book, are variably researchable. Increasingly, the largest foundations are members of their national foundation association, with the very largest joining the European Foundation Centre. But this leaves a long tail of mid-size and smaller foundations that are much harder to find. This tail includes some large foundations that chose not to join the associations. In most of continental Europe, foundations register, like companies, with a government register or a chamber of commerce. In many countries (Spain, France for example) foundations also register with a government ministry that is their 'protectorate'. A very few ministries publish details of the foundations under their protection; generally this information is of little use.

Finding the new philanthropists

At the Researchers in Fundraising Conference in London, November 2015, Philip Beresford, the venerable journalist behind the 27-year-old Sunday Times Rich List illustrated a common situation with a story; he had been talking to a man who had recently sold out of his £350 million business and who had suddenly been inundated with requests for charitable donations, all of which he had turned down. In contrast, a private equity firm boss whom the newly enriched individual contacted about investments, was able to say that he had been 'waiting for this call for ten years'.

Philip highlighted the lesson from this story; if you want to raise funds from a newly wealthy individual you must do as the private equity boss had done, and cultivate their interest over many years. Trying to build a relationship with a newly wealthy individual the day after he sells out of his business empire will get you nowhere.

Increasing transparency in corporate data in Europe makes it easier to spot people on the way up. Sources such as Bureau van Dijk or Dun & Bradstreet can help you identify people relevant to your cause (for example in biotechnology if your cause is health related) who own substantial shares in fast-growing firms. Some of these people come out as philanthropists at an early stage – check out the Cercle des Jeunes Mécènes (www.louvre.fr/remerciements-aux-mecenes/cercle-de-jeunes-mecenes) at the Musée du Louvre, or the founders of donor-directed funds at the King Baudouin Foundation (www.kbs-frb.be), for example. Develop a relationship over the long term, and allow for the fact that some entrepreneurs will fail to expand their business as fast as they might want.

As we saw in Chapter Four, many new philanthropists create foundations. These new foundations are identifiable – in most countries in Europe the government's official newspaper (*Bulletin Oficiel*) records the creation of each new foundation, and research agencies in England do the same.

You are likely to find new philanthropists in the hazy frontier area between philanthropy and impact investing. A search through the membership of the European Venture Philanthropy Association will be fruitful, as will a review of impact investment funds in Europe. Attending the EVPA or European Foundation Centre conference will also put you in contact with people who are new philanthropists.

Finally, and this is unfortunately only anecdotal, the author has met a number of new philanthropists who send test gifts to organisations. Typically in the range around €1,000 to €5,000 (so, well above the median gift size, but not a 'major gift'), these are designed to test out the reactions of the non-profit. How long do they take to respond? What form does their response take (is it a call or a letter, and is the letter personalised)? Do they take the time to find out who the donor is and to respond appropriately? There are still non-profits in Europe that are sending out standardised thank you letters (literally – meaning that they start 'Monsieur/Madame' or 'Dear Sir or Madam' and contain the same block of boilerplate text for a €10 donor as they do for a €10,000 donor!). As Dr Beth Breeze has shown, donors appear to use direct mail as a proxy for establishing the efficiency of the organisation: 'common proxies for assessing competence include the frequency and estimated cost of charity mailings'. She quotes one donor as saying that "If they send too many I feel they're just wasting the money, not spending it properly and so we cut them out" (Breeze, 2010). So the new philanthropist who receives a boilerplate thank you letter addressing her as 'Monsieur/Madame' is unlikely to give again. By contrast, the organisation – Age UK is an example – that systematically identifies these much larger than median donations, and that acts on the information, is likely to uncover new philanthropists at an early stage in their philanthropic development.

Abide by the rules

Europeans are cautious with personal data. We have laws that protect this data – laws that were drawn up by people[4] with bitter memories of the last century when knowledge of a person's religious or political beliefs, ethnic origin, sexuality or health was used by fascist regimes to single them out for discrimination or death.

I will not attempt a treatise on the protection of personal data here, there are many good sources on the topic starting with the European Union's data protection website (http://ec.europa.eu/justice/data-protection/). Data protection legislation is one of the reasons why the range of sources available to prospect researchers in Europe is much more limited than that in the USA. But this legislation is on balance helpful because it forces all of us who carry out this research to consider carefully the data that we gather on individuals. We cannot store data that is defined as 'sensitive' – this includes topics such as religion and sexuality as mentioned above. We have to gather data fairly and store it securely. We cannot gather data for one purpose and then use it for another. And at some point in the process we have to ask the data subject – the person – for her or his informed permission to allow us to store that data. Break these rules and you face a fine, with the national data protection authorities ramping up the level of these fines each year.

Data protection legislation is not the only control on what researchers find, and how they find it. Researchers have also created their own ethical statement (www.aprahome.org/p/cm/ld/fid=110) and many organisations have developed internal policies and protocols for research and data handling.

The result is that data held by non-profits is more secure than in any other sector – at least on one measure. The UK Information Commissioner (the person responsible for regulating personal data use in the UK) fined 75 organisations (data from the UK Information Commissioner, www.ico.org.uk, analysed by the author, November 2015) in the period November 2010 (the date of the first 'Civil Monetary Penalty') to November 2015. Total fines over that period were £8.7 million; 42% of these fines were paid by business, and 28% by local government, the two biggest offenders – the National Health Service was next. Just one charity was fined over this five year period, representing just 2% of the total fines applied by the Commissioner. On this measure, personal data held by a charity is much, much more secure than the data held by your supermarket, bank, local council or hospital.

Non-profits and their researchers know that the personal data that they hold on donors is one of their most precious assets. They will continue to guard it zealously.

Many borders, many languages

The central challenge in prospect research in Europe is its frontiers. There are, at July 2016, 28 member states each with one, two or more official languages. While there are similarities (the government newspaper seems always to be called the 'Boletin Oficiel' or something similar) there are many differences, and the sources that one would use to research an individual philanthropist in France are different from those used to research a person in Sweden – that is, if you happen to be clever enough to read both French and Swedish. Or Danish and Italian. Or German and Catalan. Or any other combination that would allow you to carry out research across Europe's many linguistic, cultural and knowledge borders.

At this very early point in the development of fundraising from high-value philanthropists, our grasp of research tools is enough to be able to deliver key information on European prospects to our fundraising colleagues. But that is not enough. We need specialists who know the German market in depth and who can access and understand the obscure data sources that all countries contain, who know the names of the wealthy families and can use local newspaper information to find them. We will need specialists in Italy, France, Switzerland, Spain – and eventually in Northern Italy or Southern Sweden.

The numbers of prospect researchers in Europe is still tiny, so the sector is some years from having this capability. But judging by the rate of growth of prospect research in the UK we should expect that by 2025 there will be a widespread base of researchers across continental Europe, with specialists based in most of the leading European economies.

Worth researching

The development of prospect research as a distinct profession is in line with three of the significant changes underlined in this book; increasing transparency, the growth of the Internet, and increasing professionalism.

In this chapter I have described the work of specialist prospect researchers as they identify high-value partners for non-profits, and ensure that they are assessed and managed professionally. There are far too many organisations, especially in continental Europe, that are either failing completely to identify these prospects or that are attempting to manage relationships without research support. As philanthropy becomes more visible in Europe the arguments in favour of doing nothing are becoming increasingly untenable.

Notes

1. Associations for prospect researchers:
   - APRA, the Association of Professional Researchers for Advancement, www.aprahome.org/
   - Researchers in Fundraising, www.institute-of-fundraising.org.uk/groups/sig-researchers/

2. The Central Register of the Federal Commercial Registry Office had started a database in 1990. The date shown is the earliest sighting of the website in the Wayback Machine (https://archive.org/web/).

3. The author is grateful to the Helen Brown Group (www.helenbrowngroup.com) for links to sources of rich lists.

4. Adrian Beney of More Partnership, a specialist in data protection legislation for non-profits, notes this connection in his presentations on the topic.

PART EIGHT

Preparing for change

SEVENTEEN

Strategic responses

Introduction

'Successful strategy is contingent on appropriate interpretation of environmental conditions and organizational response to those conditions', say Brown and Iverson in a 2004 paper on non-profit strategies and leadership (p 378). This was never more challenging than in developing strategies for partnerships between high-value philanthropists and non-profits, because as we have seen repeatedly in this book we barely know what the 'environmental conditions' are. This chapter will offer some pointers to strategies that work.

Strategic choices

Enter the search term 'major donor fundraising strategy' in a well-known search engine and you will see more than 160,000 references, including strident, instructional titles such as '7 Absolutes for Major Gift Fundraising Success' or '7 Must-Haves for Major Gift Fundraising'. Why there are only seven, and not 70 or 700 requirements for success is not clear. What is clear is that there is a wide range of choices in strategies for fundraising.

There is a wide range of choices in part because we are dealing here with a relationship between a person, the philanthropist, and an organisation, the non-profit. These relationships contain as many variables as any human-to-human connection; some of these relationships are distant, some have a chain of intermediaries (philanthropist–bank–philanthropy adviser–consultant–non-profit) and some are very close. Some are one-time, single events while others run over many years.

In Europe, and particularly in continental Europe, these relationships are largely happy accidents; the donor who responds to a news programme on the television by sending €50,000 to a brand-name non-profit, or the non-profit in Switzerland which is selected by a donor in Norway because she has funds domiciled there that she wishes to use philanthropically. Very few non-profits in continental Europe employ staff dedicated to relationships with high-value philanthropists, so we can safely say that most non-profits simply react to a large gift – they do not go out and seek it. This chapter will offer some directions for organisations wanting to take a more proactive approach to their relationships with high-value philanthropists.

A strategic choice of name

Judith Nichols noted, back in 2004 (p 163), that 'too many fundraisers continue to employ the same old methods even when the outcomes are disappointing' and quotes Albert Einstein as saying that 'insanity is doing the same thing over and over and expecting a different result'.

As we saw in Chapter twelve, we continue to refer to 'major donors' even although we know that their financial 'donation' is only part of the story. The private wealth managers don't refer to their clients – at least in public – as 'big spenders'. UBS does not have a 'Head of Major Savers' or a 'Bring in the Bling' department. They use the term 'wealth' with all its nuances: of 'a wealth of [knowledge, experience, connections]'.

This is despite the life experience of non-profit managers, who know that the relationship with a high-value philanthropist is full of colour and variety, that it goes much further than just the monetary donation. High-value philanthropists have, in Paul Schervish's term, 'hyperagency' – the capacity to establish the institutional framework in which they and others live (Herman and Schervish, 1991). Most have a wealth of knowledge, experience and connections, many have influence and some have power. With the right partnership, a philanthropist can help the non-profit achieve strategic objectives that go beyond a single project. This has been amply and publicly demonstrated by Bill and Melinda Gates in the USA, but examples are not hard to find in Europe: Frédéric Jousset, who made his fortune as co-founder of www.webhelp.com and then became one of the Jeunes Mécenes of the Louvre. His support for the Musée du Louvre is partly financial.

But Jousset, who is quoted by Virginie Seghers (2009) as saying "I'm one of the Internet generation", supported the Louvre by helping them develop their Lupicatule web animation project for children. His support – financial but also practical – helped the Louvre to reach a new younger audience; it was a strategic partnership.

It is time for a new terminology, and the new thinking that goes with it, amongst non-profits in Europe. Some have made the change; Cancer Research UK has a 'Head of High Value Supporter Partnerships' and VSO has a 'Head of Philanthropy and Partnerships'. Many more have yet to make this paradigm shift. A term such as 'Strategic Partner' encompasses much better than 'major donor' the benefits that high-value philanthropists bring to their relationships with non-profits.

Strategic adaptation

Almost 40 years ago, Raymond Miles, Charles Snow and Alan Meyer (1978, p 549) proposed a structure for understanding the ways that organisations – their article is focused on for-profit organisations in publishing, electronics, food processing and healthcare – adapt to a changing environment. They identify three linked problems that management must solve in order to adapt:

1. The 'entrepreneurial problem', which relates to how an organisation develops 'a specific good or service and a target market' (p 549). This requires that the management commit resources to a defined product-market domain.
2. The 'engineering problem' is the challenge of making the management's solution to the entrepreneurial problem operational; how do we make it work?
3. The 'administrative problem' is posed in terms of rationalising and stabilising the organisation's internal systems, or creating new systems to enable it to continue to innovate – in other words to be entrepreneurial. The solution to this problem completes what the authors call the 'adaptive cycle'.

From here, the authors classify organisations as:

1. 'Defenders', which react to the entrepreneurial problem by 'seal[ing] off a portion of the total market in order to create a stable domain'

(p 550). With a limited range of products, they use competitive pricing and efficient distribution and administration systems. Their primary risk is that of being unable to respond to a major shift in their market environment.

2. 'Prospectors' focus on locating and developing product and market opportunities by maintaining a constant watch on environmental conditions, trends and events. Their engineering challenge is how to avoid long-term commitments to a single type of process, and their administrative problem is about allowing and encouraging change.

3. 'Analysers' combine elements of Defender and Prospector, aiming to 'locate and exploit new product and market opportunities while simultaneously maintaining a firm core of traditional products and customers' (p 555). This duality 'forces the organisation to establish a dual technological core'.

4. 'Reactors' respond inappropriately to environmental change, principally by not adapting. The authors identify the reasons for this as management failing to articulate the organisation's strategy, and failing to shape the structure and processes in order to fit the strategy. They 'maintain the organisation's current strategy-structure relationship despite overwhelming changes in environmental conditions' (p 558).

We can apply this lens (as did Brown and Iverson, 2004, in a different context) to the ways in which non-profits in Europe have reacted to the changing environment in high-value philanthropy.

Many, depressingly probably most, are Reactors. Given the significant number of conferences, training events, books and magazine articles about high-value philanthropy it is difficult to imagine that management in these organisations is unaware of the topic. But ask ten mid-size continental European non-profits for their strategy on high-value philanthropy (or just 'major donors') and eight or nine will tell you that they do not have one. For consultants working in this field this is of course good news. But for the non-profit sector and for philanthropy in Europe it is not.

Without a strategy, Reactors face all sorts of practical problems with high-value philanthropy. Can she visit the hospital ward she is sponsoring? How should we deal with our new donor's demand for her name on our project? Is it my job to work with her, or is it the Director who should do this? She wants to talk to our social worker, who says he is very busy; what do I do? Should we still send her our normal direct mail appeal? If you are someone engaged in philanthropy or fundraising you may laugh at such questions as naïve. But for many non-profits these are the real-life challenges posed by high-value philanthropy. Most if these challenges are internal issues for the organisation; the philanthropist is ready to give but the organisation is not ready to respond. The result is a load of time wasted as the non-profit works out an individual response to each new individual situation.

Some organisations are semi-Reactors. Aware of a shift in the market they respond by offering a new product: a 'middle donor' programme that asks, through direct mail, for a little bit more from their supporters. 'Middle donor' or 'value added' programmes can be very effective and organisations in culture and the arts have been quick to take them up.

But semi-Reactors have not grasped the strategic implications of high-value philanthropy, and they have certainly not adapted internal structures to meet the market. This, as we saw with the Hierarchy Foundation in Chapter Eleven, includes changes at staff and board levels. A staff-level adaptation, for example, would be to move the fundraiser from her current lowly position in the organisation's hierarchy to a senior post, alongside the chief executive. That would enable her to bring the experience of the philanthropist to bear on management issues. A board-level adaptation would be to invite the philanthropist to join the board and thus to share her or his knowledge, networks and influence – something that many European non-profits would find very hard to do.

There are Analysers and Prospectors amongst Europe's non-profits. Oxfam Intermón in Spain, for example, has analysed the high-value philanthropy market and identified a niche – impact investing – that it can fill. So it has allocated staff and resources to that area, developed a programme and is actively promoting it amongst the venture philanthropy community. SOS Children's Villages in the Netherlands (in Dutch, SOS Kinderdorpen) could be classified as Prospectors: they noted the trend in other markets for donor-directed funds and, after analysing their supporters and market, launched a successful programme to recruit philanthropists (www.soskinderdorpen.nl/help-mee/bijzondere-giften/waarom-een-fonds-op-naam/).

Analysers in the non-profit world in Europe have faced the same challenge as their for-profit counterparts: a 'dual technological core' or, in plain English, a double database. Until very recently there was no affordable, straightforward database software for managing the complex relationships that non-profits have with high-value philanthropists. There was software for direct mail programmes provided, in many continental European countries, by direct marketing agencies or their partners. But this technology, whilst good enough to manage mailing programmes and donors' responses, was no good at the multiple relationships, at the relationship planning, that is part of building a partnership with a high-value philanthropist. The consequence, until recently, was that a strategic donor was recorded as a donor on the NGO's mainstream direct marketing database, while her account manager at the NGO kept a completely separate dataset, often on a spreadsheet, in order to track the relationship with her. A 'dual technological core' that caused duplication and sometimes errors.

European non-profits have been slow to get onto the 'adaptive cycle' that will help them develop new products for high-value philanthropists, to make these products work in the market, and to adapt internally to the market. They are now trying to catch up.

Building relationships

Professor Adrian Sargeant, Amy Eisenstein and Rita Kottasz (2015) have written a useful guide to relationship building for non-profits with incomes of US$10 million or less. The report is written for a US audience, but is relevant to us here in Europe. They describe why high-value philanthropists give, and note research from a 2014 Bank of America survey in the USA, showing that 74% of high net worth donors give because they are 'moved at how a gift can make a difference'. This response combines two ideas: impact – an implication that the person has seen evidence that her gift made a difference – and 'being moved' – implying an emotional or empathetic link with the cause. As more than two-thirds (68%) referred to the efficiency of the organisation – in other words its capacity to effect change in proportion to its income – and as more than half (53%) of respondents also reported volunteering for the organisation, this combination of impact and emotional connection seems important.

To what extent can professionals influence all of this? Can a fundraising professional, or a professional philanthropic adviser, make a difference? Whilst our colleagues in the USA and, largely, in the UK, have decided that the answer to the first question is 'plenty' and to the second it is 'yes', here in Europe these questions are still being debated. The lack of data is, as we have found so often in this book, part of the reason.

We can extract two conclusions from the work by Sergeant, Eisenstein and Kottasz (2015). First, the motivations of a high-value philanthropist are complex and nuanced (yes, they are complex and nuanced amongst all donors, but at the high-value end those complexities are playing on a lot of money). Knowledge of the philanthropist and of the organisation is going to be vital in managing any relationship. Second, building partnerships in this market will require management to commit resources to developing services for this target market: the first part of the 'adaptive cycle', and the first step toward a solid, strategic response.

Knowledge and relationships in high-value philanthropy

Relationships between high-value philanthropists and non-profits are complicated. They are likely to occur at many levels, through many nodes of connection: she is sponsoring a project, and she is a close friend of our Treasurer, went to school with another donor, knows a mother whose child has benefited from our programme, was a volunteer with our youth programme many years ago and follows us on Twitter. They are driven by a mixture of motivations and objections: "I want to help, but is this the best organisation to do the work?" "I like the project but the organisation feels very political." "I think they are good but I can't get the Director to reply to my emails." As we saw with Sargeant and colleagues (2015) this mix of motivations and objections is difficult to detect, and individual.

One person, the account manager, is meant to know all of this about all of her high-value donor clients. She needs to know about the quality and quantity of relationships, and to hear and see the subtle signals that a donor gives out that indicate where their motivations and objections lie.

To get to this level of understanding of an actual or potential donor requires an extraordinary flow of knowledge from the individual to the organisation and vice versa. The knowledge might come from a remark at a cocktail party, a comment in the press, an email to the Board Treasurer, a Tweet about refugees. Any one of these always-open channels might deliver the information to the account manager that tells her to move ahead with a relationship, or to the donor to help her decide to give. This happens at all levels of relationships between people who give and non-profits, but at the high-value end of the market the decisions that are taken on the basis of knowledge, or the lack of it, can have a significant impact, strategic and financial, on the non-profit. A simple misunderstanding ("I thought you could offer me a place on the board, but now I learn that you cannot") can not only turn off the donor but, because he or she is influential, can result in other donors turning away.

Boards and leadership are central in this flow of knowledge in high-value philanthropy. In Europe, this is where it frequently breaks down. This author has personal experience of a large brand-name non-profit in Europe where the CEO issued a decree to staff saying that on no account were board members to be contacted, except with her written permission. This effectively blocked the account manager/fundraiser from using her strongest network, the board. As we saw in Part four, hierarchies can develop in even relatively small organisations that can split the account manager/relationship manager from the board or leadership, creating useless stores of information. The CEO knows that François Philanthropist likes educational programmes but that information has never reached the account manager, who persists in trying to pitch a women's rights project to him. Or the account manager knows that George Good is interested in changing the way we educate kids, but when the Board President meets George at a cocktail party she does not, and so bores him with school book-buying programmes.

The result – again, the living experience of this author – is that there is a minority of very frustrated fundraisers in Europe. Recruited to raise large gifts from wealthy individuals, they find their paths blocked to all of the people in their President's circle. They are soon caught in a vicious downward spiral where they fail to raise the income that their board, unrealistically, expects and as a consequence lose the confidence of the board, the very people whose confidence is most required if a major donor programme is to function. As Sargeant, Eisenstein and Kottasz (2015) remind us, 'A huge part of successfully creating a culture of philanthropy at your organization depends on having engaged and effective board members, who are advocates and leaders for your organization.'

This issue of knowledge, its capture, storage and exchange, is one of the reasons why Miles, Snow and Meyer's work is still relevant. Organisations entering the high-value philanthropy market are, at least for this market segment, 'Prospectors' that need a substantial flow of knowledge in order to function, have 'product or project structures characterised by a low degree of formalisation, decentralised control [and] lateral as well as vertical communications' (p 553). They are flexible, adaptive organisations. Jean-Marie Destrée described Fondation Caritas France in these terms:

> 'the Fondation is like a start-up – an agile structure, independent of the sometimes bureaucratic processes of Secours Catholique, so decisions are fast. Our donors like the collegial management between Pierre Levené, Director General and me [Jean-Marie Destrée is Assistant DG]. They like the fact that they meet the DG or the Assistant DG.'

What are we to do?

So how should non-profits in Europe respond to the shifting sands of high-value philanthropy? Writing in 2013 about what was then the most advanced market in Europe for high-value philanthropy, the UK, Beth Breeze and Theresa Lloyd (2013, p 197) said that 'not enough [non-profits] have been willing to develop the corporate culture of engagement, not invest in and oversee the institutional changes required to underpin successful long-term fundraising from the wealthy'. They make a series of recommendations for charities (having done the same for government, for philanthropists and for advisers) including becoming better at asking, ensuring that the donor's experience of giving is positive, integrating legacy programmes, developing matched funding schemes, and addressing the lack of confidence in charities' own competence and efficiency.

I agree with all of these recommendations, but I would add some of my own.

First, some non-profits will decide not to enter the high-value philanthropy market at all. It's complicated, messy, can be controversial and does contain some sharks, so for some organisations it is safer out than in. But on one measure at least, many organisations want in: the demand for seminars and training sessions on the subject across

Europe is substantial – masterclasses on high-value philanthropy at the International Fundraising Congress (www.resource-alliance.org/ifc/) are sold out, often months in advance. Organisations want to learn how to respond to the market.

But how? How can we prepare for the future of philanthropy? I hope that this book has given you some of the answers. The stand-out lessons are:

- Analyse: Become an Analyser
- Restructure, for knowledge: Revise internal structures to get people talking
- Impact, impact, impact: What difference do we make?
- Segment: Don't send everyone the same offer
- Include: Include donors in what we are doing
- Invent: New methods of giving and investing
- Spinoff: Create new or subsidiary entities to generate permanent income
- Defend: Protect non-profits against government removal of tax status, and marauding tabloids

Analyse

Europe is uncovering its philanthropic culture, slowly exposing the good that is done around the continent to the public gaze. This process is likely to speed up as the forces discussed in this book, including government policy, changing attitudes to wealth, and the professionalisation of philanthropy take effect. So now is a good time to start analysing this market in preparation for the day in which your organisation, too, will have a 'High-Value Philanthropy Partnerships' strategy.

Out in the market, you can gather basic data on wealth in your country from your national statistics office, from Eurostat (http://ec.europa.eu/eurostat) or from the Luxembourg Wealth Study Database (www.lisdatacenter.org/). For more granular information, look out for your national wealth list (see Chapter Sixteen), or gather news and data on directors' salaries.

Data on philanthropy is much more limited in Europe, but there are some clues. Your national foundation centre, or the network of academic research centres in Europe (for both, see Chapter Sixteen) may now be publishing information.

Then look inside – at your supporter database and your stakeholders. Simple database searches (outlined in Chapter Sixteen), such as a search based on streets or districts with high-value houses (what the Dutch call the 'gold coast'), will give you the first indications of whether or not your existing supporters include some with greater financial potential than others.

Set up a tracking system for this data – with modern online search tools this is easy – so that you are receiving, and disseminating internally, information on this market.

Analyse your systems, the machinery that will, or will not, help you run your programme efficiently. Basic back-office functions ("it takes us two weeks to send a receipt for a donation") can become a significant blockage to developing a programme.

Test your products in the market. Your organisation already does this with its direct marketing, using A/B split tests to see which works better. Qualitative testing of your product – your project and the way you have packaged it – is increasingly possible in Europe as the number of specialist consultants in this field grows.

You are not going to be able to perform a full market analysis in high-value philanthropy in Europe because the data does not exist, so don't start with that objective. At the most, you will gather a little hard data and some clues. If yours is a very risk-averse organisation, and your manager likes to know all the facts before she comes to a decision, then you are in for a long wait. If your organisation is at the Prospector end of the scale, then, given a reasonable amount of information, a positive product test, and systems that work, you'll take the risk.

Restructure for knowledge

Building a partnership with a high-value philanthropist in Europe depends on informal information. As we saw above (in the section on Knowledge and relationships), this in turn depends on a close working relationship between the account manager and the principal sources of that information, who are likely to be amongst the board and leadership. Not necessarily though. In the case of one client in France it was the receptionist who came up with the link to a philanthropist.

She remembered that he had volunteered with the organisation as a young man, 20 years previously.

Structure your account management team so that they can maximise this flow of information. That means giving the team access to the board, having them work alongside the Director, and involving them in the senior management team.

It also means employing a prospect researcher. Organisations of all sorts, from the University of Oxford to Cancer Research in the UK, and from HEC to Médecins Sans Frontières in continental Europe, have discovered the benefits of employing a person dedicated to capturing, storing, interpreting and disseminating information on potential high-value partners. Essentially this is a question of efficiency, as we saw in Chapter Sixteen: it is more cost-effective to have a prospect researcher uncover the knowledge inside and outside your organisation than to have your highly paid account managers (fundraisers) do it.

Impact, impact, impact

Impact is the pot of gold at the end of the rainbow. As we saw in previous chapters, it is hard to measure and even when you do there is no internationally agreed standard against which to measure your measures. But high-value philanthropists are especially interested in impact, and for many the pot of gold would be to be able to monetise impact; to be able to say: 'I invested €1 million in education and generated €25 million in social value.'

Many NGOs have much of the data that they need to start measuring impact – the baseline study that inspired the creation of the project, or the annual survey with partners that they carry out for their principal government funder. Some have partnered with academics to carry out studies on the cost of the social problem that is the focus of the project; some neglected tropical diseases such as Yaws and Buruli Ulcer have been researched in this way. So it should not be a very big step to calculate impact. But the lack of a standardised system (and, despite what I have written above, the lack of data for many NGOs) holds organisations back from measuring and publishing impact.

A few non-profits have taken the step of employing people to work on impact; CREAF, the terrestrial ecology research centre at the Autonomous University of Barcelona has one (www.creaf.cat/), as do Mencap, Scope and NSPCC amongst others in the UK. There are impact people in venture philanthropy funds and advisers of course; Wolfgang Hafenmayer, one of the interviewees for this book, is the 'Head of Societal Impact Advisory' at Trusted Family (www.trustedfamily.net), for example.

Demonstrating impact and monetising impact are key strategies for non-profits working with high-value philanthropists. This will require resources, and agreements to define impact amongst the non-profits of Europe.

Segment

Whether or not you consider that the market is changing, you'd be a fool not to segment. It is a lesson that those elegant Swiss private bankers learned years ago, but one that the non-profit sector in Europe has not fully assimilated.

Segmentation is a very basic part of marketing – and yet too many non-profits in Europe still send out – or phone out – the same appeal to their entire donor database asking for the same gift for the same project. Why? We know that each of those individuals is different, we know that their interests, their financial situation, their understanding of giving, their motivations for giving and the types of giving that attract them are different, and yet we ask for the same gift, the same scripted way. This is no longer a question of data. We have access – just as the banks and the supermarkets do – to increasingly cheap, increasingly dense data. Nor is it a question of novelty: there are a growing number of stand-out non-profits, leading brands and smaller organisations that are successfully segmenting. There are technology questions: some non-profits are still limping along with very rusty customer relationship management software. But above all it is a question for management. If your local supermarket can gather customer data and segment, why won't you?

What segments? That is a question for a more technical marketing book than this one. But the attitudinal segments we saw featured in the research by the Fondation de France (Chapter Four; de Laurens and Rozier, 2012) would be a useful starting point. Differentiating a 'daughter of the revolution' from an 'inheritor of philanthropy' is vital to knowing how to talk to her, what to focus on, how much she might give and even who should speak to her; don't put your stuffy, conservative Treasurer into a meeting with a daughter of the revolution. She'll be more interested in your politically active, edgy, Programmes Director.

Include

Non-profits, especially the bigger NGOs, have developed over many years powerful but rigid systems for project management. These are the result of forces in their universe – principally the requirement from government funders to show auditable financial processes. Governments want to show value for money to the taxpayers (something they are not so motivated to do in other areas of their work) and so they need full accountability from the NGOs they fund, down to the bills of quantity mentioned by Arnout Mertens in Chapter Thirteen. This has all been good for governments but has created a certain rigidity for philanthropists. A philanthropist – even an enthusiastic one – can't just walk into a NGO and suggest that they create a new programme or project. That is the job of the programme team. This is part of the reason why philanthropists in Europe have been setting up their own foundations; to win the freedom to create their own programmes. Viewed in this light, the thousands of new foundations created by people of wealth in recent years in Europe is a failure of the rest of the non-profit sector; we have simply not been able to offer these powerful, energetic, entrepreneurial philanthropists the home that they seek for their money.

To win over the philanthropists, non-profits will have to start including them in their plans. Not just asking them to support a prefabricated project, but right at the start, when the problem that lies behind the project is being considered and analysed, when strategies are being discussed and a theory of change being developed. This approach has been successful in the educational field – Factary, my firm, has carried out many pre-project studies for higher education organisations in Europe in which philanthropists are consulted and involved in the very early stages of a new educational project. But the technique is still not adopted by the big development cooperation NGOs.

This is not as simple as it sounds. It involves a fundamental rethink of roles within the non-profit because we are putting the donor in charge or at least inviting her to the management table. It dramatically alters the role of the fundraiser. Seen previously as the person at the end of the corridor who brought in the money, she now becomes central to the development of the organisation as a whole – its strategic direction, its new programmes and its growth.

Invent

Non-profits are creative marketers. On limited budgets they come up with a wide range of ways in which an individual can be philanthropic. Donors, as we saw in Chapter Fourteen can give their support in an increasing variety of ways.

Clever, inventive marketing staff at non-profits in Europe will continue to come up with new ideas, and then test them in the laboratory of the market. But a better strategy would be to learn something about the market first, to innovate and then test: market research, and product development. As Europe gradually unveils its philanthropy, and as data and research become available, this becomes a realistic proposition.

"No one is financing research and development in the social sector", says Miquel de Paladella, CEO and co-founder of UpSocial. "For example, social impact bonds. There are only 60 – there should be much more." The lack of investment in R&D may be the result of lower financial returns on social purpose investments, suggests Miquel. "If you invest in 500 start-up companies and only three survive but one of those three is a WhatsApp, then you are happy. But there is nothing as big as WhatsApp in social purpose investments."

Inventions in the frontier between philanthropy and investment are a key area for growth – for example La Bolsa Social (www.bolsasocial. com) which reported raising €498,207 from 134 investors (www. bolsasocial.com/blog/, blog 19 February 2016) for two companies in biotech and workspace leasing. The Social Stock Exchange (www. socialstockexchange.com), or Ethex (www.ethex.org.uk/) in the UK offer a range of savings and investment schemes with social purposes including transferable charity bonds, shares and depository receipts that finance loans in the developing world.

Some of these products are regulated (La Bolsa Social, for example, is licensed by Spain's investment authority) but some are not. In time, just as with other financial products, we can expect some form of regulation in this market; we might want, for example, to clarify where the boundaries of 'social impact investment' lie so that the term continues to apply to investments which create measurable social change that benefits society.

Spinoff

In a basement laboratory on the campus of the University of Barcelona, I met Teresa Tarragó, founder of iProteos. iProteos is a spinoff from the university, and the first equity crowdfunded biotech company in Spain. The company raised €100,000 in 2014 from 41 investors. Teresa told me that her investors were individuals. She estimated that around half were investing for return, and half for the social impact of the company, which is working on treatments for schizophrenia.

iProteos is based in the Parc Científic de Barcelona (Barcelona Science Park), the first science park in Spain, founded in 1997 and now home to more than 70 companies and non-profits, and 2,000 researchers. The Park is controlled by Fundació PCB, whose Board President, its two Vice Presidents, and two Secretaries are all representatives of the university.

Barcelona is not, of course, alone in having a science park and hosting spinoff companies. Many other universities around Europe and the world do the same. The universities enjoy a symbiotic relationship with their science parks and companies, creating workplaces for their alumni, attracting prestigious academics and drawing in investments.

So it is surprising that other non-profits don't follow this trend. Some NGOs and UN agencies gathered in locations such as Geneva, London, The Hague and Copenhagen share office space. Many share similar problems – how to feed large numbers of people simultaneously in a disaster, how to register tens of thousands of migrants moving across a border, how to get clean water to scattered rural populations, how to grow resistant crops. Some have devised ingenious solutions; UNICEF has used its power in the mosquito net industry – it is one of the world's largest buyers of nets, purchasing 26.4 million nets in 2014 (www.unicef.org/supply/index_59717.html) – to license technology for the manufacture of these nets from Japan, and to transfer the licence to African manufacturers. But this is a rare example of a spinoff (in this case of a licence) in the NGO world. Spinoffs aimed at solving problems at the bottom of the pyramid are the subject of much discussion amongst impact investors and philanthropists. But they are not yet a reality for NGOs.

Defend

Europe's non-profits have very special relationships with their donors. During 2015/16 I was working with a brand-name international organisation. It had sent out a mailing to its more generous supporters. The mailing described, on the front page, the nutritional needs of children in the Global South, and invited readers to donate for nutritional packs. On the back page it explained the cost of the packs – €47 each. When we reviewed the results of the mailing – it raised a few thousand euros – I realised that none of the donors had given a multiple of €47. They had given €500 or €1,000 or whatever, but simply as a donation, without apparently even turning the letter over to read what they were giving to. These donors were giving as a statement of faith in the organisation. There is an often repeated and possibly apocryphal tale in the fundraising world of an A/B split test (where the recipients of a mailing are randomly allocated to receive either mailing A or mailing B, and the results compared) in which the printer failed and letter B was entirely blank, aside from its printed donation form. Letter B raised more money than letter A, says the story.

These stories illustrate the absolute faith that many donors have – despite the news stories, despite the interest in impact measurement – in our non-profits. This faith creates enormous value – in increased donations and decreased effort – for Europe's non-profits.

In the high-value philanthropy field there are a number of pressures that have the potential to undercut the close relationship between donor and non-profit recipient. The first is for-profit market entry. Donor-directed funds run by Fidelity in the USA are now larger than community foundations there (Cohen, 2014). With many of Europe's banks now entering the space we can expect similar competition here – and these competitors are powerful, well capitalised, determined and inventive.

The second is the internal pressure to be opaque, when what the market demands is transparency. This goes far beyond publishing annual reports (although in some countries even that would be a good start) because the scandals that knock the trust out of the sector – scandals about 'high' salaries for non-profit CEOs, or scandals about 'aggressive' fundraising techniques – are created from the public's lack of understanding of how non-profits work. We have not been clever enough at educating our stakeholders in what we do and why. The woman on the Clapham omnibus does not understand why non-profits use cold-call telephone fundraising or why we buy in data to help us segment our market. She knows that her insurance company, supermarket or bank do this, but it seems wrong in a 'charity'. The result? The sort of feeding frenzy enjoyed by the UK press led by the *Daily Mail* during 2015, which resulted in stricter regulation of the UK fundraising sector.

To hold out against the for-profits, and to educate our high-value stakeholders, non-profits will have to develop new strategies that emphasise our added value and our openness. As with so much in high-value philanthropy, that can mean substantial changes in the way we work, in our structures and our relationships with donors and investors.

Conclusion

This chapter has been a strategic checklist for people working in non-profits in Europe. By deciding whether this is the market for you and then focusing on these strategic elements – analysis, knowledge, impact, segmentation, inclusion, creativity, spinoffs and defence – we can prepare our non-profits for this market.

EIGHTEEN

Conclusions and future

There are four spheres of change in philanthropy in Europe.[1] The first is the demographic sphere, where we can see new wealth and growing poverty and need. The second is the radius of what we know – substantially expanded in recent years by the advent of the Internet. The third is the government, or layers of government, that try to mould what we do. The fourth is the practical sphere – the stuff that actually happens and the technicians who make it happen. The coincidence of change in all of these spheres is behind the evolution, or revolution, that we can all see but find so hard to measure. In this chapter we will review these spheres and then project them into the future.

The demographic sphere

We can find good hard data in this sphere – it is the equivalent of a rocky planet, the antithesis of the gas giants that will follow.

More wealth – obvious from the proliferation in Europe of wealth lists, the thick, fast-selling, glitzy versions of normally staid business or news magazines – is a key demographic. My 2011 edition of the Dutch *Quote* rich list runs to 302 pages and weighs 830 grams, while my 2015 edition comes in at 374 pages and just over 1 kilogram; a 20% increase in reported wealth-weight in four years. We are all wealthier than ever before, and a few are much wealthier than the rest of us. As Schervish (2000, p 4) points out using US data, more wealth means more philanthropy: 'within the 1% of highest-income families are the 0.08% of families with income of $1 million or more that contribute 22% of all the charitable dollars'. Edwin Venema notes a similar statistic from the Netherlands, where "20% of Dutch households are responsible for 80% of all gifts to charities. The few very wealthy people are responsible for the biggest gifts."

In here is the new wealth. In 1989 'around two-thirds [of the Sunday Times Rich List] was inherited wealth' (Beresford, 2016). By 2015 these proportions had reversed: 80% of the people in the Sunday Times Rich List in 2015 were self-made millionaires or billionaires against 20% inherited. This is a dramatic demographic shift; does it have an effect on attitudes to wealth? The answer (see Chapter Four) is an unscientific 'yes'.

Here, too, are women. Women have always been involved in philanthropy and, as I showed in Chapter Five, have been a major force in philanthropy at various points in history. Now women of wealth – women of self-made wealth as well as women who have joined families of wealth – are creating different structures for their philanthropy than the men who still dominate the large institutions.

This sphere includes the wealth gap – the growing distance between rich and poor. Here too, as we saw in Chapter Four, we have data. For example, we know that in 2016 the share of the wealth of the richest 1% of the population exceeded that of the remaining 99% of people for the first time in history (Cukier, 2015).

And here are poor people, excluded people, people in danger or need, abused people, people who are ill. Here is the orphan in Ghana, the girl in Barcelona enslaved for the sex trade, the family at the foodbank in Edinburgh and the woman in Berlin whose cancer is killing her. We are in philanthropy because we are surrounded by need; there is a moral imperative to give.

The known sphere – the radius of our knowledge

The places we can see, hear, feel and even touch are bigger and wider than ever before in human history. "There is a growing level of understanding of the causes and interconnectedness" of social problems says Miquel de Paladella. "There is more data on social issues than before." In the last 25 years we have developed the world's largest library of human knowledge and made it increasingly easy to read. The Internet, according to *The Economist*, entered the 'zettabyte era' in 2016, with the amount of data being transmitted now exceeding one zettabyte (a trillion gigabytes) per annum (Cukier, 2015).

Social media has exploded and is becoming our new home, our new hearth. It is almost becoming our new country; combining states and social networks, the world population ranking is shown in Table 18.1.

Table 18.1 World population rankings

Ranking	Economy	Population (thousands)
1	Facebook	1,550,000
2	China	1,364,270
3	India	1,295,292
4	WhatsApp	900,000
5	QQ	860,000
6	Facebook Messenger	700,000
7	Qzone	653,000
8	WeChat	650,000
9	Instagram	400,000
10	United States	318,857
11	Twitter	316,000
12	Baidu Tieba	300,000
13	Skype	300,000
14	Indonesia	254,455
15	Viber	249,000
16	Tumblr	230,000
17	Brazil	206,078
18	Pakistan	185,044
19	Nigeria	177,476
20	Bangladesh	159,078

Source: Table built by combining World Bank population data for 2014 (Anon, 2016c) with data on the numbers of users of social media (Anon, 2015j).
Note that none of these economies, real or virtual, is based in Europe.

Thanks to the Internet we can watch what is happening in Accra or Zanzibar from our apartment in Inverness. We can have a one-to-one chat with a doctor in a refugee camp in the Sudan, see what she sees, hear what she hears, meet the people she treats, without leaving our comfortable home. This visibility through the Internet must have an effect on our capacity to identify with a cause in a different country or a different culture. 'Identification' is one of the often cited motivations for philanthropy (for example, Schervish, 2000), and the Internet helps us to identify with people we would have been very unlikely to meet in the pre-Internet age.

Impact has become more measurable and more visible thanks to the Internet. As a donor we can confirm from open access academic studies that a specific conservation plan will, indeed, function, and we can then see the forests we are saving with satellite imagery transmitted via the Internet. We know that the sense of impact is an important motivator for philanthropy, so it is reasonable to argue that the greater visibility of impact through the medium of the Internet should create more philanthropic support. Except, of course, where the Internet allows us to see that the impact has not occurred or, worse, that the funds have been diverted to a secretive tax shell in the British Virgin Islands.

In fundraising, the Internet allows us to understand our financial supply chain. This is led by the skill, new to Europe, of the prospect researcher (see Chapter Sixteen), who helps us identify, understand and eventually approach a potential supplier of finance for our new venture. She will also help us carry out the due diligence that is increasingly necessary in supply chain management; she can only see this due diligence information because the Internet carries it to her. The Internet means she will see things "that could be papered over no longer" in the words of a Dutch philanthropist and social investor.

The sphere of our knowledge has grown thanks to the Internet. But in philanthropy in Europe we have seen one other revolution in knowledge: the increasing visibility of wealth, and of philanthropy. In Part four I discussed transparency in its various forms, and the forces that are continuing to open up our sector. As a result of that transparency we already know more than we could have known a few years ago – think for example of the Coutts Million Dollar Donors Report (Anon, 2015h), or the publication by French business school HEC of the names of key donors. We have data which is relevant to high-value philanthropy from the Geven in Nederland (http://test.geveninnederland.nl/onderzoek/geveninnederland/) study, from agencies (the 'Phi' dataset on UK donors published by my agency Factary, for example), banks, and foundations (such as the studies by the Fondation de France and its Observatoire). There are still many gaps, and there is frustration that foundations will not fund more studies, but the sphere of our knowledge is growing.

Greater visibility, or perhaps the sense that we can be transparent about things we used not to talk about, has also meant that more scandals have been reported in the non-profit sector. We saw in Part four that journalists in the 21st century are willing to do what their earlier sisters and brothers were not, and to report – relentlessly – the snowball of scandal surrounding the Spanish royal family and Fundación Nóos. This greater visibility of scandal may be one of the reasons behind the demonstrable decline in the trust in which the public holds our non-profits. And this lack of trust in established non-profits may, in turn, help explain why many people of wealth now prefer to set up their own foundation rather than rely on giving via others.

The effects of the expansion of the knowledge sphere are felt all over the non-profit sector. We have a clearer idea of what is happening in foundations – which seems only fair given that in most of Europe we sacrifice taxable income to allow them to do their good works. We can compare and then share information on campaigns, social problems and effective non-profits. And in the world of high-value philanthropy we are starting to be able to see a 'giving standard' (Wiepking, 2008), the norm about levels of giving in specific situations that people in different income groups share. This latest development is the most exciting, the most positive change for the better in philanthropy in Europe. People of wealth will be able to see what their generous peers give. That, if the sociologists are correct, could encourage them to give at their peers' generous level.

The government sphere

The ways in which governments in Europe deal with philanthropy have changed. Some of this has been for the good and some not. At the positive end of the scale, governments have encouraged philanthropy with tax breaks, new structures (new types of foundation and social enterprises) and cash. They have also – despite the rhetoric of cuts – continued to provide a solid line of funding for the non-profit sector in the form of contracts for services.

But governments have also worked in the opposite direction. Most European governments appear to be stuck in the tramline of neoliberal politics. As a result they have done little or nothing to use redistributive taxation to rein in wealth and to support the poor. Private philanthropy cannot meet the needs of widespread poverty; only governments have that scale and reach.

Governments have also struck at the freedom of expression of the non-profit world, muzzling their lobbying and campaigning. And sometimes – most notably during the attack on fundraising by the British government during summer and autumn 2015 – Governments have actively undone the goodwill and trust that existed between donor and charity.

The practical sphere

How philanthropy works – what actually happens on the ground – has changed in Europe. In this sphere are the tools of philanthropy – structures, rules, systems of taxation – and the mechanics who use them – advisers, wealth managers, fundraisers and researchers.

High-value philanthropists have 'hyperagency', 'the enhanced capacity of wealthy individuals to establish or control substantially the conditions under which they and others will live … [to] create for themselves a world of their own design' (Schervish, 2003, p 21). In Europe that hyperagency has been, for many, frustrated. They have the money, they want to do good, but the non-profits they approach will allow them to give, but not to do; many European NGOs have stuck to a model based on 'give us the money and we'll do the good'. Philanthropists in Europe express great frustration at the inability of non-profits to allow participation by donors in projects and programmes. As wealthy individuals have become more aware of their hyperagency in social, environmental and educational spheres so they have become more frustrated with the limitations imposed by the non-profits. And the consequence has been that they have taken their hyperagency elsewhere, creating new foundations across the continent.

The growth of these foundations has been supported by governments (see Chapter Eight) which have made them easier to register and manage, and by professional advisers who encourage their HNWI clients to develop their philanthropy using a growing toolset to build philanthropic vehicles of increasing complexity. The professional might be a private banker, a philanthropy coach, a consultant or a fundraiser but they are all engaged in the mechanics of philanthropy. There are more of them now than ever before, and the trend is for continued growth. Foundations have increasing numbers of professional staff, banks across the continent have recruited philanthropy teams, and the numbers of fundraisers working on 'major donors' is growing. Are they having an impact? Anecdotally, yes of course – HEC would not have raised €112 million from its 2008-2013 campaign had it not been for the professional team working there, nor would UBS Optimus Foundation have raised 2015's CHF57 million without the bank's professional management (Anon, 2016d). But we lack hard data on the impact of professionals in the sector, hard proof that employing professionals works. Which is emphatically not the same as saying that it does not. Just that we do not have the data.

The growing toolset for philanthropy is beginning to sparkle in Europe. We have Social Impact Bonds, we have crowdfunding, soft equity, loans, new types of foundation and Community Interest Companies. We have impact and Social Return on Investment, Programme Related Investment and venture philanthropy. We have donor-directed funds at national and Community Foundation level, and we have donor circles, networks and clubs – we've had them for a long time, but not in these numbers. Whether you want to pledge, give, get, invest or lend there are clever tools to do that and cleverer people who will help you construct your dream machine.

These four spheres – demographic, knowledge, government, practical – are coinciding in other parts of the world too. The Gulf States, an area of particular interest for this author, has seen similar demographic shifts amongst people of wealth, and the growth of the mechanics of philanthropy. Transparency is still a brake on development, but the sector knows that and it cannot be long before that sphere too is fully functioning. India, parts of Africa and Latin America – note the work of the Mexican Centre on Philanthropy (www.cemefi.org/) for example – are all heading in the same direction. Europe has the head start given to it by an established civil society but others will catch up, and perhaps overtake, soon.

Back to the future

We established at the start of this book that we are not dealing with truly new philanthropy. We are dealing with ideas that are endlessly recycled through the centuries from an Al-Andalusian ruler to a venture philanthropist. I also issued a warning in the Introduction (Chapter One) about trying to predict the future from a Europe that is, as I write, in turmoil: 'looking into a misty future from a foggy present'. But it is hard to resist the urge to make a bid for a better future; I take full responsibility for any mistakes here.

Philanthropy, here to stay

Despite concerns that philanthropy might be ending, or might be lost to 'impact investing', the evidence of its survival through endless revolutions and reinventions is a good base for predicting its continuity. In his wide-ranging look into the future, Jacques Attali (2008, p 273) writes about '*transhumains*' – people who 'understand that their happiness depends on that of others ... altruists' – who will lead us into the age of 'hyper-democracy'. As a Dutch philanthropist and social investor told this author:

> 'The basic drivers are the same. It's about wanting to do something good. Ours is inherited wealth – there is a moral obligation to do good. We have to strike the balance between wealth and responsibility. Our parents infused us with their value system; I share that ambition with my family. It is value driven, about the things we care about.'

For Karen Wilson, philanthropy is inbuilt, but that does not mean it is unchanging:

> 'I really think it is here to stay. But there is a fundamental shift in how people see business and philanthropy. The old model was "you are the philanthropist, you are a business person and you do not mix the two". Now it is different. People will pick where they want on the scale from philanthropy to for profit investment.'

Jean-Marie Destrée is also positive about the future generations of philanthropists.

> 'The changes [in philanthropy] are not coming from the wealthiest people. It is the young people, the middle

philanthropists, who are more in touch with [social] reality. Our most recent new fund was created by a 30 year old, an inheritor. He had decided that he did not want to live as a *"rentier"* so he put 50% of his inheritance in a foundation. He asked us to arrange a visit for him to [the refugee camp in] Calais, "The Jungle" as a volunteer, like any other volunteer. Young people are looking for sense, for implication. For a young person with money, philanthropy like this is natural.'

So we can make at least one confident prediction: philanthropy is here to stay for at least as long as there is a humankind to love (with apologies to Wiepking, 2008).

The wealth gap

Unless there are dramatic changes in European politics, we are likely to see the continuing growth of the wealth gap. Dramatic changes – think of Podemos in Spain or the SNP in Scotland – are conceivable but the neoliberal status quo and its mistaken belief that wealth 'trickles down' will be hard to shift, and the wealth gap in the UK, Spain and other European countries will not start to close during the lifetime of this book.

The relationship between the wealth gap and philanthropy is contradictory, as we saw in Chapter Four. The existence, side by side, of wealth and poverty may encourage people of wealth to give more, although this is not at all a certain hypothesis. In that sense it may be good for philanthropy. But it means that people are poor, the antithesis of what philanthropic people and the non-profits they support want. Poverty in Europe is far too big a problem for philanthropy to solve alone, so this creates a second dilemma, that private philanthropy needs state intervention, state partners, if it is to have any effect on Europe's poor millions, let alone the much larger numbers of poor people in the Global South.

Structured philanthropy

"More and more people are setting up their own foundation. It's a second career. They are having great fun doing this", says Theresa

Lloyd. The numbers bear out her assertion, with more foundations in Europe than ever before. This appears to be a move toward a more structured, strategic philanthropy, a more professional way of creating social change. The form that these structures take is becoming standardised, suggests Karen Wilson. "In Europe there is a convergence led by the European Commission as to what it means to be a foundation. Europe has very variable models for foundations, so expect a convergence of rules across Europe."

Given that the EU was unable to agree a common model for a foundation despite years of lobbying by the European Foundation Centre, this might be an optimistic view. But foundations are popular with governments, so we can expect that it will become easier, faster and cheaper to establish them, and that numbers will continue to grow.

This is good news if it is combined with increasing transparency, so that we can see who is in control, what they are supporting and thus determine how the tax relief we offer foundations is being used.

The growth in corporate-originated donor-directed funds (UBS' Optimus foundation has grown from an income of CHF12 million in 2012 to CHF57 million in 2015 – Anon, 2016d), brings advantages and disadvantages: strong, skilled, well-resourced competition for non-profits, and concerns that we are losing transparency.

Investing for impact

There are a number of clues that indicate that investing for a mix of impact and profit is going to grow.

Governments are interested; the UK's Department for International Development set up its £75 million Impact Fund in 2012 to focus on long-term 'patient capital' investments, in the range £5-£15 million, in services for poor people, including food, water and sanitation (Martin, 2016). In July 2016 the Cabinet Office announced the launch of a £80 million Life Chances Fund to support social impact bonds and other payment-by-results contracts involving 'socially-minded investors' (Sharman, 2016).

The corporate sector is interested. Dr Lisa Hehenberger notes that "in impact investment there is a lot of growth. Some multinationals are setting up impact investment funds." There are many motives for companies investing in this way, but Dr Hehenberger points out that "part of the interest amongst corporate investment funds is to source ideas from outside the business". The manager of a group of Dutch family foundations talks in a similar vein; "Business and philanthropy will merge". Non-profits will increasingly enter the business sphere and "we will have many more companies that think about doing social investments".

The foundation sector is also entering the field, and we have seen multimillion Euro impact investment funds from foundations such as Fondazione Cariplo. Foundations in Europe could light the touch paper to a potentially explosive area of growth here, by shifting part of their endowments into Programme Related Investment (PRI). Bear in mind that the last estimate of the total assets of the European foundation sector was between €350 billion and €3 trillion (Hopt, von Hippel and Anheier, 2009), and remember that this estimate is based on only a partial view of the sector, the part that is visible, and you can see the potential were foundations to allocate even a modest percentage of their portfolios to PRI.

Wolfgang Hafenmayer looks further ahead, suggesting a conundrum for philanthropy: "people are thinking about shifting their whole [investment] portfolios into impact investing. This could create a revolution in the financial system, when people move all their investment to impact." He suggests that this might be helped by legislation, or a shift in the way we measure costs such as environmental costs. "If companies were not allowed to create negative externalities then it would have enormous consequences. No one wants to invest to destroy the environment. We are only at the very beginning of this playing out." He notes the irony that if the bulk of investments were to shift toward impact investing then the logical conclusion would be that "the field of philanthropy could become much smaller. In theory there should then be no need for philanthropy."

The demand for investments looks likely to continue to grow, although there are brakes on its development. We do not have a clear definition of impact, or a standard methodology for assessing it. There are no limits to 'impact'; we can describe almost any investment, from a hamburger restaurant to a conservation project as having a 'social impact'. This leads to some confusion when businesses that are profit first, impact second pitch to venture philanthropy investors. The lack of a pipeline of investment-ready projects is a constant complaint in venture philanthropy circles. But Ramón Bernat is hopeful: "There are more and more social entrepreneurs", he says. "We see the sector as very strong, with entrepreneurs who are more positive, and better prepared. The projects – the business plans – are better prepared. The sector is getting more professional."

Impact will not happen quickly. A Dutch philanthropic manager cited one of the world's leading philanthropists: "People from a business background tend to be more in a hurry, but social change needs time. As Warren Buffet has said, '[I] can be very patient. No matter how great the talent or effort, some things just take time: you can't produce a baby in one month by getting nine women pregnant'."

Unless there is some overwhelming economic crisis in Europe, impact investing will grow, and we will see more foundations supporting it through Programme Related Investment. We will also see an increasingly fuzzy frontier between giving and investing for social and environmental change, and will perhaps suffer a reputationally damaging crisis when some large 'impact' fund of the future turns out to be a profit wolf dressed as a social lamb. That future event will spur us to create clearer definitions, and to wish that we had done so earlier.

Goodbye government?

In the future, "governments will not have more money to give", says Serge Raicher, co-founder of EVPA, "so we all have a collective responsibility [to society]. I must hope that the growth of social investment is not temporary or short term. The change of mind-set is a key element. We have gone from a militant-driven social sector to one where there is more heart and head and accountability. That is here to stay."

Serge is making a point that many in the non-profit sector repeat: that governments across Europe are withdrawing from social responsibilities, some of which are then contracted out to non-profits. Can I safely predict that this trend will continue? I am a specialist in philanthropy, not in politics, but governments do not have a good recent track record with the social causes that non-profits support, and with an ageing population and a load of other concerns including the continuing economic doldrums there seems little prospect that they will shift their position and invest properly in poverty, health or education, let alone in environment and culture. I see many years yet of cuts and social deprivation. As I have pointed out repeatedly, philanthropy, even high-value philanthropy, cannot fill these gaps left by government. But many of us will continue to try.

In a horrible confluence of circumstances and political beliefs, Europe's non-profit sector might be caught between two dark forces; cuts in government expenditure on welfare, environment and culture on the one hand, and criticism and control on the other. The heavy-handed reaction of the Westminster government to the press campaign against fundraising in 2015, the gagging of charity campaigning (see Chapter Eight), and the concerns in France that a new government might reduce the tax breaks for donations, may be indications of a growing duplicity toward the non-profit sector – of biting the hand that you feed.

Goodbye, good causes?

It is a minority view, but an interesting warning of change ahead. The causes are varied; the growth of the foundation sector, the programme specialists being employed by larger foundations, the increasingly blurred frontier between the commercial and non-profit sectors, the trend for 'direct-to-beneficiary' giving both in the high-value philanthropy space and at the consumer end of giving (witness the growth of Kiva for example). The result of these forces could be that large, broad NGOs might not survive.

> 'A lot of classic NGOs will not be there. There will be focused NGOs with very specific goals. The big generalist NGOs will lose out. Family foundations will become the competitors for NGOs. The family foundations are growing wealthier, and have a lot of money. They will hire their own people and set their own agenda.'

The view of one experienced manager of Dutch family foundations might sound fantastical. Big NGOs have a huge social base to call upon; some have millions of members and donors across Europe. They have shown they can innovate – the creation by Greenpeace Austria of 'Direct Dialogue' or street-level face-to-face fundraising is a successful example. But they are beginning to face stiff competition from powerful and wealthy philanthropists who are determined to carve their own path in creating social change, to deal directly with beneficiaries and to meld giving with investment. Many of these new entrants – at least at the venture philanthropy end of the spectrum – favour partnerships with smaller specialist non-profits where they can have some positive influence and a clear view of where their investment is going. The biggest NGOs have been slow to respond to the changes in high-value philanthropy in Europe.

That does not mean the end of the large multipurpose NGO. Their wide consumer base of faithful supporters and their track record in winning government funding should save them. But it is unlikely that high-value philanthropists will spontaneously turn to the big NGOs for partnerships, and more likely that they will do it themselves or with smaller specialist partners. The big NGOs will have to make an increasingly strong case to philanthropists if they want to build partnerships, and win investors with this segment of the market.

A clearer view

This book has touched often on the subject of transparency, defined in Part four as visibility, the 'degree to which information is complete and easily located', and inferability, the 'extent to which it can be used to draw accurate conclusions' (Michener and Bersch, 2013). In the professional lifetime of this author Europe has opened up – in some places dramatically – its philanthropic archives for public inspection. Encouraged by the threat of scandals, of money laundering and of tax evasion, and supported by a public who believe they have a right to know what is going on with their public funds, governments across Europe have opened registers and published lists. Karen Wilson believes that this new clarity is here to stay: "In the future there will be transparency on financial returns and full transparency on impact."

There are still huge dark pools in the information – readers should take the test suggested in Chapter Ten to discover just how much light is being shone, or not, on Italian foundations. Looking across the European landscape we still know very, very little about how non-profits function, where the money comes from, where it goes and why. Even in Europe's most culturally and politically open countries – the Netherlands for example – there are still debates over whether or not foundations should expose their financial frills to the breeze of public view. Government policy there is only going in one direction, as the manager of a group of family foundations in the Netherlands told me. "The Ministry is closing in on the sector", he said, predicting regulations that would bring further financial disclosure amongst Dutch foundations.

But transparency in high-value philanthropy could be at a turning point, as we saw in Part four. The growth of corporate-originated charitable funds amongst the banks of Europe could push back the advances being made in openness elsewhere. These funds are growing in number and in staff; it is reasonable to assume that this growth will continue, meaning that we could know less about more high-value donors in the future.

And the gorilla in the corner?

High-value philanthropy in Europe is influenced by developments in the USA, and we can expect that to continue.

This is not at all surprising. Philanthropy in the USA is out there in the public domain, loud, transparent and proud. Academic researchers, prospect researchers, philanthropists, fundraisers and bankers have a wealth of data on giving and getting and there is a temptation to take the conclusions that they draw and apply them to Europe. I hope that I have shown in this book that high-value philanthropy in Europe is different, that it requires a specific approach, specific strategies to unlock its potential.

The end of the beginning

In this book I have tried to capture what is happening now in Europe in high-value philanthropy. There is never a perfect time to portray philanthropy and now, in the midst of economic stagnation, migration, a restless Russia, a changing climate and an EU that is tottering on its foundations is as good as any. The almost complete lack of hard data is a minor hindrance in comparison to these other factors. I am not complaining – all of these elements help to make philanthropy interesting and to make high-value philanthropy – the canary in the generosity goldmine – more challenging still.

My image is blurred and smudged, but I hope that it has given you at least a glimpse of the human goodness in Europe.

Notes

[1] I am not the first person to come up with spheres and circles as metaphors to explain philanthropy and its environment. The first edition of *Why Rich People Give* (Lloyd, 2004) includes circles of influences on giving including 'Belief in the Cause', 'A Catalyst for Change', 'Self-Actualisation', 'The Moral Dimension' and 'Relationships'.

References

Abrams, B.A. & Schmitz, M.D., 1984. The Crowding-Out Effect of Governmental Transfers on Private Charitable Contributions: Cross-Section Evidence. *National Tax Journal*, 37(4), pp 563–568.

Aillagon, J.-J., 20003. Mécénat, associations et fondations: Discussion d'un projet de loi. Paris, France. Available at: www.senat.fr/seances/ s200305/s20030513/s20030513001.html#int39.

Aknin, L.B., Dunn, E.W., Sandstrom, G.M. & Norton, M.I., 2013. Does Social Connection Turn Good Deeds into Good Feelings? On the Value of Putting the 'Social' in Prosocial Spending. *International Journal of Happiness and Development*, 1(2), pp 155–171.

Andreoni, J. & Payne, A.A., 2010. *Is Crowding Out Due Entirely to Fundraising? Evidence from a Panel of Charities*, National Bureau of Economic Research. Available at: www.nber.org/papers/w16372.

Andreoni, J., Payne, A. & Smith, S., 2014. Do Grants to Charities Crowd Out Other Income? Evidence from the UK. *Journal of Public Economics*, 114, pp 75–86.

Anheier, H.K., 2001. *Foundations in Europe: A Comparative Perspective*, London: LSE.

Anon, 2004. *Campaign Review: The Giving Campaign 2001–2004*, London: The Giving Campaign. Available at: www.fundraising. co.uk/files/campaign_review.pdf.

Anon, 2006. The Birth of Philanthrocapitalism. *The Economist*. Available at: www.economist.com/node/5517656.

Anon, 2008. Les fondations en France en 2007: fondateurs, secteurs d'interventions, poids économique, Paris: Fondation de France. p 13. Available at: www.fondationdefrance.org.

Anon, 2011a. ¿Crees en la nueva filantropía? *Ethic*. Available at: http:// ethic.es/2011/11/%C2%BFcrees-en-la-nueva-filantropia/.

Anon, 2011b. *Charities and Investment Matters* (CC14), Charity Commission, London, October 2011.

Anon, 2012a. *High Net Worth Individuals and Sustainable Investment 2012*, Brussels: Eurosif AISBL. Available at: www.eurosif.org/wp-content/uploads/2014/05/1.-report_hnwi.pdf.pdf.

Anon, 2012b. *Review of Philanthropy in UK Higher Education: 2012 Status Report and Challenges for the Next Decade*, Dundee, Scotland: More Partnership. Available at: www.morepartnership.com/library/Review_of_Philanthropy_in_UK_Higher_Education.pdf.

Anon, 2012c. Anuario del Tercer Sector de Acción Social en España, Fundación Lluis Vives. Available at: http://plataformaong.org/fichaBiblioteca.php?id=13&p=1&t=anuario+del+tercer+sector

Anon, 2012d. Anuario del Tercer Sector de Acción Social en España. Resumen Comparativo 2010-2012, Fundación Lluis Vives. Available at: www.plataformaong.org/ARCHIVO/documentos/biblioteca/1366037195_004.pdf.

Anon, 2014b. *Verzeichnis der Deutschen Stiftung*, Berlin: Auflage. Available at: www.stiftungen.org/index.php?id=253.

Anon, 2015a. *Les Fonds et Fondations de 2001 à 2014 en France*, Paris: CFF – Centre Français des Fonds et Fondations. Available at: www.centre-francais-fondations.org/fondations-fonds-de-dotation/le-secteur/les-fonds-et-fondations-en-france/panoramas-des-fonds-et-fondations-depuis-2005/les-fonds-et-fondations-de-2001-a-2014-en-france/view. p 7.

Anon, 2015b. *La nueva filantropía – Atarecos*. Available at: www.canarias7.es/blogs/atarecos/2015/07/la_nueva_filant.html.

Anon, 2015c. *Future of Foundations*, Stuttgart: Robert Bosch Stiftung. Available at: www.bosch-stiftung.de/content/language1/downloads/RBS_Studie_Zukunft_des_Stiftens_en.pdf.

Anon, 2015d. World Wealth Report 2015. Capgemini. Available at: www.capgemini.com/thought-leadership/world-wealth-report-2013-from-capgemini-and-rbc-wealth-management.

Anon, 2015e. *Comparative Highlights of Foundation Laws: The Operating Environment for Foundations in Europe*, Brussels: European Foundation Centre. Available at: http://efc.issuelab.org/resource/comparative_highlights_of_foundation_laws_the_operating_environment_for_foundations_in_europe.

Anon, 2015f. *2015 Donor-Advised Fund Report*, Jenkintown, PA: National Philanthropic Trust. Available at: www.nptrust.org/daf-report/index.html.

References

Anon, 2015g. *The Art of Adaptation: Why Talking Philanthropy Transforms the Adviser–Client Relationship*, Kent: Charities Aid Foundation. Available at: www.cafonline.org/.

Anon, 2015h. *Million Dollar Donors Report 2015 – Philanthropy – Executive Summary & Trends*, London: Coutts. Available at: http://philanthropy.coutts.com/en/reports/2015/executive-summary.html.

Anon, 2015i. *Wellcome Trust 2014 Annual Report*. London: Wellcome Trust, 19 February. Available at: www.wellcome.ac.uk/About-us/Publications/Annual-review/index.htm.

Anon, 2015j. Global Social Networks by Users 2015. *Statista*. Available at: www.statista.com/statistics/272014/global-social-networks-ranked-by-number-of-users/.

Anon, 2015k. *CAF World Giving Index 2015. A Global View of Giving Trends*, London: Charities Aid Foundation. Available at: https://www.cafonline.org/about-us/publications/2015-publications/world-giving-index-2015.

Anon, 2015l. *UK Giving 2014*, West Malling, Kent: Charities Aid Foundation. https://www.cafonline.org/about-us/publications/2015-publications/uk-giving-2014.

Anon, 2016a. Bilancio di Missione Esercizio 2015, Fondazione Cariplo. Available at: www.fondazionecariplo.it/it/la-fondazione/dati-di-bilancio/rapporto-annuale-bilancio-di-missione.html.

Anon, 2016b. *Poverty and Income Inequality Scotland 2014–5*, Edinburgh: The Scottish Government. Available at: www.gov.scot/Publications/2016/06/3468.

Anon, 2016c. *Population Ranking*. The World Bank. Available at: http://data.worldbank.org/data-catalog/Population-ranking-table.

Anon, 2016d. *Annual Review 2015 UBS Optimus Foundation*, Zürich: UBS. Available at: www.ubs.com/microsites/optimus-foundation/en/about-us/annual-report.html.

Antoine, C., 2003. *La Empresa informativa y su tratamiento de las informaciones sobre el Patrocino Empresarial a la Cultura*. In 1° congreso internacional de ética y derecho de la información, 1° congreso internacional de ética y derecho de la información. Valencia: Fundación COSO, pp 117–128. Available at: www.fundacioncoso.org.

Archambeault, D.S., Webber, S. & Greenlee, J., 2015. Fraud and Corruption in U.S. Nonprofit Entities A Summary of Press Reports 2008-2011. *Nonprofit and Voluntary Sector Quarterly*, 44(6), pp 1194–1224.

Arenal, C., 1894. *La Beneficencia, la filantropía y la caridad*, Madrid: Libr. de Victoriano Suárez.

Arutyunova, A. & Clark, C., 2013. *Watering the Leaves, Starving the Roots*, Toronto, Canada: AWID. Available at: www.awid.org/publications/watering-leaves-starving-.

Attali, J., 2008. *Une brève histoire de l'avenir*, Paris: Librairie générale française.

Bagwell, S. et al, 2013. *Money for Good UK: Understanding Donor Motivation and Behaviour*, London: New Philanthropy Capital. Available at: www.thinknpc.org/publications/money-for-good-uk/.

Bekkers, R., 2006. Keeping the Faith. Presentation at NCVO/VSSN conference. Available at: http://www.rug.nl/research/portal/publications/keeping-the-faith(9a8b5018-d512-4b48-bda7-907fc4ce9859).html.

Bekkers, R., 2012. Limits of Social Influence on Giving: Who is Affected When and Why? In *Social Influences and Charitable Giving*. Royal Overseas League, London: Center for Philanthropic Studies, VU University Amsterdam. Available at: www.giving.nl/2013/09/limits-of-social-influence-on-giving-who-is-affected-when-and-why-rene-bekkers/.

Bekkers, R. & Mariani, E., 2009. Is the Charitable Deduction in the Netherlands Treasury Efficient? In *Economics of Charitable Giving Conference*, Mannheim, p 26. Available at: http://test.giving.nl/wp-content/uploads/2013/09/Bekkers_Mariani_09-2.pdf.

Bekkers, R. & Smeets, P., 2014. Wealth and Giving in the Netherlands. Available at: https://renebekkers.files.wordpress.com/2014/12/14_12_18_wealth-and-giving-in-the-netherlands.pptx.

Bekkers, R. & Wiepking, P., 2011. Who Gives? A Literature Review of Predictors of Charitable Giving Part One: Religion, Education, Age and Socialisation. *Voluntary Sector Review*, 2(3), pp 337–365.

Bekkers, R.H.F.P. & Wiepking, P., 2015. *Giving in the Netherlands: A Strong Welfare State with a Vibrant Nonprofit Sector*, London: Palgrave MacMillan. Available at: http://dare.ubvu.vu.nl/handle/1871/53075.

Bekkers, R., Janssen, B.A.S. & Wiepking, P. 2010. Geefgedrag van vermogende Nederlanders: een verkennende studie. Available at: http://dare.ubvu.vu.nl/handle/1871/48189.

Bekkers, R., Boonstoppel, E. & de Wit, A., 2013. *Giving in the Netherlands Panel Survey – User Manual* (version 2.2), Amsterdam: Center for Philanthropic Studies, VU University Amsterdam. Available at: http://test.giving.nl/wp-content/uploads/2013/11/GINPS_user_manual_v2_2.pdf.

Benyza, Y., 2015. Takaful 2015 Fifth Annual Conference on Arab Philanthropy and Civic Engagement. Available at: http://aucegypt. edu/research/conferences/takaful-2015-fifth-annual-conference-arab-philanthropy-and-civic-engagement.

Beresford, P., 2015. The Sunday Times Rich List. Available at: www. thesundaytimes.co.uk/sto/public/richlist/.

Beresford, P., 2016. Philip Beresford: The Sunday Times Rich List Compiler on 27 Years of Wealth Watching. *Management Today*, 24 April, p 1.

Bisbal Galbany, A., et al, 2013. Manual Practic sobre els Impostos Directes a Andorra. Andorra: Cambra de Comerç, Indústria i Serveis d'Andorra. www.ccis.ad.

Bishop, M. & Green, M.F., 2010. *Philanthrocapitalism: How Giving Can Save the World*, London: A. & C. Black.

Booth, C., Leary, K. & Vallance, F., 2015. *Qualitative Research to Understand Charitable Giving and Gift Aid Behaviour amongst Better-off Individuals*, London: Ipsos MORI Social Research Institute. Available at: www.gov.uk/government/publications/charitable-giving-and-gift-aid-behaviour-amongst-better-off-individuals.

Bourdieu, P., 1977. Cultural Reproduction and Social Reproduction. In *Power and Ideology in Education*. New York: Oxford University Press, pp 487–511.

Brademas, J., Robinson, O., Freeman, R. & Riley, C.A., 1993. The New Philanthropy for the New Europe. In *The Arts in the World Economy: Public Policy and Private Philanthropy for a Global Cultural Community*, London: University Press of New England, pp 17–25.

Brand, M. & Kohler, J., 2014. Private Equity Investments. In *New Frontiers of Philanthropy: A Guide to the New Tools and New Actors that Are Reshaping Global Philanthropy and Social Investing*, Oxford: Oxford University Press, pp 395–423.

Breeze, B., 2010. *How Donors Choose Charities: Findings of a Study of Donor Perceptions of the Nature and Distribution of Charitable Benefit*, University of Kent. Available at: www.cgap.org.uk/uploads/reports/HowDonorsChooseCharities.pdf.

Breeze, B., 2011. Is There a 'New Philanthropy'? In *Understanding the Roots of Voluntary Action*. Brighton: Sussex Academic Press, pp 182–195.

Breeze, B. & Lloyd, T., 2013. *Richer Lives: Why Rich People Give*, London: Directory of Social Change.

Brown, E. & Ferris, J.M., 2007. Social Capital and Philanthropy: An Analysis of the Impact of Social Capital on Individual Giving and Volunteering. *Nonprofit and Voluntary Sector Quarterly*, 36(1), pp 85–99.

Brown, W.A. & Iverson, J., 2004. Exploring Strategy and Board Structure in Nonprofit Organizations. *Nonprofit and Voluntary Sector Quarterly*, 33(3), pp 377–400.

Brunet, J.M. & Gilabert, D., 2016. Una infanta al banc dels acusats. *La Vanguardia*, 10 January, pp 28–29.

Cameron, K.S. & Quinn, R.E., 2011. *Diagnosing and Changing Organizational Culture: Based on the Competing Values Framework*, 3rd edition, San Francisco, CA: Jossey-Bass.

Cantwell, M., 2014. *21st Century Barriers to Women's Entrepreneurship: Majority Report of the US Senate Committee on Small Business and Entrepreneurship*, Washington, DC: United States Senate. Available at: http://www.sbc.senate.gov/public/?a=Files.Serve&File_id=3f954386-f16b-48d2-86ad-698a75e33cc4.

Carballeira Debasa, A.M., 2012. Aproximación a las donaciones piadosas en el Islam Medieval: el caso de al-Andalus. In *Las donaciones piadosas en el mundo medieval. Asturiensis Regni Territorium*. Oviedo: Alfonso García Leal.

Carnegie, A., 2006. *The 'Gospel of Wealth': Essays and Other Writings*, edited by D. Nasaw, New York: Penguin Books.

Carnie, C., 2015. *Trust Women*, Bristol: Factary. Available at: http://factary.com/blog/.

Carnie, C., 2016. *I Want to be in America*, Factary. Available at: http://factary.com/2016/02/i-want-to-be-in-america/.

Carnie, C. & Whitefield, W., 2013. *The Venture Philanthropists*, Bristol, UK: Factary. Available at: http://factary.com/2013/11/venture-philanthropists-uk/.

Carrington, D., 2009. *Doing Good – Done Better*. Available at: http://new.davidcarrington.net/articles-talks/.

Chahim, H. & Carnie, C., 2015. Entre Mirage et Réalité, Presentation to the Association Française de Fundraising Annual Conference, Paris, 25 June.

Chiang, Y.-S., 2015. Good Samaritans in Networks: An Experiment on How Networks Influence Egalitarian Sharing and the Evolution of Inequality. *PLoS ONE*, 10(6), p e0128777.

Cingano, F. & Förster, M., 2014. *Trends in Income Inequality and its Impact on Economic Growth*. Available at: www.oecd.org/social/inequality-hurts-economic-growth.htm.

Çizakça, M. , 2000. *A History of Philanthropic Foundations: The Islamic World from the Seventh Century to the Present*, Istanbul: Bosphorus University Press.

Clotfelter, C.T., 1992. *Who Benefits from the Nonprofit Sector?*, Chicago: University of Chicago Press.

Cohen, R., 2014. Corporate-originated Charitable Funds. In *New Frontiers of Philanthropy: A Guide to the New Tools and New Actors that Are Reshaping Global Philanthropy and Social Investing*, Oxford: Oxford University Press, pp 255–290.

Cronin, J., 2011. Success and Failure in Scottish Convalescent Homes, 1860-1939. In *Understanding the Roots of Voluntary Action*, Brighton: Sussex Academic Press, pp 137–154.

Cukier, K., 2015. Charting Change. *The Economist*, December, p 89.

Cullen, F., 2016. *Scottish Charity Accounts and Trustees' Names*. UK Fundraising. Available at: http://fundraising.co.uk/2016/05/16/scottish-charity-accounts-trustees-names/.

Davies, R., 2015. *Public Good by Private Means: How Philanthropy Shapes Britain*, London: Alliance Publishing Trust.

De Laurens, O. & Rozier, S., 2012. *La philanthropie à la française. L'engagement au service du progrès social*, Paris: Fondation de France. Available at: www.fondationdefrance.org/Outils/Mediatheque/Etudes-de-l-Observatoire/La-Philanthropie-a-la-francaise.

Debbasch, C., 1987, Les Fondations, un mécénat pour notre temps? Economica, Paris, cited in Parés i Maicas, M., 1994. La Nueva filantropía y la comunicación social: mecenazgo, fundación y patrocinio, 2nd edition, Barcelona: PPU.

de Wit, A. & Bekkers, R., 2016. Government Support and Charitable Donations: A Meta-Analysis of the Crowding-out Hypothesis. *Journal of Public Administration Research and Theory*. Available at: http://jpart. oxfordjournals.org/content/early/2016/07/28/jopart.muw044.

Diario de Navarra, 2014. Available at: www.diariodenavarra.es/ noticias/mas_actualidad/nacional/2014/07/04/quot_fin_aizoon_ era_desviar_los_fondos_del_instituto_noos_quot_166177_1031. html.

Duijts, S., 2015. *Fondsenboek 2015 and Fondsendisk*, Zutphen: Walburg Pers.

Eagar, C., 2014. The Rise of Boutique Philanthropic Advisors. Financial Times 'How To Spend It' supplement, 21 March.

El País, 2012. Una ONG convertida en entramado, *El País*, Madrid, 24 February 2012. Available at: http://politica.elpais.com/ politica/2012/02/24/actualidad/1330090807_263996.html.

Etzel, M., 2015. Philanthropy's New Frontier – Impact Investing. *Stanford Social Innovation Review*. Available at: http://ssir.org/articles/ entry/philanthropys_new_frontierimpact_investing.

Farouky, N., 2016. The State of Arab Philanthropy and the Case for Change. *Development in Practice*, 26(5), pp 637–645.

Fiennes, C., 2012. *It Ain't What You Give, It's the Way That You Give It: Making Charitable Donations That Get Results*, Great Britain: Giving Evidence.

Ford, J., 2016, The Taxman, Google and the Benefits of Fiscal Voyeurism. *Financial Times*, 21 February.

Fowler, J., 2011. Scientific Philanthropy and the Society for Bettering the Condition and Increasing the Comforts of the Poor, 1796-1824. In *Understanding the Roots of Voluntary Action*, Brighton: Sussex Academic Press, pp 171–181.

Frumkin, P., 2006. *Strategic giving: the art and science of philanthropy*, Chicago: University of Chicago Press. Available at: http://www. press.uchicago.edu/ucp/books/book/chicago/S/bo3775602.html.

Gaudiosi, M.M., 1998. The Influence of the Islamic Law of Waqf on the Development of the Trust in England: The Case of Merton College. *University of Pennsylvania Law Review*, 136(4), pp 1231–1261.

Gautier, A. & de Nervaux, L., 2015. *La France qui donne: Etat de la recherche sur le don en France*, Paris: Essec. Available at: www. fondationdefrance.org/sites/default/files/atoms/files/la_france_qui_ donne_dec_2015.pdf.

Gutiérrez, M., 2006. Desarollo: La caridad es historia, surge nueva filantropía. IPS Agencia de Noticias. Available at: www.ipsnoticias. net/2006/06/desarrollo-la-caridad-es-historia-surge-nueva-filantropia/.

Hagen-Dillon, A., 2014. *The Business Case for Women's Economic Empowerment: An Integrated Approach*, Berlin: Oak Foundation. Available at: http://dalberg.com/documents/Business_Case_for_Womens_Economic_Empowerment.pdf.

Haibach, M., 1999. Contemporary Women's Philanthropy in Germany, ISTR. Available at: https://c.ymcdn.com/sites/www.istr.org/resource/resmgr/working_papers_geneva/Haibach.pdf.

Handy, C., 2006. *The New Philanthropists: The New Generosity*, London: William Heinemann.

Hartnell, C., 2015. Individual, Family and Corporate Philanthropy: Common Trends. *Alliance*, 20(3), September. Available at: www. alliancemagazine.org.

Herman, A. & Schervish, P.G., 1991. Money and Hyperagency: The Worldly Empowerment of Wealth. Available at: http://dlib.bc.edu/islandora/object/bc-ir:104112.

Hines, F., 2005. Viable Social Enterprise: An Evaluation of Business Support to Social Enterprises. *Social Enterprise Journal*, 1(1), pp 13–28.

Hogan, C., 2004. *Prospect Research: A Primer for Growing Nonprofits*, Sudbury, MA: Jones & Bartlett Publishers Inc.

Hopt, K., von Hippel, T. & Anheier, H., 2009. *Feasibility Study on a European Foundation Statute: Final Report*, Heidelberg: Max Planck Institute for Comparative and International Private Law, and CSI, Universität Heidelberg. Available at: http://ec.europa.eu/internal_market/company/docs/eufoundation/feasibilitystudy_en.pdf.

Ibrahim, B. & Sherif, D., 2008. *From Charity to Social Change: Trends in Arab Philanthropy*, Cairo, Egypt: American University in Cairo Press.

John, R., 2006. *Venture Philanthropy: The Evolution of High Engagement Philanthropy in Europe*, Oxford: Oxford University. Available at: http://eureka.bodleian.ox.ac.uk/745/.

Johnson, P., 2010. *Global Institutional Philanthropy: A Preliminary Status Report*, WINGS. Available at: http://wings.issuelab.org/resource/global_institutional_philanthropy_a_preliminary_status_report.

Kania, J., Kramer, M. & Russell, P., 2014. Strategic Philanthropy for a Complex World. *Stanford Social Innovation Review*, (Summer 2014). Available at: http://ssir.org/up_for_debate/article/strategic_philanthropy.

Kingma, B.R., 1989. An Accurate Measurement of the Crowd-out Effect, Income Effect, and Price Effect for Charitable Contributions. *Journal of Political Economy*, 97(5), pp 1197–1207.

Koele, I.A., 2007. *International Taxation of Philanthropy: Removing Tax Obstacles for International Charities*, Amsterdam: IBFD Publications.

Kopczuk, W., 2015. Recent Evolution of Income and Wealth Inequality: Comments on Piketty's 'Capital in the 21st Century'. Paper prepared for Fourth Annual NYU/UCLA Tax Policy Symposium, Columbia University. Available at: http://cobe.boisestate.edu/allendalton/files/2015/04/Kopczuk_PikettyNYU.pdf.

Laybourn, K., 2015. The New Philanthropy of the Edwardian Age: The Guild of Help and the Halifax Citizens' Guild, 1905-1918. *Transactions of the Halifax Antiquarian Society*, 23, pp 73–94.

Leal, J., 2014. Los ricos españoles, un 3,5% más ricos en 2014. *El Mundo*, 31 December, p 1.

Letts, C., Ryan, W. & Grossman, A., 1997. Virtuous Capital: What Foundations can Learn from Venture Capitalists. *Harvard Business Review*, 75(2), pp 36–44.

Li Perni, G., 2016. *La Filantropia degli High Net Worth Individuals in Italia – 2015*, Rome: UNHCR. Available at: www.unhcr.it.

Lloyd, T., 2004. *Why Rich People Give*, London: Association of Charitable Foundations.

Maas, K. & Liket, K., 2010. Talk the Walk: Measuring the Impact of Strategic Philanthropy. *Journal of Business Ethics*, 100(3), pp 445–464.

Macadam, E., 1934. *The New Philanthropy. A Study of the Relations between the Statutory and Voluntary Social Services, etc*, London: G. Allen & Unwin.

MacDonald, N.A. & Tayart de Borms, L., 2008. *Philanthropy in Europe: A Rich Past, a Promising Future*, London: Alliance Publishing Trust.

Manzoor, S.H. & Straub, J.D., 2005. The Robustness of Kingma's Crowd-Out Estimate: Evidence from New Data on Contributions to Public Radio. *Public Choice*, 123(3/4), pp.463–476.

Magnani, E., 2009. Almsgiving, Donatio Pro Anima and Eucharistic Offering in the Early Middle Ages of Western Europe (4th–9th Century). In *Charity and Giving in Monotheistic Religions*, Berlin: Walter de Gruyter.

Martin, M., 2016. *Building the Impact Economy: Our Future, Yea or Nay*, Springer International Publishing. Available at: http://link.springer.com/10.1007/978-3-319-25604-7.

Meehan, W.F., Kilmer, D. & O'Flanagan, M., 2004. Investing in Society: Why we Need a More Efficient Social Capital Market – and How We Can Get There. *Stanford Social Innovation Review* (Spring). Available at: http://ssir.org/articles/entry/investing_in_society.

Meijs, L., Roza, L. & Vermuelen, M., 2014. Contemporary European E2P: Towards an Understanding of European Philanthrepreneurs. In *Handbook of Research on Entrepreneurs' Engagement in Philanthropy*, Cheltenham: Edward Elgar Publishing. Available at: www.rsm.nl/about-rsm/news/detail/3340-handbook-of-research-on-entrepreneurs-engagement-in-philanthropy/ or at http://www.e-elgar.com/shop/handbook-of-research-on-entrepreneurs-engagement-in-philanthropy

Mernier, A. & Xhauflair, V., 2014. *Les Fondations en Belgique*, Brussels: Réseau Belge des Fondations. Available at: www.reseaufondations.be/fr/POD-Fondations-FR.pdf.

Mesch, D., 2009. Women and Philanthropy: A Literature Review. Unpublished manuscript. Available at: https://philanthropy.iupui.edu/files/file/women_and_philanthropy_literature_review.pdf.

Mesch, D.J., Brown, M.S., Moore, Z.I. & Hayat, A.D., 2011. Gender Differences in Charitable Giving. *International Journal of Nonprofit and Voluntary Sector Marketing*, 16(4), pp 342–355.

Michener, G. & Bersch, K., 2013. Identifying Transparency. *Information Polity*, 18(3), pp 233–242.

Milanovic, B., 2013. Global Income Inequality by the Numbers: In History and Now. An Overview. *Global Policy* 4(2), pp 198–208.

Miles, R.E., Snow, C., Meyer, A. & Coleman, H.J., 1978. Organizational Strategy, Structure, and Process. *The Academy of Management Review*, 3(3), pp 546–562.

Milner, A., 2015. Does Impact Rule with Donors? *Alliance Magazine*, 20(3). Available at: www.alliancemagazine.org.

Morera Hernández, C., 2015. Mecenazgo, relaciones públicas y filantropía: «Fendi for fountains» análisis de caso / Patronage, Public Relations and Philanthropy: 'Fendi for Fountains' Case Study. *Vivat Academia*, 0(133), pp 80–124.

Morvaridi, B., 2015. *New Philanthropy and Social Justice: Debating the Conceptual and Policy Discourse*, Bristol, UK; Chicago, IL: Policy Press.

Murray, S., 2015. Donors Recognise the Benefits of Outsourcing. *Financial Times*, 18 September. Available at: https://next.ft.com/content/d6858f18-56be-11e5-9846-de406ccb37f2.

Napier, C., 2010. United Kingdom. In *A Global History of Accounting, Financial Reporting and Public Policy: Europe*, Bingley: Emerald Group Publishing, pp 243–273.

Nichols, J.E., 2004. Repositioning Fundraising in the 21st Century. *International Journal of Nonprofit and Voluntary Sector Marketing*, 9(2), pp 163–170.

Nickson, J., 2013. *Giving is Good for You: Why Britain Should be Bothered and Give More*, London: Biteback Publishing.

Odendahl, T., 1989. The Culture of Elite Philanthropy in the Reagan Years. *Nonprofit and Voluntary Sector Quarterly*, 18(3), pp 237–248.

OECD, 2014. Poverty Rates and Poverty Gaps. In *OECD Factbook 2014*, Paris: OECD Publishing. Available at: http://dx.doi.org/10.1787/factbook-2014-table57-en.

Ogden, T., 2015. Are Today's Donors Different. *Alliance Magazine*, 20(3). Available at: www.alliancemagazine.org.

Oliver Arbós, C.M. & Contreras, J., 2012. *Obligacions fiscals i comptables de les associacions, fundacions i federacions [de Andorra]*. Available at: www.lidera.ad/arxius/84_ca.pdf.

Ostrower, F., 1997. *Why the Wealthy Give*, Princeton, N.J.: Princeton University Press.

Palin, A., 2015. UBS to Offer Social Investment Fund. *Financial Times*. Available at: https://next.ft.com/content/4be9a404-3ce0-11e5-8613-07d16aad2152.

Parés i Maicas, M., 1994. *La Nueva filantropía y la comunicación social: mecenazgo, fundación y patrocinio*, 2nd edition, Barcelona: PPU. Note that the first edition, in Catalan, was titled simply *Mecenatge, Patrocini i Comunicació*. This second edition carries the moniker 'new'.

Parker, S., 2014. *Opening Up: Demystifying Funder Transparency*, Washington, DC: Foundation Center. Available at: www.grantcraft.org/guides/opening-up.

Payne, A.A. & Smith, J., 2015. Does income inequality increase charitable giving? *Canadian Journal of Economics/Revue canadienne d'économique*, 48(2), pp 793–818.

Payton, R.L. & Moody, M.P., 2008. *Understanding Philanthropy: Its Meaning and Mission*, Bloomington, IN: Indiana University Press.

Pearson, A., 2009. Generosity is Natural for Kind-hearted People. *New Scientist*, 21 December. Available at: www.newscientist.com/article/dn18311-generosity-is-natural-for-kind-hearted-people/.

Peerdeman, V., 2015. *Filantropie in Nederland. Grote Gever onderzoek 2015. Conclusies en Aanbevelingen*, Jazi Foundation, Nassau Fundraising. Available at: www.filantropieinnederland.nl/wp-content/uploads/2015/11/Filantropie-in-Nederland-Grote-Gever-Onderzoek-20151.pdf.

Penn, A., 2011. Social History and Organisational Development: Revisiting Beveridge's Voluntary Action. In *Understanding the Roots of Voluntary Action*, Brighton: Sussex Academic Press, pp 17–31.

Peretz, P., 2012. *Pratiques du don. La Vie des Idées*. Available at: www.laviedesidees.fr/Pratiques-du-don.html.

Peri, O., 1992. Waqf and Ottoman Welfare Policy. *Journal of the Economic and Social History of the Orient*, 35(2), pp 167–186.

Pharoah, C., Jenkins, R. & Goddard, K., 2015. *Foundation Giving Trends 2015*, London: Association of Charitable Foundations. Available at: www.acf.org.uk/downloads/publications/Foundation_Giving_Trends_2015.pdf.

Piketty, T., 2015. *L'économie des Inégalités*, 7th edition, Paris: La Découverte.

Pluyette, C., 2016. Le nombre d'assujettis à l'ISF a encore progressé en 2015. *Le Figaro*.

Porter, M.E. & Kramer, M.R., 2011. Creating Shared Value: How to Reinvent Capitalism and Unleash a Wave of Innovation and Growth. *Harvard Business Review* 89(1-2), 62–77.

Ragin, L.M., 2014. Overview: The New Tools of 'Philanthropy'. In *New Frontiers of Philanthropy: A Guide to the New Tools and New Actors that Are Reshaping Global Philanthropy and Social Investing*, Oxford: Oxford University Press, pp 311–313.

Rathgeb Smith, S. & Gronbjerg, K., 2006. Scope and Theory of Government-Nonprofit Relations. In *The Nonprofit Sector: A Research Handbook*, New Haven, CT: Yale University Press, pp 221–242.

Reed, D., Fechner, P., Baic, A., Houedenou, G., Strack, R., von Funck, K., Wilms, S. & Ziegler, B., 2016. *Gauging Long-Term Impact in the Social Sector: A Cutting Edge Approach*, Boston, MA: Boston Consulting Group. Available at: www.bcgperspectives.com/content/articles/innovation-strategy-gauging-long-term-impact-social-sector/.

Reich, R., 2013. Rich people's idea of charity: Giving to elite schools and operas. *Salon.* Available at: http://www.salon.com/2013/12/14/the_wealthy_give_to_charity_elite_schools_and_operas_partner/

Reich, R., 2016. Repugnant to the Whole Idea of Democracy? On the Role of Foundations in Democratic Societies. *PS: Political Science & Politics*, 49(3), pp 466–472.

Rishi, V., 2016. Palliative or Catalyst? Defending the Space for Civil Society. In *The Shrinking Space for Civil Society*, Brussels: European Foundation Centre. Available at: www.efc.be.

Rubio Guerrero, J.J. & Sosvilla Rivero, S., 2014. *El sector fundacional en España: atributos fundamentales (2008–2012): segundo informe*, Madrid: Asociación Española de Fundaciones. Available at: www.fundaciones.org.

Rubio Guerrero, J.J., Sosvilla Rivero, S. & Méndez Picazo, M.T., 2015. *El Perfil del Donante Tipo en España 2002–2010*, Madrid: Asociación Española de Fundaciones.

Salamon, L.M., 1992. Social Services. In C. T. Clotfelter, ed. *Who Benefits from the Nonprofit Sector?.* Chicago: University of Chicago Press, pp. 134–173.

Salamon, L.M. (ed), 2014. *New Frontiers of Philanthropy: A Guide to the New Tools and New Actors that Are Reshaping Global Philanthropy and Social Investing*, Oxford: Oxford University Press.

Saltuk, Y., El Idrissi, A., Bouri, A., Mudaliar, A. & Schiff, H., 2015. *Eyes on the Horizon: The Impact Investor Survey*, London: J.P. Morgan. Available at: www.thegiin.org.

Sargeant, A. & Shang, J., 2011. *Growing Philanthropy in the United Kingdom. A Report on the July 2011 Growing Philanthropy Summit*, Bristol, UK: University of the West of England. Available at: www.plymouth.ac.uk/schools/plymouth-business-school/centre-for-sustainable-philanthropy.

Sargeant, A., Eisenstein, A. & Kottasz, R., 2015. *Major Gift Fundraising: Unlocking the Potential for Smaller Nonprofits*, Plymouth, UK: Plymouth University. Available at: http://masteringmajorgifts.com/report/thanks.php.

Scheerboom, C., 2013. The Philanthropic Revolution: Changing the Game of Giving. *ECSP Insight*, 4(1st Quarter), pp 16–18.

Schervish, P., 2000. *The Modern Medici: Patterns, Motivations and Giving Strategies of the Wealthy*. Boston, MA: Boston College Social Welfare Research Institute. Available at: www.bc.edu/content/dam/files/research_sites/cwp/pdf/usc1.pdf.

Schervish, P. 2003. *Hyperagency and High-Tech donors: A new Theory of New Philanthropists*, Social Welfare Research Institute. Available at: https://www.bc.edu/content/dam/files/research_sites/cwp/pdf/haf.pdf.

Schuyt, T.N.M., 2010. Philanthropy in European Welfare States: A Challenging Promise? *International Review of Administrative Sciences*, 76(4), pp 774–789.

Seel, K.E., 2006. *The Statute of Charitable Uses and the English Origins of American Philanthropy*. PhD thesis, University of Calgary. Available at: www.mtroyal.ca/cs/groups/public/documents/pdf/npr06_bound_thesis.pdf.

Seghers, V., 2009. *La Nouvelle Philanthropie*, Autrement. Available at: www.autrement.com/.

Seghers, V., Delson, X., Gautier, A. & Le Brun, F., 2015. *Les Fondations Actionnaires: Première Étude Européenne*, Paris: Essec and Prophil. Available at: http://philanthropy-chair.essec.edu/research/research-reports.

Shah, S., McGill, L.T. & Weisblatt, K., 2011. *Untapped Potential: European Foundation Funding for Women and Girls*, New York: Foundation Center. Available at: www.mamacash.org/publications/report-untapped-potential/.

Shang, J. & Croson, R., 2009. A Field Experiment in Charitable Contribution: The Impact of Social Information on the Voluntary Provision of Public Goods. *The Economic Journal*, 119(540), pp 1422–1439.

Sharman, A., 2016. Charity Finance News – £80m Payment-by-results Life Chances Fund Launched. *Civil Society*, 4 July, p 1.

Shaw, A., 2015. *Understanding Strategic Engagement: An Exploratory Study of Perspectives on Philanthropic Investment in Programmes for Children and Youth in Ireland*. PhD thesis, NUI Galway. Available at: https://aran.library.nuigalway.ie/handle/10379/5757.

Shaw-Hardy, S., Taylor, M.A. & Beaudoin-Schwartz, B., 2010. *Women and Philanthropy: Boldly Shaping a Better World*, Chichester: John Wiley & Sons.

Shoard, C., 2016. The Fine Example Set by One English Village Begs the Question: Why Can't the Season of Goodwill Carry On for 12 Months, and Not Just 12 Days? *The Guardian Weekly*, 15 January, p 48.

Sibille, H., 2008. *Voyage dans la nouvelle philanthropie américaine (suite)*. Available at: http://alternatives-economiques.fr/blogs/sibille/2008/12/11/voyage-dans-la-nouvelle-philanthropie-americaine-suite/.

Simmons, C., 2013. *Present Law and Background Relating to the Federal Tax Treatment of Charitable Contributions*, Washington, DC: Joint Committee on Taxation. Available at: www.jct.gov/publications.html?func=startdown&id=4506.

Simmons, R., 2014. *The 2014 U.S. Trust Study of High Net Worth Philanthropy*, Indiana University Lilly Family School of Philanthropy.

Spinney, L., 2015. Roots of Brutality. *New Scientist*, 228(3047), pp 40–43. Available at: https://www.newscientist.com/article/mg22830471-000-syndrome-e-can-neuroscience-explain-the-executioners-of-isis/.

Steenbergen, R., 2008. *De nieuwe mecenas: cultuur en de terugkeer van het particuliere geld*, Amsterdam: Uitg. Business Contact.

Surmatz, H., 2014. *Country Profile: Sweden*, Brussels: Transnational Giving Europe. Available at: http://www.transnationalgiving.eu/en/country-profiles/.

Tchernia, J.-F., 2014. *Baromètre de la générosite France générosités, Paris: Centre Français des Fonds et Fondations*. Available at: www.centre-francais-fondations.org/ressources-pratiques/donner-a-un-fonds-ou-une-fondation/Statistiques-sur-les-dons-des-particuliers-et-des-entreprises/dons-des-particuliers/barometre-de-la-generosite-france-generosites-cerphi-2014/view.

Thibaut, 2008. *La philantropie en France: Valeurs en hausse*, Paris: Fondation de France. Available at: www.fondationdefrance.org/.

Vecchi, V., Casalini, F., Balbo, L. & Caselli, S., 2015. Impact Investing: A New Asset Class or a Societal Refocus of Venture Capital? In *Public Private Partnerships for Infrastructure and Business Development: Principles, Practices, and Perspectives*, London: Palgrave Macmillan.

Verduyn, L., 2015 De Rijkste Belgen – Ranking van de Rijkste Belgen. *De Rijkste Belgen*. Available at: http://derijkstebelgen.be.

References

Von Hippel, T., 2014. *Taxation of Cross Border Giving in Europe after Persche and Stauffer – From Landlock to Free Movement*, Brussels: European Foundation Centre. Available at: http://www.transnationalgiving.eu/en/article/2014/10/13/cross-border-philanthropy-in-europe/4/.

Wagner, L. (2002). The 'New' Donor: Creation or Evolution? *International Journal of Nonprofit & Voluntary Sector Marketing*, 7(4), pp 343–352.

Weisbrod, B.A. & Cordes, J.J., 1998. *Differential Taxation of Nonprofits and the Commercialization of Nonprofit Revenues*, Rochester, NY: Social Science Research Network. Available at: http://papers.ssrn.com/abstract=1856640.

Wiepking, P., 2008. *For the Love of Mankind: A Sociological Study on Charitable Giving*, Amsterdam: Vrije Universiteit.

Wiepking, P., 2010. Democrats Support International Relief and the Upper Class Donates to art? How Opportunity, Incentives and Confidence Affect Donations to Different Types of Charitable Organizations. *ResearchGate*, 39(6), pp.1073–1087.

Wilson, K.E., Silva, F. & Ricardson, D., 2015. *Social Impact Investment: Building the Evidence Base*, Rochester, NY: Social Science Research Network. Available at: http://papers.ssrn.com/abstract=2562082.

Wit, A.D. & Bekkers, R., 2016. Exploring Gender Differences in Charitable Giving: The Dutch Case. *Nonprofit and Voluntary Sector Quarterly*, 45(4) pp 741–761.

Wolff, E., 2001. The Economy and Philanthropy. In *Philanthropy and the Nonprofit Sector in a Changing America*, Bloomington, IN: Indiana University Press.

Zeekant, J., 2015. Ideëel en ondernemerschap: samen sterk voor people en planet. *Vakblad Fondsenwerving*, (100), p 3.

Appendix: Interview questions

This document was sent out prior to each interview.

Questions

1. **Thank you for participating**
   a Would you prefer attributed, or off-the-record?
   b Can I confirm that we have 40 minutes?
2. **The focus of the book is on high-value private philanthropy in Europe.** That means gifts, partnerships and investments by people and foundations, mostly in the range over €25,000. It includes social impact, or 'social first' investments. My hypothesis is that philanthropy in Europe is changing and my objective is to find out what is happening, and why.
3. **Change, or not?**
   a Has high-value philanthropy in Europe changed over the last 10/20/30 years?
   b What have been the most important changes?
   c What has not changed?
   d Was there a watershed event or year when philanthropy changed?
4. **Why has it changed?**
   a The person
      i Wealth?
      ii Demographics (e.g. age at which people start high-value philanthropy)?
   b Beliefs
      i Religion?
      ii Political views?
      iii Personal tastes and preferences?
   c Engagement and personal experience
      i Engagement in volunteering?

      ii Awareness of need?

      iii Solicitation (asking – being asked more, or asked differently)?

      iv Awareness of impact

      v Perception of efficacy, or value for money?

  d Information and advice

      i   Transparency in the social sector in Europe?

      ii Professional philanthropic advisers?

  e Economic environment

      i   Economic stability?

      ii The wealth gap?

      iii Fiscal encouragement of giving?

          1) How does this work, in the minds of the philanthropists?

             a) It is cheaper to give?

             b) It sets a new social standard?

             c) If the government thinks it is a good thing, I do too?

  f New structures and tools?

      i   (Foundations, social enterprises, donor circles, venture philanthropy, Social Impact Bonds, loans...)

  g Other factors?

5. Trends, future

  a Are these shifts temporary?

  b Are they part of a cycle that we have seen before?

  c What next, in high value philanthropy?

6. Your age, or your decade of birth?

  a Number of years involved (volunteer, paid) in the non-profit or social purpose sector.

7. Could you suggest anyone else I should speak to?

8. Thank you for taking part in this study.

Index

Index

Printed and bound by CPI Group (UK) Ltd, Croydon, CR0 4YY

16/04/2025

14658341-0001